THE FOURTH AMERICAN FAITH

THE
FOURTH
AMERICAN
FAITH

★ ★ ★

Duncan Howlett

BEACON PRESS
BOSTON

To
CAROLYN

CONTENTS

Introduction   vii

CHAPTER I   CONTEMPORARY UNBELIEF   1

　　　　　　　1. Some Sobering Statistics   2
　　　　　　　2. Unbelief Among the Clergy   9
　　　　　　　3. Heresy Trials   14
　　　　　　　4. The Ecumenical Movement   22

CHAPTER II   THE FOURTH FAITH   28

　　　　　　　1. The Copernican Revolution and the
　　　　　　　　　Church   29
　　　　　　　2. American Religious Pluralism   41
　　　　　　　3. Secularism   47
　　　　　　　4. The Fourth Faith   54

CHAPTER III   THE FAITH OF STABILITY   62

　　　　　　　1. Judaism   63
　　　　　　　2. Roman Catholic Faith   72
　　　　　　　3. Protestant Liberalism   83
　　　　　　　4. Modernism   93

CHAPTER IV   THE RETURN TO ORTHODOXY   101

              1. Karl Barth and the Return to Orthodoxy
                 in Europe   102
              2. Reinhold Niebuhr and the Return to
                 Orthodoxy in the United States   106
              3. Neo-Orthodoxy's Debt to Fundamentalism 113
              4. Paul Tillich   119

CHAPTER V   THE HOUSE BUILT UPON THE SAND   127

              1. Biblical Theology   128
              2. The Paradox   137
              3. You Can Believe if You Want To   143
              4. God in History   147
              5. The Authority of Self Assertion   155

CHAPTER VI   THE FAITH OF ADVENTURE   168

              1. A Second Look at Adam   169
              2. The Heaven Stormer   176
              3. The Heretic   183
              4. The Last Question   193
              5. The Battle of the Assumptions   200
              6. The Quest for Ultimate Meaning   208

Notes   217

Index   233

Introduction

The fourth American faith was first identified back in the 1950's. During the early part of that decade certain Protestant, Catholic, and Jewish writers began to note the fact that pluralism was becoming the American way in religion. The three great organized faiths, Protestantism, Catholicism, and Judaism, they pointed out, had by that time become a kind of accepted religious "establishment" in this country, a socioreligious subculture, a way of belonging religiously. This situation came about, they said, because the three established faiths, different as they were from each other, had so much in common.

SECULARISM AND HUMANISM

These writers then went on to identify a fourth faith, which seemed to them to threaten the other three because its basic premises were different. Their descriptions of this faith varied widely, and they gave it many names. They called it civic or civil religion, religion in general, the American culture religion, religiosity, and, most commonly, secularism and humanism. Generally, however, they agreed that the fourth faith, whatever it was, had no name, no body of doctrine, and certainly no organization.

The present volume is a paperback edition of a book I published in 1964. It was an attempt to delineate the fourth American faith to which these writers pointed. Among their various descriptions of it I usually recognized myself. But there was also much in their descriptions that I rejected. The fourth faith, I discovered, was a theological wastebasket into which these writers dumped all the trends and movements that seemed to them to stand against the three established faiths.

Any one of the multifarious movements included in their fourth faith concepts might have come forward and claimed to be the faith they were talking about. Why, then, is the point of view espoused in this book entitled to make such a claim? There are two reasons why: first, because the point of view I shall describe and try to defend, usually called "secularism" or "humanism," received by far the most attention from these writers and hence was obviously their central concern. Secondly, because secular humanism is increasingly seen to be one of the most basic trends in Western culture.

If the American people were to give the recognition to a fourth religious body they have already granted to Protestantism, Catholicism, and Judaism, that fourth body would undoubtedly be the Eastern Orthodox Church, by far the next largest religious group. But those who speak of a fourth American faith are not undertaking a numerical classification of organized religions in this country in order of size or influence, or origin. They seek instead to show that a new faith is now becoming articulate, which is different from the three major groupings into which religion in America is now divided. Speaking in terms of numbers, this fourth faith is probably held by more people than are to be found in any of the organized religious bodies in this country.

This book, then, is my attempt to state the faith of a great number of people who, like myself, realize that the faith of their fathers is theirs no longer. It is a statement made on behalf of those who know they are not men of little faith even though they can no longer accept the religious traditions in which they were reared. My purpose is to say to them that they are not faithless, nor are they alone. Instead, they belong to a vast company who today seek a faith of integrity which the mind can accept and which the heart can also acclaim.

The New Theological Outlook

A noticeable change in the theological scene has occurred since this book was first published. An English Bishop's proposal that we be "honest to God" has been hailed by even the most conservative; a "God is dead" movement streaked through the theological sky and sputtered out; and just now a call to "Christian secularity" enjoys the latest wave of ecclesiastical popularity. In the Roman Catholic Church, under the influence of Pope John XXIII and the Second Vatican Council, a ferment of growth and change which had long been latent bubbled up into a series of reforms in the structure, practice, and belief system of the Church. At the same time, the mood of the Church in the United States and in many other countries as well has suddenly changed. Now cooperation is easy where once it was difficult. Mutual recognition and respect have replaced the clashing assertions of ecclesiastical primacy and exclusiveness common only a generation ago. Platform and living room dialogue have replaced separateness. Aggiornamento is the order of the day.

Another new development in contemporary religion, most conspicuously in the United States, but not alone here, is to be seen in the "hippie" assertion of personal freedom, of being yourself, of attention to the senses, and of living the doctrine of love. The rising interest in eastern religions, the use of mind-expanding drugs as a means of achieving religious experience, and the religious and moral character of much popular music point in the same direction. The new ascendance of the guru is the current phase of the movement that brought about a revival of interest in Buddhism a decade or more ago. Yesterday it was Zen, today it is Yoga. Who knows what new phase of popular religion awaits us tomorrow?

These current theological phenomena are evidence of the deep and widespread dissatisfaction with organized religion which gave rise to the fourth American faith. It is heartening that the clergy at last are beginning to deal with the questions it raises.

We can only applaud their acknowledgment that we no longer believe in the traditional God of Judaism and Christianity. The liberals, clerical and lay, have been saying this for a long time. It was an enormous gain when the clergy generally began to say so too. It is in that sense that God is "dead." The movement that took its name from Nietzsche's startling assertion was a natural outgrowth of the widespread acceptance of Bishop Robinson's thesis. His popular book title, by its brevity and slightly profane implication, cast in a single phrase the yearning of many a devoutly religious person. If we cannot be honest with ourselves in our thought about God, what is it that we really worship?

We can only applaud, too, the effort of the death-of-God movement to disentangle the figure of Jesus, the man who lived and died in Palestine, from all the theologies that have since been heaped upon him. And certainly the new involvement of the churches in the life of the world which marks "Christian secularism" is a matter for the greatest rejoicing. It is the theological rationale for the active participation of the churches in the civil rights movement and in inner city problems.

No Basic Change

These new developments would be exciting indeed if they foreshadowed a basic change in organized religion as it exists in this country today, a change from the position of the three established faiths to that of the fourth. But there is no sign that any such change has taken place. The new theological developments appear to be but a continuation of the earlier liberal movement described in this book, particularly in Chapter V. So far, they appear to be but the latest phase in the steady retreat of traditional religion before the onward march of human knowledge and understanding.

The "honest to God" movement, for example, began once more the slow relaxing of Christian dogma that the neo-orthodox movement had interrupted. It is essentially a neo-liberalism. The "death of God" movement, especially in its return to the historical Jesus, also reverts to the older liberal position. The "Christian secularists" on their part offer a latter-day development of the social gospel that dominated Christian thought earlier in this century. This, too, was an important aspect of the liberal movement.

To illustrate, Harvey Cox, the leading spokesman of the Christian secularizers, like Walter Rauschenbush before him, bases his argument on the Bible. That the Bible is a theological addendum, unnecessary to Cox's argument, seems to show his traditionalism. He does not break with the biblical tradition even though his argument is in fact quite independent of it. Nor apparently does he desire to. His purpose seems rather to be to show that the advance of secularism does not and should not damage traditional religion. Christians and Jews need not be frightened, he seems to be saying. Modern secularism is not necessarily antireligious: we should claim it as our own, for at its best it is really derived from the biblical faith.

Nothing has changed, really, although some concessions have been made. The basic position of the established faiths remains the same. If to the casual observer it should appear that these recent theological developments have brought into the three established faiths all the distinctive values the fourth might claim for itself, we will find on closer examination that it is not so. The change in outlook sought by the people of the fourth faith is not here. The names have been changed but the characters in the drama are still the same. The central problem remains unresolved. The three "established" faiths still have a body of doctrine or tradition or religious truth which they believe they possess by virtue of a revelation from God. The fourth faith, on the contrary, holds that truth in religion is not handed down from heaven but that it comes through a process of discovery. It holds that whatever truth is attained is always partial, always subject to further amplification, modification, even rejection.

There is nothing novel in this position. The designation "fourth faith" is but a new name for a movement that is far older than Christianity and Judaism. To recognize its validity is to see that inquiry is basic to the nature of man. It is to see that the desire for growth, development, and change is as much a part of man's nature as his reverence for the past. It is to see that given the chance man would use his past not to bind himself down, but as a means of understanding the present and charting his course in the future.

Alfred North Whitehead, turning to philosophy after achieving a worldwide reputation in mathematics, called Western culture "a great adventure in the region of thought." Summarizing his views in his *Science and the Modern World*, he wrote: "The tale is the epic of an episode in the manifestation of reason. It tells how a particular direction of reason emerges in a race by the long preparation of antecedent epochs, how after its birth its subject-matter gradually unfolds itself, how it attains its triumphs . . . and finally how at its moment of supreme success its limitations disclose themselves and call for a renewed exercise of the creative imagination."

This is where religion stands in the culture of the West in our time. The Judeo-Christian tradition has been supremely successful judged by its impact upon Western culture and the degree to which its institutions, its thoughts, and its practice are woven into the fabric of that culture. But now, in our time, the limitations of that tradition have disclosed themselves. Yet our religious institutions seem to be unable or unwilling to modify their beliefs and practices sufficiently to meet the new demands being made upon them. In the resulting vacuum a so-called fourth faith has made its appearance.

Adopting Whitehead's concept, we call the fourth faith the faith of adventure. We contrast it with the three established faiths which together we call the faith of stability. This is not because Protestantism, Catholicism, and Judaism have no important differences from one another. It is not because any of them lacks an adventurous spirit. It is because the three established American faiths have a single fundamental characteristic in common which the fourth faith rejects. Each of them possesses an orthodoxy based on a revelation from God — a tradition, a body of right thinking and practice by which adherents are identified and accepted into membership. These standards have been continued from generation to generation, honed over the centuries until they have become very sharp and clear. The resulting tradition permits a decreasing opportunity for change within itself. In spite of the ferment of our present day, continuity, loyalty to the traditions of the elders, stability, and orthodoxy are still the chief marks of Protestantism, Catholicism, and Judaism in our time despite their denials that this is so.

THE FAITH OF ADVENTURE

The faith of adventure rejects the orthodox approach. It rejects the idea of orthodoxy itself. The faith of adventure holds that no church may arrogate to itself the right to declare what is right and what is wrong, what is true and what is false. It holds that no one knows the answers to ultimate questions, and that insofar as answers may be found they are to be reached by men in community testing their ideas and convictions against one another. But in this process, no answer shall have any final authority. The faith of adventure holds that any man or group of men may do no more than declare what they believe to be the truth, to say why, and to invite men generally to assent to it and to do so on the strength of the case it presents. This is the sense in which the fourth faith is marked by adventure. It cannot remain fixed, for the mind and spirit of man are never still. Always man seeks clearer understanding, greater insight, wider knowledge. To the extent that he succeeds, the reformulation of what he already supposes himself to know becomes necessary.

Will Herberg, one of the first to point to the fourth American faith, states the difference between the first three faiths and the fourth in this way. "Jewish-Christian faith is God-centered." It is to be contrasted with "sinful egocentricity," with man pursuing a faith for living "in self-sufficiency, relying on his own virtue, wisdom or piety." Such a faith finds "not God but an idol," he asserts, "some aspect of the self writ large." The Jewish-Christian God "discloses Himself in the divine-human encounter of which Scripture and the tradition of the believing community are witness," he says. This is the sense in which the three established faiths differ from the faith of adventure.

The faith of stability starts with truth already in hand, the biblical faith, Scripture, the beliefs and traditions of a believing community to which the members bear witness. The faith of adventure starts where it believes every man must start, from where he is, from what he knows and what he is able to find out, not in arrogance and not as a self-idol but in humility, joining with all the millions who would seek the truth and right and are ready to help each other on the way. One who accepts the faith of adventure seeks to move from ignorance to understanding. His faith is that continuous discovery will reward his efforts, and not his alone, but his in concert with the efforts of his fellowmen, the results of each checked against all the rest. Confronted by those to whom "God has disclosed himself," such a man grows wary. Too many of the world's ills can be attributed to those to whom God was said to have disclosed himself. The faith of adventure thinks it better to test all such claims against the wisdom and experience of men.

As we shall see in Chapter I, this faith is held by vast numbers of people. As we shall also see, it is a very old faith. It goes far back in the cultural history of man. It was articulate in ancient Greece and found expression once more at the time of the Reformation. It became more articulate in the Enlightenment, and in the thought of certain of our great national leaders, men like Thomas Jefferson and Abraham Lincoln.

RELATION TO UNITARIANISM AND UNIVERSALISM

Many people, inside and outside my own Unitarian Universalist denomination, have asked me why in this book I did not relate the faith of adventure to the church in which I am an ordained minister. Obviously, the book is a statement of your own personal beliefs, they said. Doubtless it also states the position of many other Unitarian Universalists today as well. If so, why not say so? Such a statement is very much needed.

Indeed it is, but this book is not a denominational tract, and was never intended to be. It was and is intended to be a statement of faith, valid in its own right, to which any church or individual may aspire, but concerning which none can boast full possession, or authoritative control. What I have written is no more Unitarian because I happen to be a Unitarian minister than Bishop Robinson's book is Episcopal because he is a member of the hierarchy of the Church of England.

Nevertheless, the question is legitimate. How does the fourth American faith relate to my particular denomination? The answer is, very closely, and more closely than to any other organized religious group. Reading the works of Protestant, Catholic, and Jewish scholars who have written about the fourth faith, I found that each seemed to describe, at least in part, the faith that Unitarians and Universalists share, the goal our denomination strives to implement in a religious institution, in a church. I readily saw, too, as did these writers, that the faith of adventure enjoys very wide acceptance. It is by no means confined to the Unitarian Universalist denomination. It is held by millions who still maintain formal adherence to Protestantism, Catholicism, and Judaism, and by an even greater proportion of the vast body of those who have no church affiliation at all. The Unitarian Universalist denomination, the result of a merger of the Unitarian and Universalist churches nearly a decade ago, is not the fourth American faith. To make any such claim would be presumptuous in the extreme, though some Unitarians and Universalists have made it.

Nevertheless, Unitarian Universalist churches comprise the only religious movement in the United States that rejects the faith of stability and yet seeks to express its aspirations through an organization of churches. Have they succeeded? Can anyone succeed, or are the faith of adventure and organized religion irreconcilable? Will any attempt to institutionalize the faith of adventure inevitably result in the establishment of yet another sect holding yet another orthodoxy? How can those who choose the faith of adventure be drawn together with sufficent cohesion to enable them to work together? Must they be fractured by diversities or be forced to a definition of their common bonds which will defeat the unfettered spirit of adventure they seek together?

Speaking for my own denomination, I can only say that so far we have been able to hold to both of these standards at the same time, however imperfectly we may have applied them. Ours is a viable, unified body of churches, as are our local churches, with few exceptions. At the same time we preach and practice the faith of adventure to the highest degree we can attain. It is a tenet of this faith that it can be institutionalized in a church as the democratic ideal can be institutionalized in government. The faith of adventure holds that religion can survive only if it acknowledges that the truth toward which men strive is not delivered from the heavens, but is slowly and painfully discovered here on earth.

Today, more than when this book was first published, a theological logjam blocks the course of man's spiritual development. The ancient beliefs of the church, flowing easily down the river of history, are now locked between the two headlands of ecclesiastical conservatism and the fear that Western culture will stand or fall with ancient dogma. Meanwhile, still pouring down the stream of man's thought and experience are new discoveries, new convictions, new attitudes, and new beliefs. Each piles the total mass higher and locks it tighter. Unless new discoveries, new conceptions, new ideas, are permitted to follow those that have gone before, soon there will be no alternative but an explosion or the convergence of natural forces to sunder the logjam, and who shall say what destruction will follow?

The headlands of ecclesiastical and social conservatism will remain, but the stack of religious ideas and practices now locked between them must be broken. It is the thesis of this book that the faith of adventure, a basic faith, emerging in contemporary religious thought and striving for recognition in our religious institutions, points the way.

CHAPTER I

Contemporary Unbelief

> Faith of our fathers, holy faith
> We will be true to thee till death.

Thus concludes the refrain of a beloved old hymn of the church. Yet a great many of those who sing it, including many devoted church members, while they honor the faith of their fathers, do not hold it. Others who profess the traditional faith "interpret" it in such a fashion that only the form remains, the meaning having been so changed that the fathers, were they to return, would have none of it.

We have said that the fourth faith has made its appearance in America because the other three do not meet the religious needs felt by many of the men and women of today. This situation is not new. A generation ago Walter Lippmann, writing about "those who no longer believe in the religion of their fathers," observed that "an increasing number feel that there is a vacancy in their lives." A host of others have written in the same vein.

The churchmen have, of course, long been aware of this change. And now, even for those who have discounted it, our modern proclivity for opinion-sampling no longer leaves any room for doubt. The literature based upon polls of religious belief is enormous. Fortunately, we need not attempt a survey of it, for it all points the same way. A few samples will serve well enough to show what all the polls show—an ever-widening discrepancy between the creeds of the churches and the convictions that animate the members; an ever-increasing departure from the faith of our fathers. They extend over a number of years, enough to make it clear that what might once have been looked upon as a temporary trend, can now be seen as one of the major movements of thought in our time. And in addition to the polls, there are a number of other pointers that indicate the degree to which the gulf between official doctrine and the beliefs of the people has widened in our time.

1. Some Sobering Statistics

In 1951 a young Episcopal clergyman in Richmond, Virginia, decided to find out how far the beliefs of his people diverged from the creed they professed to believe as members of his church. So he made up a questionnaire and sent it to the mailing list. His poll was significant for the very reason that it was neither large nor professional. For this reason it gives us deep insight into the heart of a single congregation as typical as any we might find—neither the most sophisticated nor the most unlettered, neither the richest nor the poorest, neither the most liberal nor the most conservative, neither the most urban, suburban, or rural. The young rector got a high percentage of returns to his questionnaire which showed that there was a very real interest in the subject. But to his dismay the response also showed that many of the members of his church quite candidly rejected the doctrinal position of the Episcopal Church. Many more who did not reject these doctrines outright revealed serious doubts about them.

A summary of the results from 307 out of 550 members indicated that the congregation generally rejected the idea of man's innate depravity, although the Prayer of General Confession which each of these men and women said together on Sunday morning contained the statement that they had so grievously sinned that there was no health in them. Some 272 said they believed that "God is personal"; but 66 of these said they held this belief only "with a feeling that probably it was the right one." They were not sure about it, even though this has been a central teaching of Christianity from the beginning. An equally large majority said they believed in the divinity of Christ. Nevertheless, the tabulation showed that 19 did not. One member did not believe that Jesus ever lived at all.

Although the Bible is the foundation stone of Christianity, the survey showed that Bible-reading was infrequent with more than half the congregation. Ideas of immortality, also a central Christian teaching, were extremely vague, although about half said they thought that at death the soul "separates from the body and lives on forever in the spirit world." An unbelievable 119 thought "other religions are as good as ours"; and that "we should not disturb other people in their beliefs," although Christianity has always maintained that it is unique among the religions of men, and for this reason has throughout its history been characterized by intensive missionary activity.

The congregation that responded to the foregoing survey with such candor is no isolated instance of rampant skepticism. Similar results could have been obtained from such a questionnaire in thousands of other Protestant churches in this country then or now. A study of over 500 children between the ages of 12 and 18 conducted at Syracuse University and representing a typical cross section of a typical American city bears this out. The study showed that skepticism as to the truth of traditional religious teachings set in very rapidly during the teenage years. Many religious teachings were almost completely discarded by the time these young people had reached the age of 18. Among them were the belief that "every word in the Bible is true"; that "God is someone who watches over you and who punishes you if you are not good"; that "there is a Heaven"; that "people who go to church are necessarily better than those who do not"; that "Hell is a place where you are punished for your sins on earth"; and that "it is necessary to attend church to be a Christian."

"As the child approaches maturity," the Syracuse investigators concluded, "his doubts, uncertainties and perplexities regarding religion tend to multiply. He faces problems which he needs help to solve. His main difficulty seems to be in getting such help. He finds that most conventional religious programs are unsatisfying." Some might argue that these beliefs should never have been taught to the children at all. Others would argue that they should not be presented in so bald a form, that Protestantism now understands these teachings in a more symbolic than literal sense. What is important for our purposes, however, is the fact that as these children move toward adulthood, they came to the point where they no longer believed much of what their churches were still teaching as God's truth.

Surveys of the religious opinions of college students show that the same trend toward skepticism continues at the higher educational levels. A study of 1,100 freshmen and seniors at six different colleges and universities, made by psychologists at Ripon College, showed that belief in the Ten Commandments as a law for life dropped from 92 per cent among the freshmen to 76 per cent among the seniors. Belief in the power of prayer dropped from 75 per cent among the freshmen to 66 per cent among the seniors. Concluded the investigators: "on virtually all questions of religious belief, the seniors expressed appreciably greater skepticism than the freshmen."

In 1959 the editors of the *Harvard Crimson* published a survey of college opinion on religion as it prevailed among Harvard and Radcliffe students. Some results: 21 per cent of the Roman Catholics and 25 per cent of the Jews reported that they had "apostasized." Of the "middle-ground" Protestants, 39 per cent said they had fallen away. Of the Protestants, only 31 per cent (as against 74 per cent of the Catholics) said they believed in immortality. Only 45 per cent regarded Jesus Christ as "divine": 40 per cent considered him "only a very great prophet or teacher." Of all those answering the questionnaire, 24 per cent said they believed in "a God about whom nothing definite can be affirmed." Only 18 per cent said they believed in an "infinitely wise, omnipotent, three-person God who created the universe and who maintains an active concern for human affairs."

In England a similar departure from the faith of our fathers appears to have taken place. Of those interviewed in a public opinion poll published in 1960, 83 per cent thought it would be a good thing if people were to take an increasing interest in the Christian religion and its activities, yet only 50 per cent thought people were taking such an interest in fact. Only 19 per cent thought the Old Testament of divine authority, so that its commands should be followed without question. Only 41 per cent were willing to concede divine authority of any kind to the Old Testament. They thought that "interpretation" was necessary if the Old Testament was to be used as a guide for living; 22 per cent thought it a mere collection of fables; 18 per cent had no view at all, which as far as the acceptance of Christian doctrine is concerned, is tantamount to total rejection, for Christians have always held themselves to be believers. The statistics for the New Testament were about the same except that there was a little greater willingness to attribute divine authority to it and there were fewer who were willing to write it off as a collection of myths and fables.

Evidence of the discrepancy between official dogma and the beliefs of the heart is to be seen in many ways in addition to opinion surveys, official and unofficial. A church bulletin picked up at random contains an announcement which speaks eloquently of the problem the average Protestant confronts as he tries to accept the beliefs required of him as a church member. The notice is by no means exceptional. Similar announcements appear in thousands of church calendars all across the country annually during the Lenten season. This particular one read as follows: "STUMBLING BLOCKS IN THE CREED is the topic for consideration at the next meeting of the Inquirers' Class being conducted by the Rector, this Sunday afternoon at 4:45 in the parish house. Must we take the creeds literally? What do they really mean to affirm? Why not revise them? Why bother with creeds when it is action that counts? These are some questions to be considered." How plainly they reveal the credal dilemmas of the faithful.

Religious opinion polls among Catholics are seldom published, but their views may be surmised as they appear scattered through more general polls. The evidence indicates that with Rome, too, the gulf between personal belief and official faith, while not nearly so wide as in Protestantism, exists and is growing. Private conversations with individual Catholics also indicate that this is so. The large number of Roman Catholics now joining Protestant churches further indicates a departure from official teachings, for Rome includes among her dogmas the primacy of her own church. Roman Catholic converts to Protestantism are, by their own admission, people who can no longer accept the beliefs Rome requires of them.

Protestant conversions to Catholicism might seem to indicate that Rome was, numerically at least, restoring the faith of as many as fall away. Other evidence, however, indicates that the gulf between official dogma and the convictions of the heart plagues Catholicism along with all other branches of Christianity. In 1961 a news dispatch from Bologna reported: "A crusade against indifference has begun here in the wake of the first full-scale survey of religious activity ever made in an Italian city. Giacomo Cardinal Lercaro has ordered the building of thirty parish churches in this ancient university city as the first step in a program to combat a drift from religion revealed by a two-year survey. Cardinal Lercaro ordered the survey in 1959. It showed that only 102,647—or 21.2% of the city's 415,424 inhabitants—could be considered practicing members of the Roman Catholic Church."

With Judaism, too, it is the same, as again the opinion polls show, for Jews are no more reluctant to state their religious views to pollsters than are Protestants. In 1961 *Commentary,* a magazine published by the American Jewish Committee, gave the results of a questionnaire it had conducted. "Have you ever considered the possibility that your children may convert to another religion?", the magazine asked in a kind of symposium. The question was addressed to thirty-one Jews, medical doctors, novelists, professors, poets, journalists. Here are some of their answers:

"I do not regard Jewishness as primarily a matter of religious belief. . . . I do not practice any religion. . . . Being both Jewish and in a sense an opponent of all religion, . . . I don't understand the religious impulse. . . . I would be discomfited were a child of mine to convert to any religion. . . . I would be puzzled if [my children] became religious Jews. . . . Religious conversion in America reflects more on the emotional instability of the person involved than on the merits of the religions. . . . As an atheist, I hope my children will have no need for any 'religion,' Judaism included. . . . Better they should stay off both religion and fried foods. . . . [It is] quite incredible that anyone should actively believe in a body of religious dogma. . . . I do not now consider religious participation an important arena for personal commitment or action. . . . I find myself indifferent to the faith of my fathers. . . . I am not a believer. . . . All religions rest on false assumptions. I hope any children I have will become atheists. . . . I find . . . conversion *to* Judaism . . . inexplicably absurd. . . . I don't feel allied. . . . The conversion of my children would be no more calamitous than their religious adherence to Jewish liturgy, ritual, and supernatural dogma. In either event I would have failed as their father, teacher and friend."

One of the ways in which the problem presents itself is not so much in a conscious departure from the faith as in a failure to understand or to value what the faith is in any unique sense. A survey of the concerns of Protestant families published in 1961 showed that the impact of the church on the family was either insignificant or not susceptible of measurement. It was a small, yet carefully planned survey, and the researchers concluded that the faith of their subjects "had no unique qualities which could not be duplicated among other worthwhile efforts. . . . Only a scattered few [of those surveyed] realized that theological connections lie between what one believes and how one lives in relationship to others."

Perhaps the most alarming evidence of the gulf between personal faith and official dogma was pointed up in a survey of religious bestsellers. Published in 1958, it was an analysis of the religious inspirational books that had been the most popular in this country since 1875. The authors, Louis Schneider and Sanford M. Dornbusch, included in their list books by Protestants, Catholics, and Jews alike. The bestsellers, they concluded, generally blurred the conflict between the individual and the social code and produced a religion of escape which was meaningless. In this sense, they said, most so-called "inspirational" literature is actually antireligious. It does not confront men with any moral decision, and they might have added, it amounts to a rejection in fact of the teachings of the churches they attend, for all three of the standard American faiths make very considerable demands upon their adherents.

There is a vast amount of evidence for contemporary unbelief besides statistical surveys of individual belief. Another growing body of literature within which such evidence appears has been supplied by the churchmen themselves and by sociologists interested in the church. These men find the church a nearly empty replica of the vital institution it pretends to be. Its recent rapid growth in numbers and in power is, to these men, but proof of its hollowness and of the unbelief that pervades it. They include Gibson Winter *(The Suburban Captivity of the Churches)*; Peter Berger *(The Noise of Solemn Assemblies)*; A. Roy Eckardt *(The Surge of Piety in America)*; Martin Marty *(The New Shape of American Religion)*, and many more. Their case is far from proved, but the materials they have amassed provide impressive substantiation for asserting that the gulf between personal belief and official dogma is widening very rapidly.

This vast array of evidence, and much that I have not mentioned, is not to be ignored. There is no sign that it will diminish. Rather, it increases every day and as with the new studies in the sociology of religion just mentioned, it now appears in unexpected quarters and in new contexts. The literature of explanation, of interpretation and defense, is not succeeding. All the apologetics and exhortations to the faithful appear to be in vain. The rejection of dogma advances apace among our people. Christians down the ages have rejoiced to say with Paul the Apostle, "I have fought the good fight. I have finished the race. I have kept the faith." Increasingly today the rank and file churchgoer finds these words difficult to repeat with any real sense that they represent what has actually taken place within him.

The difficulty is, our contemporary loss of faith is not without serious consequences. A recent college graduate summed it up in the following penetrating and truly alarming manner. "One of the bitter criticisms I have of manifest Christianity," he wrote, "is that by postulating and enforcing what is absurd and contrary to life, and at the same time posing as a complete and final authority, it leads men to reject morals altogether, thus allowing their pursuit of life to become a heedless following of appetite and fortuitous opportunity." Too many of us, in our contacts with present-day students, can corroborate this judgment. Into the vacuum left by an unbelievable theology an increasing number of students are putting the philosophy of hedonism.

"We are waiting," say the students of the present day. This is the conclusion of Professor William E. Hordern after surveying in person student religious opinion on several campuses. They are waiting for a religion that makes sense to them, that can make some kind of demands upon them and that can elicit from them some kind of commitment.

2. UNBELIEF AMONG THE CLERGY

Perhaps the most arresting evidence for the increasing gap between official creeds and personal beliefs is to be found in the fact that the clergy themselves often do not believe the teachings of the churches they serve. Again, to turn to some sample surveys, Professor David E. Lindstrom of the University of Illinois, in 1959 made a survey of the beliefs of Methodist ministers as compared with the beliefs of the laity. He discovered that some 85 per cent of the laymen believe that "Jesus' resurrection is our pledge of assurance of eternal life," but only 78 per cent of the ministers accept this completely. More than a quarter of the ministers doubt that necessary marks of the true church are the preaching of the Gospel and the administration of the sacraments, while less than a fifth of the laymen express similar doubts. Half the ministers doubt that the value of the sacrament of Communion depends entirely upon the attitude of the participant, while less than 20 per cent of the laymen show any uncertainty. Sixty per cent of the ministers reject the belief that if a person takes Holy Communion, "he is automatically a better person," but only 46 per cent of the laymen reject the idea completely.

It would be easy to account for these differences between clerical and lay views of Christian doctrine. The survey may well mean nothing more than that the clergy have thought about these questions while the laity have not. It could mean nothing more than that laymen are willing to accept on faith much of what their churches teach while the ministers are not. But whatever else this survey may mean, it must be perfectly clear that it means Methodist ministers as well as Methodist laymen do not believe all that their church officially teaches.

This is, of course, not a problem that is confined to the Methodists. Another survey, published in 1960, corroborates this data for the Episcopal clergy. It reported that one out of eight priests does not believe in the virgin birth. A spokesman for the church defended this finding as follows: "Disbelief in the virgin birth is not likely to get a

priest excommunicated today," he said, "even if he confesses it publicly. A great many Anglicans do not believe in the biological meaning of the virgin birth, but [they do believe] in the theological
interpretation that the person of Christ was a result of divine action
or divine initiative."

In June, 1963, Canon John Pearce-Higgins of Southwark Cathedral
created a sensation during his installation ceremony when he ob-
jected to having to give his assent to the Thirty-nine Articles in
which the Anglican creed is declared. "The Articles are a theological
fossil embedded in the Constitution of the Church of England,"
said the canon. Less than two months later, he set the Modern
Churchman's Conference in Cambridge on edge when he attacked
the status of the Bible as the word of God. "The theological professors cannot help asking themselves," he declared with obvious relish,
"what evidence they have that the Bible is any more or less the
word of God than any of the other ancient holy books of the world.
. . . The Bible is only one among the holy books of the world . . .
Christian scholars must state fearlessly that there is much in the
Bible that if taken literally is just plain wrong. . . . St. Paul was completely wrong in his idea of a Second Coming and the sudden
transformation of the bodies of the still living into etheric or spirit
bodies."

What this means was indicated by the comment of another spokesman for the church who said that freedom of belief prevailed in the
Episcopal Church so long as "the central belief of the church, Jesus
Christ is God and Man," was not under attack. "It is not impossible
to believe in the divinity of Jesus and disbelieve in the virgin birth,"
he said. Another took the position that the virgin birth was "theological" not "physical."

For the average layman, unaccustomed to theological subtleties,
that is another way of saying that the event designated by the doctrine never took place, which in its turn is, for the average layman,
a denial of the doctrine itself, a doctrine in which minister and
people declare their belief as they recite the Apostles' Creed together each Sunday morning. And this is by no means an Anglican
phenomenon. Increasingly today belief in the virgin birth is being
given up by Protestant leaders. "We would have to look a long
time," remarked one of them recently, "to find a Protestant congre-

gation that cared one way or the other whether or not its minister believed in the virgin birth."

In support of these observations, the director of the Rockefeller Brothers Theological Fellowship Program reported in 1955 his startling conclusion that many young men who have considered the ministry as a career, turn aside because of what they have observed in the churches and in the clergy that serve them. "I have been persuaded reluctantly," wrote Robert Rankin, "that some of our fine young people do not respond to the vocation [of the ministry] because they believe they see hypocrisy, arrogance and incompetence in the pulpit. Worst of all, some are under the impression that such characteristics are essential for success in the ministry."

In 1947 the Committee of Evangelism of the Chicago Congregational Association sent questionnaires to fifty Congregational ministers in regard to their beliefs. The results diverged widely from the beliefs of Congregationalists as stated in books and manuals written by Congregational clergymen. Answers to the questionnaire revealed that of the fifty ministers polled, two did not believe that Christ ever lived on earth. Twelve considered the Crucifixion a "noble example"; only twenty-three believed that it was "Divine redemption for sinful men." Eight denied the doctrine of original sin; thirty decided that there was "a tendency toward evil in human beings." Seven did not believe in the Resurrection, but half the ministers considered Jesus a "necessary mediator between God and man." Only eight of the fifty held the Bible authoritative in matters of faith, rather than merely a guide. Thirty-five counted the church as indispensable; thirteen rated it "helpful." These were not the views of old men, long in the ministry, who have not kept up on the latest theological developments, but of a wide cross section.

What might be called the blockbuster in this area came in 1961 when *Redbook* magazine published a survey of the beliefs of students for the ministry. It was made by a public opinion research firm of unquestioned reputation. The sampling of opinion was scientific. Researchers talked with over a hundred students in eight different theological schools. Some results: "Only 44% believe in the virgin birth of Christ. Only 29% believe there is a real heaven and hell. Only 46% believe that Jesus ascended physically whole into heaven after his crucifixion. 89% answered yes to the question, 'Do you believe in the divinity of Jesus?' A number, however, wanted to define the word 'divinity' to suit themselves."

Although each of these doctrines is derived from explicit Bible texts, many of the students said that "a major failure of today's churches is the failure to promote Bible study." Ninety-six per cent of the students saw no danger to religion from psychiatry. Again, apparently they were unaware that psychiatry proceeds from a set of assumptions entirely different from orthodox Christianity.

Of course, there was a loud outcry from the more conservative Protestants upon the publication of the *Redbook* article, so great in fact, that the magazine was forced to publish a sequel containing a number of letters of rebuttal. But when it was all over, whoever desired it had before him yet more extensive evidence of the widening distance between the official faith of the churches and the beliefs which actually are held by deeply religious men and women.

Again, let me illustrate by recounting in some detail a case known to me at first hand. A young minister, conducting a catechism class for those who were to join his church, found himself teaching: "We believe that God, on the sole ground of the perfect obedience and sacrifice of Christ, pardons those who by faith receive Him as their Savior and Lord." He had long known this particular statement by heart. But now suddenly he found he did not believe it. Eventually he resigned from the church and left the ministry of that denomination. Reporting later on the reasons for his resignation and subsequent suspension from his church, he wrote: "When it came time to discuss with the class what the Doctrine says is the sole ground of salvation, I realized it had lost all meaning whatsoever."

It is well known that such feelings commonly occur among the clergy. What is not so well known is how these problems are resolved. Some insight into this particular matter is gained through the following letter which the minister in question received from an elderly colleague at the time of his resignation. It read:

Dear Mr. _____:

My first thought on reading your two letters is one of regret over the step you have taken and I wish that you had written me sooner. I could at least have given you a glimpse into my own life and ministry in which my departures from the formal doctrines of the Church have been much more radical than yours appear to be. Yet I have had a very happy and on the whole, successful ministry.

First of all, when I was licensed to preach and afterwards ordained, I paid no attention at all to the questions that were put to me. These questions and the whole body of doctrine which they represent are based on what is called Theology, but Theology became obsolete at least four hundred years ago, but certain official persons, especially in colleges, do not seem to be aware of its decease. But surely the life of mankind is a large enough phenomenon, large enough and rich enough to provide us with aspects of it for our discourses Sunday after Sunday.

I have not used the word "God" nor the word "Jesus Christ" in the pulpit for fifty years, both of these being theological terms and therefore, meaningless. I have both at my own university and at another, given addresses in harmony with that which I am now stating to you, and while there has been some shaking of heads among the weaker brethren, I have gone my own way unmolested. . . .

All this I am mentioning to you, not as if I were exhibiting my own wares, but to show you how it is possible to live one's life as a minister with utter indifference . . . for those who walk in darkness or try to sit on two stools at one time. Though I have some dear friends who are as orthodox as John Knox or John Calvin, as for the "average man" of whom you speak, this is what I notice; namely, that he is more enlightened than he knows he is. The minister in the pulpit must speak, but the people in the pews remain silent. It is only when they are given an opportunity of expressing themselves that they fall back into the language of the pulpit. They have not found any other kind of utterance, but leave them alone and you will find that they have grown away from all the orthodoxy of the past. They no longer read the Bible, nor at their clubs and in other meeting places do they pay any attention to the rubbish they hear on Sundays. And as for their relationship with the minister, all they want is a pleasant, good-natured person who can make or take a joke. But now, what else can I write to you? If you were a young person at the stage of choosing your profession, I would not advise you to enter the ministry, but as you made this choice now a good long time ago, and as the Church, though in a dying condition, is still living, I do advise you to withdraw your resignation and take your place in the pulpit and in the hearts of your people.

At any rate, write me again, and I shall do the same.

Occasionally, although not very often, we see in print a clear acknowledgment of the gulf between the official beliefs of the clergy and those they really hold. An editorial in the 1957 Christmas issue of a widely read religious periodical begins with these words: "By now it is a theological commonplace that Christians will sing creeds and declarations that they will not say. They will make confessions with a tune that they would not dream of making in plain speech.

Never in the Christian year is this double standard so eagerly, even flagrantly evoked as at Christmas. Then, in carol or hymn, we happily chant all the lovely poetry and legend of the occasion, agreeing at the top of our lungs to statements that in soberer discourse we would at least want to discuss before affirming."

The author of those words was right. But in his resolution of the problem he showed little understanding of the average churchgoer. Theological subtleties, whereby the old words are given new meanings, are not for him, either by temperament or by training. If he does not believe in the virgin birth any longer, he would like to stop declaring each week on Sunday morning that he does. He is not sure what is asked of him when it is suggested that what he no longer believes is still true in a "theological" sense. And so his disbelief increases generally. So the faith of our fathers fades and unless a new one comes to take its place, we begin to get along as best we can without any.

3. HERESY TRIALS

In the year 1235 Pope Gregory IX officially established the Holy Office known popularly as the Inquisition. In that year, he appointed permanent delegate-judges in local communities, whose task it was to search out heresy wherever it might lurk within their jurisdiction. The thoroughness with which these papal judges did their work and the human agony that accompanied it bear testimony to the standards by which the Middle Ages lived and the determination of the church to maintain its position of supremacy. Torture was added in 1252 as a means of extracting confessions from the recalcitrant, and in the same year, it was decreed that officials of the state whose task it was to carry out the judgments of the church were to be excommunicated if they did not burn at the stake those whom the papal judges condemned and handed over to them for punishment.

Modern psychology may explain this sadistic vendetta as it will, but to students of the role of belief in religion and the development of the church as an institution in society its meaning is clear. The Inquisition was a device to which the church was forced to resort in an attempt to maintain the position of supremacy it had achieved in ancient times and in the Middle Ages. It was one of the means by which the church sought to bring the "medieval reformation" to a stop. The church had won its position of supremacy through the doctrine that it was God's instrument of salvation on earth. The place of the church in medieval society rested upon the universal acceptance of that teaching. The heretic accordingly, who arrogated to himself the right to challenge a part of that teaching was always a threat to the power and prestige of the church. The Inquisition was designed to maintain an outward pattern of uniformity with regard to the church's role and function. Pope Innocent III stated the position of the church exactly when he said that since "the civil law punishes traitors . . . all the more should we excommunicate and confiscate the property of those who are traitors to the faith of Jesus Christ." Heresy was, in the literal sense, treason to the church, for it threatened the position of the church more than treason threatened the state.

The thoroughness with which the officers of the Inquisition went about their work, and the terrifying methods they employed, stayed the rising tide of independent expression for nearly three hundred years. But it did not stay the rising tide of independent thought in Europe, for it could not unless it had reduced all but the most loyal churchmen to ignorance. While the public expression of heresy virtually disappeared, its private expression mounted until it burst forth as a flood in the Protestant Reformation. Despite the continued use of the Inquisition by Rome, and the extreme restrictive measures of most of the Protestants, heresy was never contained again, as the proliferation of Protestant sects that followed the Reformation clearly indicates.

The cry of heresy has not been heard from Rome for a long time, but now we are beginning to hear it among the Protestants. While merger after merger takes place among the various denominations, and the ecumenical movement gains strength, heresy trials have appeared among the Presbyterians and Lutherans. These trials are at the moment few and far between. They may portend a trend. More probably they represent an ecclesiastical aberration. But what is significant about them is the fact that they have occurred at all. They represent, as did the Inquisition long before, an attempt to enforce doctrinal conformity upon those whom argument can no longer persuade. They offer further evidence of the increasing gap between the creeds of the churches and the beliefs of men. The sudden re-appearance of heresy trials is perhaps the best evidence we have of the fact that the gap exists and why.

To illustrate, in 1952 Orange Presbytery of North Carolina appointed a Judicial Commission empowered "to investigate the situation in the Presbyterian Church of Chapel Hill." In November the Commission asked the minister of the church, Rev. Charles M. Jones, to resign his pastorate "for the welfare of the Church." The legal maneuvers that followed are too complicated to trace here. In sum, the Commission removed Jones from his pastorate in February, 1953, over the vehement protest of the minister and his church. An appeal to the General Assembly sustained the decision. In the end Jones asked leave to withdraw from the Presbyterian Church rather than stir up the row that was sure to follow if he and his church pressed their case against the Presbytery.

What kind of man was it the Presbyterians felt should resign his post "as soon as possible for the good of the Church." The Commission wrote, with admirable honesty: "The Pastor of this Church is deeply loved by the vast majority of the active officers and members. There are those who frankly consider him an embodiment of Jesus." The report continues with supporting evidence for this remarkable appraisal. "There are those who have known the comfort of his presence in trouble or sickness; those who have had mental and spiritual problems solved under his pastoral ministry. People in trouble have been taken into his home. People who needed help have found it in him. He has been a fearless champion of the ideal of brotherhood. . . . He presents a face to the world which is respected by a great many outside his immediate congregation. Many indicate that, in their opinion, he is 'the finest Christian in the community.' . . . His sermons have been variously described as the soul of the Church's spiritual life, as 'seminars in religious experience,' and as 'challenges to individual thinking.' . . . A great many of his hearers feel that he comes to grips with spiritual problems in their own experience and helps them find a way out."

The foregoing would seem to be a description of all that a minister might aspire to be and few would expect to achieve. What brought about the demand that he resign his post "for the good of the Church" sustained after an appeal to the national governing body of the church? The Commission, a model of clarity and honor in stating both its own views and those of Jones, said it was Jones' philosophy of religion that was objectionable. "This philosophy might be variously expressed," the Commission said, and gave as an example: "that being a Christian is more important than being a Presbyterian."

The Commission went on to condemn Jones for his belief "that 'religion' is in some sense prior to and independent of 'dogma' or 'doctrine.' This philosophy," said the Commission, "permits a church to embrace every shade of theological opinion and forbids it to dictate in any way to the convictions of its members, for each has an equal right to be heard. . . . In conclusion, the Commission does not feel that the Pastor, the officers of this Church or the members . . . have always been true to the Record of God's Revelation, as it is interpreted in our denominational Standards. We realize the seriousness of the charge, but it is simply a reflection of the seriousness with which we view the discrepancies in faith and polity that we have found."

In all the material that follows we shall not find a better statement of the issue between the fourth faith and the other three. Orange Presbytery felt that "discrepancies in faith and polity" were of such seriousness as to require the resignation of a minister considered by those who knew him to be "an embodiment of Jesus." The General Assembly did not see fit to question this decision. And so a comforter of the suffering, a helper of the helpless, a fearless champion of the ideal of brotherhood, the finest Christian in the community and the soul of the church's spiritual life, was asked to step down from his pastorate, because Christianity deals with Revelation and not with man's search for truth," said the Commission. "Religious doctrines—the Truth about God—are given not found." The "given" was, in the eyes of the Commission, what the Presbyterian Church said it was. And so, while the word "heresy" does not appear in the record, a godly man was in our generation, required to give up his charge because his beliefs did not appear to Orange Presbytery to conform to its understanding of God's revelation to man.

Unfortunately, the case of Rev. Charles M. Jones does not stand alone. The supremacy of traditional doctrines over the personal religious qualities and the personal religious commitment of an individual has been asserted in a number of cases. It is as old as the idea of heresy itself. In fact, from the earliest times, one of the most continually recurring characteristics of the heretic has been the elevated character of his religious life and thought. From the classic controversy between Pelagius and St. Augustine to the present day, personal virtue and high spiritual commitment have marked the heretic: "It was not an uncommon thing," observed Rufus Jones, the great Quaker mystic, "for persons in the twelfth century to be suspected of heresy when they were discovered to be living lives of extraordinary purity and simplicity."

Another contemporary trial for heresy occurred in 1955 when Pastor George P. Crist, a minister of the United Lutheran Church of Durham, Wisconsin, was found guilty of "doctrinal deviation" and was suspended. It was charged that he had taught "doctrines, opinions and surmises" in conflict with the Lutheran synod's constitution to which all its pastors must subscribe. "He has abandoned the fundamental principles of scriptural interpretation," it was charged. "He holds the doctrine of the virgin birth to be not significant, he denies the physical resurrection of Jesus; he has taught from the pulpit an interpretation different from the Lutheran doctrine of the real presence in the Lord's Supper; he does not teach or believe in the doctrinal of baptismal regeneration; he denies the 'actuality and historicity of the recorded miracles of our Lord in the realm of nature,' as well as the transfiguration and ascension of Jesus; he denies the efficacy of intercessory prayer and the value of direct address to Jesus, who he teaches does not hear prayer, and he holds that prayer possesses only that spiritual force which encourages the petitioner to help himself or be of active service to others."

Such were the conclusions reached by a committee set up to investigate the orthodoxy of Pastor Crist after a layman in his congregation had made the charge of heresy to synodical authorities. They found him guilty, but he replied: "I am innocent. A literal interpretation of Scripture and a belief in traditional church dogma are not vital to the Christian faith. Dogma should be interpreted flexibly and freely."

The proceedings were, however, supported by most of the church leaders. "It is healthy for the whole church to go on record that it will not tolerate teachings in conflict with the faith it officially professes," declared the minister appointed to serve as prosecutor at the trial, and no one rose to challenge what he said.

The case aroused a storm of controversy inside and outside the United Lutheran Church. The question was theological literalism. There was no suggestion that Crist was not otherwise fit for the ministry. How far might a man be permitted to move in his interpretation of Scripture and of the doctrines officially accepted by his church? The Northwest Synod replied emphatically, not at all. The Lutheran Church is a confessional church, the argument ran. A man may believe what he likes, but as a Lutheran, he must profess what his church professes. He is not free to offer his own interpretation of what Scripture and dogma are to be taken to mean. Two other cases which came up at the same time further underscored the anxiety in the Northwest Synod over independent thinking among its clergy. A second minister accused of heresy at the same time, Rev. John Gerberding of Menomonee Falls, Wisconsin, was acquitted, but some of his fellow ministers set up such a cry that for a time a new trial seemed inevitable. Apparently, they proposed to keep trying him until he was found guilty, observers said.

To settle the matter a special convention of the English Evangelical Lutheran Synod of the Northwest was held in January, 1956. By now a third member, Rev. Victor Wrigley, had been tried for heresy by the Synod. Like Crist, he too had been found guilty. The convention deposed and defrocked Crist, with but three negative votes as against 99 lay and 155 clerical votes in favor of his condemnation. It was the same with Wrigley except that there were a few more votes in the negative. Gerberding's acquittal, on the other hand, was sustained. The convention sensed the fact that a group of ministers, having determined in their own minds that he was guilty, proposed to pursue the matter until he was officially censured. The convention apparently would have none of it and cleared him.

In 1960 in another equally well-publicized case a Presbyterian minister, Rev. Harold J. Quigley of Haverstraw, New York, was removed as pastor of his church. Again the charge was heresy, but in this case it was the minister himself who brought the matter to the attention of his ecclesiastical superiors. Of his own accord Quigley went before the Presbytery of Hudson and told them he was "in conflict with the dogma of the the church." He could no longer accept the Bible as the word of God or Jesus as a divine being, he said. The presbytery thereupon voted 46 to 7 to divest him of office and remove his name from the roll of the church.

"Under the circumstances, there was nothing else we felt we could do," the clerk of the presbytery said. But Quigley felt he should have been allowed to remain as pastor. In other words, he boldly declared his heresy and with equal forthrightness declared his belief that heresy is unimportant, at least heresy of the sort he embraced. "The church is not just a theological community," he said. "It should be concerned more with social betterment and less with theological doctrine."

Another case in the Presbyterian Church which has nothing to do with heresy shows the increasing readiness on the part of Protestants to resort to ecclesiastical trial courts and to judge their proceedings by the standards of civil law. In the case of Rev. Maurice McCrackin, minister of West Cincinnati-St. Barnabas Church in Ohio, which had to do with pacifism and civil disobedience, the Presbytery of Cincinnati voted to bring McCrackin to trial on the following charges: "(1) The Rev. Maurice McCrackin has resisted the ordinances of God, in that upon pretense of Christian liberty he has opposed the civil lawful power, and the lawful exercise of it. . . . (2) He has published erroneous opinions and maintained practices which are destructive to the external peace and order which Christ hath established in the Church. . . . (3) He has failed to obey the lawful commands and to be subject to the authority of civil magistrates. [All these actions are] contrary to the Constitution of the United Presbyterian Church, U.S.A."

McCrackin was found guilty September 15, 1960, and appealed, as was his right according to the procedures of the Presbyterian Church, to the permanent judicial commission of the United Presbyterian U.S.A., Synod of Ohio. A year later that synod reversed the decision of the "lower court" and remanded the case for "retrial." Particularly noticeable is the judicial language used throughout. Said the judicial commission: "Two specifications, presented in evidence of the charge of publishing opinions destructive to the peace of the church, were inadequate to sustain it in that they provided neither witnesses nor other evidence whereby the prosecution could show how or to what extent the peace of the church was in fact threatened with destruction as charged. . . . He was found guilty not because the specifications presented established his guilt, but because he had not proved himself innocent."

Letters to the *Christian Century* continued the debate afterward in the concepts of Anglo-Saxon jurisprudence. Said one: "If the Mc-Crackin appeal costs us one of our greatest ministers, it may well bring home the need for United Presbyterian judicial reform. The truth is that the constitution of the Presbyterian Church still permits star chamber proceedings in our courts. Further, in civil courts selection of juries is a sacred right which was obviously denied Mc-Crackin by his presbytery. The convicting commission was selected by those who brought the matter to trial. In any civil court the veniremen would have been asked such questions as these: Do you know any reason why you cannot sit as a fair and impartial juryman? If you find for the defendant will that tend to embarrass you in your church? Do you now have an opinion on this case?"

Here as in the other sections of this chapter, the temptation is great to continue to pile up examples of the point we are making. But it is unnecessary. The movement toward heresy hunting, and the attempt to introduce judicial procedures into Protestant denominational structures, shows no sign of abating. And while it is a concomitant of the growing division between official dogma and personal belief, it is not a necessary part of it. The charges of heresy continue to mount as the clergy take greater and greater liberties to "interpret" Scripture and dogma. Today we hear an increasing demand for adherence to traditional theological principles. For example, Martin Marty, a Protestant scholar, has attempted to identify the fourth American faith because he is alarmed at the lack of concern for theological differences that marks the contemporary American mood. After devoting a book to an attack upon religion-in-general as opposed to particular confessions of faith, he admits that what he has argued for so vehemently implies the divisiveness of competing sects, and the assumption of dogmatic truth on the part of each. "Will there not be new holy wars," he asks, "if we begin once again to contend for the faith not because we believe it to be useful, but because we believe it to be true?" The record of Christian history certainly gives us reason for uneasiness on this score. In past centuries Christians have not hesitated to slaughter one another in defense of what they believed to be the one true faith. Dr. Marty believes there are certain safeguards against the "new holy wars" he predicts. But the impact of his argument savors more of Cardinal Newman who once said, "I do not shrink from uttering my conviction that it would be a gain to the world were it vastly more superstitious, more bigoted, more gloomy, more fierce in its religion than it now shows itself to be."

Church historians observed long ago that the cry of heresy and the demand for heresy trials make their appearance not in the great ages of faith, but in the ages when the faith is declining, when it no longer establishes itself in the minds of men by its own intrinsic power to persuade, but must be shored up on the outside by artificial means. The new cry of heresy in our land, coupled with the new effort to enforce doctrinal conformity, is perhaps the best evidence we have that the faith of our fathers no longer serves us as it once served them.

4. THE ECUMENICAL MOVEMENT

It might not be supposed that the ecumenical movement would provide evidence of the increasing disbelief that besets contemporary religion. Yet the problems attendant upon the drawing together of the Protestant churches of the United States with the National Council of Churches and the churches of the world into the World Council of Churches, are largely of this sort. The ecumenical movement is a denial of denominational particularism. Implicit within it is a rejection of the claims of the several member communions with regard to their own teachings. In any true ecumenical movement no mutually exclusive claims are possible. This means a very real dilemma for the member churches in their relationship with one another. By the degree to which they emphasize the eternal rightness of their own separate teachings, just by that much do they rob the ecumenical movement of any real vitality. And yet, by the degree to which the member churches participate in an inter-church movement based upon a common faith, just by that much do they deny, overtly or by implication, the eternal truth of their own church teachings, to which heretofore they had always held.

Many men have addressed themselves to this problem. Professor Robert L. Calhoun of Yale University, in the opening address of the World Council of Churches held at Evanston, Illinois, in 1954, said: "Like fellow Christians in every country and in every part of the church, we are apt to regard our own understanding of the gospel as, at least in principle, both correct, and sufficient." But, he went on, "it will not *do* to claim for any particular doctrinal tradition or current habit the infallibility of God. We are all fellow servants, none of us entitled to lord it over the rest."

Calhoun's meaning is all too plain. Hidden beneath his gracious words is the clear implication that most of the churches of Christendom tend to claim that their particular doctrinal position is correct. Thus everyone who does not agree is in error. Uncounted lesser men, the rank and file of the clergy and laity in all denominations, express themselves in a similar vein. Cried one author passionately: "Our agreements are all but destroyed by our underlying disagreements. They amount to completely different views of faith." Like many another ecumenicist, he thinks that confessional differences regarding God and Christ are not important. "What holds us back?" he asks, and answers his own question. His list of the obstacles to the ecumenical movement is impressive. He asks: "Is the Kingdom of God inside the church or elsewhere? Is the church visible or invisible? What are the requirements and rules for baptism and profession of faith? What about the sacraments: are they necessary to salvation? How many? Seven? Two? None? When should baptism come? early? late? Is Christ actually present in the Eucharist? When are the sacraments valid and when invalid? Who has the authority to say? In regard to the ministry: when is ordination valid? how? by whom? what kind of laying on of hands? congregational witness?" and so on.

Said another: "Only ministers, ecclesiastical authorities, and a few leading laymen cling to the traditions of denominationalism. The average churchmember sees no appreciable difference between churches. . . . Protestants of America are becoming one people regardless of denominational distinctions. On the level of the rank and file of our churches, we have a practical church unity in American Protestantism."

Yet another attacked the problem of doctrinal differences between the denominations by pointing to the doctrinal differences that prevail within each of the denominations.

"Do all Episcopalians see alike on apostolic succession," he asked, "or the sacraments, or the ministry? Manifestly, no. . . . do all Presbyterians see alike on the Westminster Confession? By no means. . . . do all Baptists and Disciples see alike on immersion baptism? Far from it."

Henry P. Van Dusen, with mounting impatience at the repetition of ecumenical cant by those who go on insisting upon denominational differences, said this practice was "our gravest heresy." To dramatize his point, he called for "a moratorium on the use of the mighty 'Prayer for the unity of Christ's Church.' Then," he said, "we might . . . recognize how unreal is our present reiteration, with such meagre effort to do anything . . . about these 'unhappy divisions,' which we so readily, so glibly bewail."

Most of these differences have successfully been ignored so far, even if the result has been to rob the ecumenical movement of any great power or effectiveness. But the issue has had to be met in regard to the Eastern Orthodox Church which takes a much more narrowly doctrinal position than most Protestant churches. The problem was stated cogently by Dr. John Baillie, a president of the World Council, when he reported to the Evanston meeting the dissent of the Eastern Orthodox to the report on Faith and Order as submitted to the Conference. Said Baillie: "We have long understood that we can only keep the Orthodox within the World Council if we allow them to express their dissent on this point. They want to stay in, and we want to keep them in. They agree with us in so much that we have to say but they must be allowed to express their dissent on certain points. It is on these terms that they are in and we are happy to have them on these terms until we can present a more united front."

But if the doctrines which now divide the Protestant denominations from one another are to be given up or reduced to a secondary status in the interest of church unity, what meaning can they be said to have had heretofore? What status can any of them be said to have now? Can any and all of them be washed out in an attempt to achieve some larger unity? Some aspect of the "basis formula" of the ecumenical movement—the Lordship of Christ—answers the first of these questions. Church unity extends to those who will accept *that* doctrine. But the second question remains unanswered. The ecumenical movement is virtually silent on the status of other credal matters. Few have remarked upon the threat to credal Christianity lurking in ecumenicity. But to the untutored layman, the suggestion that he might give up certain doctrines his church had taught him to accept suggests that other doctrines his church still wants him to keep may also be given up. What of them?

For most Protestants these considerations become real, not in the ecumenical movement in the large, but in the combining of the denomination to which they happen to belong with some other in the widespread merger pattern now in process in the United States. In working out such unions, and there have been many of them, worshipers have been asked to give up doctrines they had once been asked to cherish. In the talks begun among the Episcopalians, Presbyterians, Methodists, and the United Church of Christ the operation of this principle is clear. On the doctrine of apostolic succession, and attendant beliefs about the authority of the church and its clergy, there are sharp differences of opinion. Had the merger been effected, this central doctrine would have to be adopted as part of the official teaching of the church or it would have to be abandoned. Whichever course was chosen, those who believe in it would find themselves having to give it up, or those who reject it would find themselves having to adopt it. In either case, the result could only be to teach believing Christians that doctrines they once looked upon as eternally true because divinely set forth are, in fact, man-made formulas to be accepted or rejected by majority vote.

Church leaders may claim, as they surely will, that whatever decision is reached comes through the inspiration, if not the direct intervention, of the Holy Spirit. But those who engage at first hand in the struggle that precedes the vote will not be likely to give the Holy Spirit undue credit for the part he plays in the final outcome. Sound judgment will also play its part in the outcome, but the end result of such a process can only be skepticism or outright unbelief. If one set of doctrines can be arrived at in that fashion, cannot all? And cannot all, then, be equally called in question?

In Britain the Annunciationists, an Anglo-Catholic group in the Church of England, have seen this issue clearly. They opposed the granting of intercommunion to the Church of South India in 1955 because, as a united church, it included Methodists, Presbyterians, Reformed, and others, who had not been ordained in accordance

with Anglican practices. "Such a church," said one of the Annunciationists, "cannot be called a Christian church in any hitherto definable sense of the term. . . . after today, it will be impossible to be
certain that any ordination in the Church of England is valid. This is
not just another crisis. It is a unique happening which is bound to
have historical consequences."

Despite the Annunciationists' objection, the union of the churches
of South India was continued and has proved successful. They might
have seen the weakness in their argument, had they come across a
pamphlet issued by another group of Anglican clergymen but two
years before. There the shoe was on the other foot, for in the earlier
pamphlet, English churchmen were defending themselves against
attacks upon their position expressed or implied by the churchmen
of Rome. The line of argument in both cases was virtually the same
—the church that departs from the standards of the main body is no
church at all.

The points considered in the pamphlet are worth examining in
some detail for they concern the central issue in any attempt of the
churches to join forces with one another. The pamphlet begins by
objecting to Roman Catholic exclusiveness. For example, when converts are admitted to the Roman Church, they are rebaptized. This
means, says the pamphlet, that any Anglican convert to Catholicism,
when he has been baptized, "has publicly declared that the Anglican
Bishop who confirmed him was an imposter, that the priest who baptized him, taught him the catechism, and gave him his communion
was cheating him, that he has never before received absolution,
never before received the sacrament of the Lord's Body and Blood,
never before received the gift of the Holy Spirit by the laying on of
hands. Is this not the sin against the Holy Ghost—to say that what is
of the Holy Spirit is not of the Holy Spirit?"

Apparently the Anglicans quite failed to see that when they themselves rebaptize Christians who enter the Church of England from
what they call the "nonconformist sects," they require the same
repudiation of his former church by the convert as does Rome. They
seem not to realize that the leaders of a church whose members are
rebaptized by the Church of England can feel quite as incensed at
their effrontery as do they at the effrontery of Rome in rebaptizing
Anglicans.

The Anglicans object to the Roman Catholic attitude toward their clergy. They are not true priests, says Rome. Yes they are, says the Church of England. The argument is lengthy and need not be reviewed here. But again it applies quite as well to the relationship between the Anglican and the nonconformist sects. The Anglican attitude toward nonconformist ministers corresponds exactly to the Roman position in regard to the Anglican clergy.

The pamphlet continues with arguments about what is and what is not the true church. Again the issue is the same as that between the Anglicans and sectarians. The Anglicans think Rome does not give the people a sufficient part in the government of the church. The sectarians say the same of the government of the Church of England. The pamphlet accuses Rome of duplicity because it officially opposes remarriage after divorce, yet permits remarriage in practice by means of various devices. The same argument, of course, applies to the Church of England. It forbids its clergy to marry divorced persons. Yet if divorced communicants wish to remarry, it sends them to a nonconformist minister to perform the ceremony, and then welcomes them back into the church again. In fact, some of its prominent clergymen have themselves been divorced and have subsequently remarried.

We could go on citing claims and counterclaims of those who would set the teaching of their churches over against all others. The idea of the one true church will not down. Yet whoever makes such a claim on behalf of his church automatically reduces all other churches to an inferior status. Perhaps some of the clergy are persuaded by such arrogation of authority and importance to their own church, but few laymen are. The end result is to call all doctrines in question. In short, the end result is not the belief that is sought, but its opposite—unbelief. And in the vacuum of unbelief that results the ground is laid for the emergence of a new faith.

Meanwhile, the ecumenical movement continues to grow in strength and in popular appeal. The overtures toward Protestantism, made by Pope John XXIII, elicited an astonishingly warm response in all quarters. The merging of Protestant denominations continues, for the hunger for Christian unity lies very deep. But the ecumenical movement is symptomatic also of an increasing impatience with doctrinal differences, which in turn is a tacit if not overt admission that they are not so important as they were once supposed to be.

CHAPTER II

The Fourth Faith

How are we to account for the pervasive disbelief revealed by successive surveys, heresy trials, and the uniting of the churches with one another? Disbelief is not new with us. The twentieth century from the beginning has been marked by doubt and skepticism. So were the nineteenth and the eighteenth centuries, although to a lesser degree. Unbelief was a problem among the ancients, as well, and in the Middle Ages, the so-called "age of faith," unbelief or wrong belief was considered to be one of the gravest problems faced by Western culture.

The great councils of the ancient church, Nicaea, Chalcedon, and the rest, did not solve the problem of unbelief or wrong belief for the Greco-Roman world, nor did the Inquisition, the Protestant Reformation, or any of the more recent revolts against the church solve the problem for later ages. Why? It is our purpose here to explore the historical aspects of this question, in order that we may better understand and deal with it in its contemporary form. One of the causes, surely, is the introduction into Western culture of what we know as the scientific method of thought. We shall attempt to explain and measure its impact upon traditional religious beliefs and to show the role it has played in bringing about the contemporary loss of faith we have just surveyed.

We shall then turn our attention to a new faith form which has appeared in our time in answer to the doubt and disbelief that characterizes our age, the so-called fourth faith. Here we shall attempt an appraisal of the emerging multiple faith pattern of American culture and the place of the new fourth faith within it.

1. THE COPERNICAN REVOLUTION AND THE CHURCH

The publication of Nicolaus Copernicus' theory of the revolution of the planets around the sun, together with Galileo Galilei's invention of the telescope and his polemical writings, mark a fundamental turning point in the history of Western thought. Upon this point students of the question are now generally agreed. If then we are to pick a date by which to mark the beginning of the "warfare between science and religion," perhaps 1616, the year in which Galileo was brought before the Inquisition, would be the best choice we could make. But the Holy Office of the Curia Romana, as we now know, often achieved a result opposite to that which was intended. Subjected to the appalling methods of producing pain in the human body devised by the Inquisition, people said what they were wanted to say in order that their torment might cease. Designed as an instrument for the discovery of truth, it became in fact a device by which truth was suppressed and outward conformity took its place.

The recantation of Galileo before the Holy Office might have seemed like the end of a great forward step in human thought. Instead, it marks a fundamental revolution in man's understanding of his world, for his forced denial only underscored the truth he had stated. Even the word "revolution" in its present meaning came out of that struggle. It was a part of the title of Copernicus' book *De Revolutionibus Orbis Coelestum*. There it meant literally to "revolve." But the word entered the languages of the West from its place in the title of Copernicus' monumental study because what he said was recognized at the time as "revolutionary" in our sense of the word. Alexandre Koyré remarked: "I have been forced to recognize, as many others have before me, that during this period human, or at least European, minds underwent a deep revolution which changed the very framework and patterns of our thinking and of which modern science and modern philosophy are, at the same time, the root and the fruit."

This revolution had two aspects. The first and most obvious is the rejection of the Ptolemaic system of astronomy. The second and less obvious is far more profound. The Copernican revolution established a new way of thinking. It established a new way of determining truth, the way of reason and experiment as against the older method of authority. Heretofore the searchers after truth consulted the recognized authorities in the field in which they wished to inquire. After the scientific revolution the searcher after truth, having consulted the authorities, turned to the world about him and examined that. In the process he also re-examined the reasoning of the authorities to see whether it was sound. In short, the Copernican revolution established what we know today as the scientific method of inquiry, as against the older method of consulting the authorities.

The rejection of authority in favor of the method of critical reason and experiment, of close observation and measurement, was not entirely new with Copernicus. Abélard (1079-1142) had reasoned his way to many a heresy and Averroës (1126-1198), the Arab philosopher and mathematician, had set all Europe by the ears as a result of his independent thinking. A school of Averroists grew up at the University of Paris in the thirteenth century. The church repeatedly tried to forbid the reading of his works, but without success. W. E. H. Lecky described the influence of Averroës with characteristic, but not inaccurate, color: "Among the Mahometans the panic was so great, that the theologians pronounced logic and philosophy to be the two great enemies of their profession, and ordered all books on those dangerous subjects to be burnt. Among the Christians, St. Thomas Aquinas devoted his genius to the controversy; and, for two or three centuries, most of the great works in Christendom bore some marks of Averroës. M. Renan has collected some curious evidence from the Italian painters of the fourteenth century, of the prominence Averroës had assumed in the popular mind. The three principal figures in Orcagna's picture of Hell, in the Campo Santa at Pisa, are Mahomet, Antichrist, and Averroës."

In fact, the obscurity into which Averroës' work fell was due not so much to Christian anxiety as to that of his fellow Moslems. The study of Greek philosophy, specifically the study of Aristotle, had been growing apace in Islam during the eleventh and twelfth centuries. In its import it was no less contrary to the precepts of Mohammed, now crystallized in tradition, than to the dogma and authority of the Roman Catholic Church. Averroës had no wish to undermine the Islamic faith, however. On the contrary, he undertook to show how philosophy and religion might be reconciled to each other. This of course was precisely what Rome's philosophers were doing at the same time. But where their work was accepted and made a part of the official teaching of the church, the work of the Arab philosophers was rejected. With a sudden change in the political climate, coming late in his life, Averroës' writings fell out of use and disappeared in Islam. They have come down to us through Hebrew and sometimes Latin translations. Only in the present generation is the work of this independent spirit being made available to the reading public in English.

The method of inquiry rather than the reiteration of that which had been established by authority emerged as early as the sixth century B.C. when Thales and Anaximander, Anaximines and Anaxagoras, began speculating upon the nature of the world in contravention to the then prevailing views derived from the writings of Homer and Hesiod. It came to fruition with men like Socrates, Pythagoras, and Archimedes, and died out when Greek culture yielded to the political hegemony of Rome.

To what an extent the mood of independent thinking, and the method of observation, may have survived in the West after the collapse of Hellenic civilization, we cannot say. Of late years there has been an increasing interest in the effort to trace the tradition of independent thought from ancient times to the present. All the connecting links in the chain cannot be said to have been established as yet, however, perhaps because the men who were doing the independent thinking generally sought to avoid any conflict with the church.

Students of the history of thought, who have attempted to trace the mood of independency in the West, have been greatly handicapped by the fact that such thinking went underground, so to speak. Perhaps it disappeared altogether in the intellectual conformity enforced by the Church of Rome after it gained ascendancy in the Roman Empire and codified its teachings in the succession of councils beginning with Nicaea in A.D. 325. Where this spirit next emerges, as in the Averroist School at the University of Paris, we find its immediate antecedents very difficult to discern.

The policy of avoiding conflict with the teachings of the church marks the post-Reformation years as well as the earlier period. Copernicus (1473-1543) refrained from publishing his theories during his lifetime. His posthumous editor presented them as mere alternative speculations about the motions of the planets. The great French philosopher and mathematician, René Descartes (1596-1650), referred to the Copernican system as a "fable" or a new "hypothesis."

Those who followed Galileo, men like Kepler (1577-1630) and Tycho Brahe (1546-1601), were careful as Copernicus had been not to relate their discoveries to any of the teachings of the church, although it must have been as clear to them as to Copernicus that they were demolishing the entire Ptolemaic system upon which the metaphysical aspects of medieval theology rested. They were able to go safely about their work because few outside their own circle heard about their abstruse work and fewer still understood what it meant. Consequently, there was no need to disturb them. And there was the further practical fact that the astronomers were of great assistance to the churchmen and princes alike for they knew how to cast horoscopes for an age which devoutly believed in astrology. Because they were good scientists they, better than anyone, could plot the position of the planets. On the basis of the information they provided horoscopes were read. In those days few important decisions were made without attempting first to read the supposed decrees of the stars.

But the fundamental difference between the way of science and the way of the church could not long be suppressed or ignored. The real difficulty in the case of Galileo Galilei (1564-1642), for example, was not a reluctance on his part to cast his writings into language. This is precisely what he did in his *Dialogue*. Galileo's unstated but real life crime was the invention of the telescope. Through this novel instrument, the curious, the doubter, the inquirer, all alike might look and there see with their eyes corroboration for the theories Copernicus and Galileo had tactfully stated as theoretical possibilities.

The thought structure of the church, majestic, beautiful, symmetrical, and ancient, backed by gigantic civil and political power, rooted in centuries of tradition and conceded to have been divine in origin, was not lightly to be set aside. One after another, devout men who also saw the validity in the scientific method, sought to reconcile its increasingly impressive results with the ancient dogmas of the church. Blaise Pascal (1623-1662) tried to solve the problem by distinguishing between the things which reason knows and those which the heart can discern. In other words, he proposed an ultimate dualism. Pierre Bayle (1647-1706) applied the Cartesian method of doubt to religion itself. But he was by no means one of the great scientists. We come to Joseph Priestley (1733-1804) before we find an important scientist who explicitly concerns himself with the impact of science on theology. The battle was really joined at last when Voltaire and the deists demanded that the churches come to terms with the body of knowledge then accumulating in the secular world. As a result, the churches, Protestant and Catholic alike, were forced to reassess their teachings in the light of the rapidly accumulating scientific discoveries.

The method by which the church met the threat to its position has three facets. The first two were established in the course of what has come to be called "The Medieval Reformation," a great movement of independent thought that nearly engulfed the church almost half a millennium before the time of Luther. First, the medieval schoolmen elaborated further the traditional defenses of the faith worked out by the early church fathers. Second, they began forcibly to enjoin the expression of opinion contrary to the official position of the church, the movement that eventuated in the Inquisition. The third method by which the church sought to meet the scientific revolution appeared with the Renaissance and the Reformation. As the thinking of Copernicus, Galileo, and the rest was increasingly accepted by the leading minds of Europe, the churches, both Protestant and Catholic, began slowly and with obvious reluctance to modify doctrines which heretofore it had defended not only with the debater's eloquence and the theologian's pen, but also with the rack and the wheel, the dungeon, the sword, and the torch.

Increasingly, as the years went on and the methods of persuasion replaced the methods of coercion, the churches met the issue by yielding as much ground as they were forced to, while clinging doggedly to whatever they could. Whatever remained inaccessible to the new methods of thought and demonstration was declared to be true. The rest was said to be of secondary importance or to require new understanding. But the process did not enhance either the prestige or power of the churches. The history of religion in the West since the Renaissance and the Reformation is a melancholy review of the retreat of the churches from positions previously held. That retreat has been described many times by many writers. Alfred North Whitehead, one of the earliest to make the observation, summed it up incisively. "Through the work of the scientists," he wrote, "a series of novel situations have been produced for thought. Each such occasion has found the religious thinkers unprepared. Something which has been proclaimed to be vital, has finally, after struggle, distress and anathema, been modified and otherwise interpreted. The next generation of religious apologists then congratulates the religious world on the deeper insight which has been gained. The result of the continued repetition of this undignified retreat, during many generations, has at last almost entirely destroyed the intellectual authority of religious thinkers."

We have spoken of the first and most dramatic encounter between the old and the new methods of thinking—that in which the church condemned the writings of Copernicus and Galileo. All are now aware that the church has since retreated from the position it took at that time and this change of heart is now cited as an example of the church's ability to grow and adapt itself to new conditions. But the pattern of denial, retreat, and subsequent acknowledgment of error has not changed. Still today the church goes on yielding up territory it formerly claimed as its own, while asserting with redoubled emphasis that what it yet holds is its own and remains inviolate before the onslaughts of the enemy, as if the modern mind in its independency had chosen the church as its enemy and were working purposefully to destroy it. The churchmen seem not to be able to see that in the pursuit of truth in which the Western mind is engaged, the enemy is not the church but ignorance. The mistake is made because the church insists upon placing ancient ignorance athwart the path to understanding. Thus it makes itself the inevitable object of attack, for it identifies itself with ignorance, the enemy against which the pursuit of truth is forever on the march.

The battle that raged after the discovery of the Dead Sea Scrolls provides a contemporary example of this continuing conflict. Here was one of the greatest potential threats to official Christian doctrines that had occurred since the time of Copernicus. The Dead Sea Scrolls presented the sudden possibility that documentary proof of the falsity of certain Christian dogmas might come to light. When the Dead Sea Scrolls were dated to the first century B.C. and the first century A.D. and the close relationship between the Essene Community at Qumran and the first Christian church at Jerusalem became clear, it was evident that a document might turn up at any moment relating to Jesus of Nazareth. Such a document might well contain information contrary to some of the central doctrines of the church, possibly even that of the Incarnation itself. What then, it was asked.

The men of theology had a ready answer even though subsequent searching brought no such document to light and thus the answer has been rendered unnecessary. As in previous instances, the theologians retreated one step further from the position they had previously held. Having heretofore rested their faith on the historical accuracy of the Bible, "God's Word," the theologians now began to say that their faith was not in the events that the Bible recorded, but in the Christ whom the Bible revealed. They had long been moving to this position, under the impact of advancing studies in biblical criticism and archaeology as well as in natural science. The threat posed by the Scrolls helped to accelerate and clarify the statement of the new position. Christ was Lord, they said, because the Christian faith held this doctrine to be true, not because the New Testament said so. Nothing that had been and nothing that could be discovered at Qumran could affect that faith. Such a declaration would have been unthinkable but a generation before, when the events recorded in the New Testament were still held to have happened, and in some sense also, to be the basis of Christian faith.

At the present moment the retreat of theology before the advance of human knowledge expresses itself in the problems presented by the space age. Currently, for example, Christian theologians are being asked about the impact on their position of the possible discovery of life elsewhere in the universe. If God in Christ came to save man here on Earth, what of other men elsewhere? Did he go to other planets, there to be crucified also in order to save those beings? Heretofore it has been held that Christ is Lord and that salvation comes through him. There were no exceptions or qualifications to this statement. But the theologians, old hands now at retreating from previously held terrain while defending their ancient stronghold, do not lack for an answer to this new problem.

"If there should be conscious intelligent life among other planets," wrote one divine recently, "we are assured God has not left himself without a witness there. . . . How God, through the Eternal Son or Word, reveals himself on other planets we cannot know, at least at present.

> " 'God may have other words for other worlds,
> But for *this* world, the Word of God is Christ.' "

The possibility that there is life elsewhere in the universe poses no threat to the theology of this latter-day defender of the faith. The mind of man through its discoveries may turn the universe upside down and inside out, yet still his theological position will remain intact. He will follow what is by now a well-tested formula. As necessity may dictate, he will draw his circle ever more narrowly around him. Holding that the central principle of his faith is eternal truth, he will keep it, never doubting, while explaining away whatever discoveries may seem to challenge it. And this he will always be able to do since his faith is not anchored to anything that anyone will ever be able to refute.

The continual relinquishing of prior claims on the part of Christian theologians, the "undignified retreat" noted by Alfred North Whitehead, was described in detail by Andrew D. White in his *Warfare of Science with Theology*, which he published in 1896. The conflict, however, did not begin when White supposed. It began when the first doughty skeptic asked himself how he could be sure an alleged divine revelation that had taken place long ago could be verified. It began when our first primitive ancestor sought answers to his questions in the book of nature as well as from the wise men of his tribe. The contest was on when the first man asserted the perceptions of his mind and sense against a sacrosanct dogma of his culture.

At the heart of the Western tradition of independent thought lies the conviction that every alleged truth must be constantly re-examined. Its symbol is the question mark, not the period. J. Bronowski calls it "the tradition of dissent—a tradition of questioning what is traditional." Science is heresy, it has been said, and the greatest danger to science is that it, too, will become orthodox. This has already happened, although only on certain specific occasions. The case of Pasteur's rejection by the French Academy is well known. Less well known is the storm that broke out in the Royal Society of London when Sir Isaac Newton submitted the paper that described his reflecting telescope. His experiments were accurate and his conclusions indisputable. No one questioned either. But opposition was violent because the conclusions he had drawn were at variance with the prevailing scientific views.

During the four hundred years of its life, science's concept of itself has undergone a very considerable development. Formerly it thought of itself as a method by which data was gathered, measured, tested, catalogued, and finally interpreted so that its meaning could be understood. The test tube was its symbol. Now the scientist sees himself and his task in much more fundamental terms. A typical expression is that of James Bryant Conant. He describes Science as "that portion of accumulative knowledge in which new concepts are continually developing from experimentation and observation and lead to further experimentation and observation." Science makes its greatest discoveries by the rigid testing of its own concepts. This testing often reveals inadequacies or discrepancies in findings once thought to be satisfactory. As a result newer and better concepts, formulations, and descriptions have to be devised in order to include whatever new data rigid testing produces.

A fundamental premise of the rational or scientific approach is that today's "knowledge" will become tomorrow's error. The method of science is to re-examine not only its data, but the general principles by which all data are understood. Its conclusions remain tentative, subject to constant testing and constant reformulation. In the rational approach to life nothing is exempt, nothing sacrosanct, nothing queer. Everything, religion and all its revelations included, requires to be tested and tested again as man's knowledge and understanding increases.

To relate this mode of thinking to religion is not to fall into the religion of science. "Scientism," as it is often called, is based upon the scientific theories prevailing in a given age: deism in the eighteenth century, for example, based as it was upon the theories of Sir Isaac Newton; or the evolutionary religions of the late nineteenth century based upon the thought of Sir Charles Darwin. These pseudo-scientific religious philosophies passed as soon as science itself gave up the theoretical structure upon which they were based. No one now conceives of God as did the deists, and no one now sees the role of evolution as did Herbert Spencer. A later generation than ours will undoubtedly see in some of our religious thought a too great reliance on the concepts of Albert Einstein. Such "scientism" or the "religion of science" is in point of fact quite as unscientific as traditional religion, for like them it is dogmatic. It, too, believes that it *knows*. It holds dogmatically that all things can be understood in material terms and that there is nothing else.

It is of the essence of science that it does not know with finality and does not pretend so to know. Thomas Henry Huxley was not defining science when he coined the now common word "agnostic," but in doing so, he capsuled the scientific mood as neatly as anyone could do. "When I reached intellectual maturity," he wrote, "and began to ask myself whether I was an atheist, a theist, or a pantheist; a materialist or an idealist; a Christian or a free thinker; I found that the more I learned and reflected, the less ready was the answer; until, at last, I came to the conclusion that I had neither art nor part with any of these denominations, except the last. The one thing in which most of these people were agreed was the one thing in which I differed from them. They were quite sure they had attained a certain 'gnosis' [knowledge] and had, more or less successfully solved the problem of existence; while I was quite sure I had not, and had a pretty strong conviction that the problem was insolvable.

"So I took thought, and invented what I conceived to be the appropriate title of 'agnostic'. . . . I, too, had a tail like the other foxes."

An agnostic is neither a believer nor a disbeliever. He is distinguished by a third characteristic that is different from each of the other two. He rejects the idea of gnosis itself. He does not believe that there is any special body of knowledge which God has revealed to men. He reminds us that Christianity was born at a time when most men believed in such special knowledge, and that it was nat-

ural for Chrisianity to adopt it then. But he thinks it is now time we
abandoned such a notion since we have nothing to corroborate it.

It has often been said that the difference between science and
religion is the difference between fact and faith, data and value,
observation and commitment. These are superficial differences only.
Science, like religion, has faith; and religion, like science, concerns
itself with fact; science believes in values and religion has its data;
science has its commitments, and religion makes its observations.
The mood of science is one of agnosticism and skepticism. The mood
of religion is one of credulity. The man of science likes to quote the
line from Sophocles' *Antigone*, "Don't only think your mind is the
right one." Or he may say with Oliver Cromwell, "I bid you by
the bowels of Christ to think that you may be mistaken," and in this
mood he continues his work. In the face of all those who say they
know on the authority of the claims of a religion, he remains a not-
knower and he continues his pursuit of such truth as he may know.

Science now knows itself to be an aspect of Western thought as a
whole. Thus in the widest sense, Western thought is scientific. But
we must not make the mistake of thinking that Western thought is
anchored in natural science. In the widest sense Western thought is
scientific but in no sense does it lack wider dimensions. The so-called
warfare between science and religion is not a contest between materialism and religiosity. It is not the opposition of reason to faith;
it is not a clash between things and ideals. The warfare, insofar as
there is one, is between answers and questions, between the belief
that certain fundamental questions have already been answered and
the belief that no fundamental question can ever be answered with
finality.

In point of fact, then, the Copernican revolution never entered
the church. It has been kept outside. Its effect has been, not to
change the church, but only to narrow the area it claims as its own
special province. The Copernican revolution set up a rival faith,
contrary in its basic principles to a Christianity and a Judaism that
have continued to reject it so far as religion is concerned. That faith
may be stated in many ways. It is summarized in the "Rules of
Philosophizing" of Isaac Newton. He does not begin by setting up
principles on the basis of which to explain what he cannot understand, as do the religions. Newton moves in the opposite direction.

His data are the phenomena of experience and it is with them that he begins. Principles are the goal of his investigations, not their starting point.

The Copernican revolution is but a part, although the most conspicuous part, of what has been called the Western intellectual tradition which has recently been traced in a number of histories of thought. Some of its aspects may be stated as follows: (1) Reasoned dissent has provided the motive power for progress in the West (Bronowski). (2) We cannot claim to possess the absolute truth about man or the universe: knowledge is always a waystation to more knowledge yet to come (Herbert J. Muller). (3) Our understanding of nature can never be subjective. It must be objective and achieved through dissecting, manipulating, and measuring. But this has meant an aberration from nature, a loss in the sense of participation in the process and purposes of nature (Charles C. Gillespie). (4) Human beings have been moving toward an evermore complex social structure (Carleton S. Coon). We are not yet out of the Neolithic.

Of course, it was not only the scientific revolution represented by Copernicus, Galileo, Newton, and Einstein that disrupted the majestic structure within which medieval thought had gathered all knowledge. From the anthropological and cultural point of view, the voyages of Christopher Columbus, Vasco da Gama, and the rest were quite as disruptive of the Christocentric world of Thomas Aquinas, Martin Luther, and John Calvin. Slowly, the West discovered that what had seemed eternally right in morals because it was based on natural law known to Cicero, was but the system of mores developed in the West and that there were quite different systems known to other cultures which worked very well for them, and which within those systems seemed right enough. What the early voyagers first sensed as they came in contact with cultures quite unfamiliar to them, the studies of Bronislaw Malinowski, Ruth Benedict, and Margaret Mead have since demonstrated. Truth and right are far more relative than the ancient and medieval Western mind ever dreamed possible. The revolution in the moral universe of the West wrought by Columbus and da Gama were no less shattering to the medieval mind than that wrought by Copernicus and Galileo in the physical universe.

Here, too, the church at first said "No" emphatically. The only right mores were those known to Western culture. So the Christians strove to convert the "natives" to Christian ways and to impose Western modes of thought upon them—and here again the story from the sixteenth century to the twentieth is one of steady retreat, with the churches continually giving up areas they had previously claimed as their own until today most of them, insofar as they carry on missions at all, maintain hospitals, service centers, and schools. The emphasis now is on service rather than on conversion to the Christian faith.

No human institution could withstand the erosion suffered by the Christian churches during the last few centuries. This is the heart of the problem of unbelief in our time.

2. AMERICAN RELIGIOUS PLURALISM

The refusal of the churches to accept the full impact of the Copernican and Columbian revolutions upon the thought of the West explains the deep gulf between dogma and faith we noted in the first chapter. But the nature of man accounts for the sense of loss and the deep longing that has set in as a result of it. Men want to believe. They know they need to believe and they are possessed by a haunting nostalgia for the good old days when, as they suppose, men believed the teachings of their fathers and society rested upon a foundation that was solid and dependable. As we shall see in Chapter IV, this mood appeared on the continent of Europe during and after World War I. It appeared in England and America a generation later.

Just before the outbreak of World War II a magazine which is read by the business leaders of the nation published an editorial, "War and Peace," with the subtitle "The failure of the Church to teach absolute spiritual values will undermine Christian civilization." It read in part: "We cannot enter into the great underlying conflict between God and mammon, or suggest what reconciliation there may be between them if there may be any. As laymen dedicated to the practice of Christianity, we can merely record our certainty that in order for humanity to progress, it must *believe:* it must have faith in certain absolute spiritual values, or at least have faith that absolute spiritual values exist."

For the author of that editorial, faith itself is apparently the important thing. He italicizes the need to believe, but he pays little attention to what we are to believe. He says we are to believe in "absolute spiritual values." Yet he himself is not sure what those values are, so he adds, "or at least that such values exist."

How deep was the longing for something to believe in became apparent during the war itself. During the Battle of Britain Edward R. Murrow instituted a radio program called "This I Believe," which was outstandingly successful. If listener and reader response is any measure, the need for such statements was enormous. When these personal credos were later collected and published, Murrow wrote:

"As the months wore on [in the Battle of Britain] and the nights lengthened, and the casualty lists mounted, I became more concerned to try to understand what sustained this island people: what belief or what mythology caused them to stand so steady in their shoes. In part, it was ignorance of their own weakness; in part, it was a reluctance to appear obvious by expressing doubt as to the ultimate outcome. But at bottom this calm confidence stemmed from a belief that what they were defending was good; the Englishmen had devised a system of regulating the relationship between the individual and the state which was superior to all others, and which would survive even though cold military calculations concluded that the state was doomed."

Perhaps the most significant thing about these statements was the fact that few were by clergymen. In the foreword it was stated flatly: "*This I Believe* has no connection with any church—it is run by laymen."

The religious nostalgia of the war period, coupled with an increasingly articulate lay faith, vanished in the American postwar boom in church attendance, church membership, and church building. But the boom only sharpened the pervading disbelief of the people and the anxiety of the clergy about it. The gulf between official dogma and heartfelt conviction did not lessen with the swelling activity and prosperity of the church. It increased, although people were now less concerned about it than during the cataclysm of the war.

By the 1950's these concerns began to express themselves in attacks on "secularism." The most penetrating of the many books that dealt with the problem saw much further into it. In 1955 Will Herberg published his *Protestant, Catholic, Jew.* "Secularism is on the increase," he wrote. It "pervades the American consciousness." As a result, he said, the American people are "thinking and living in . . . a framework . . . remote from the religious beliefs simultaneously professed." This, he said, was a paradox in view of the mounting religiosity of the country. Worse than that, the secularization of American faith was a great danger. Religion cannot be a part of the world, he said. It must stand over against the world.

In attempting to deal with the waning faith of religiously oriented Americans, Will Herberg dealt at length with a closely related but quite different matter, the growing acceptance of pluralism as the American religious pattern. "The basic fact defining the contemporary religious situation in this country is the transformation of America, in the course of the past generation, from a Protestant nation into a three religion country," he wrote later, summarizing the conclusions he reached in the course of his earlier work. "These three religions," he continued, "Protestant, Catholic and Jewish, while separate from each other, constitute a single over-all religious entity. . . . The socio-religious group has emerged as a primary sub-community in American society." He spoke of it as the "tri-faith system of Protestant-Catholic-Jew," and commented, "This is the kind of religious belonging that today, normally and naturally, goes along with being an American; it is, in a real sense, the nation on its religious side."

So far as I have been able to learn, George H. Williams of the Harvard Divinity School was the first to spot and state the emerging pattern of pluralism in American religious life. Participating in a symposium on "Issues between Catholics and Protestants at Mid-Century" in 1953, Professor Williams identified "American Critical Pluralism as the Emerging Middle Ground in Interfaith Relations" and urged both Catholics and Protestants consciously to adopt it. "May it be hoped," he concluded, with genuine prophetic insight, "that informed good will, firmness in charity on the issues of current tension and redoubled research on either side . . . will bring forth a significant restatement of papal instruction under the influence of the new currents flowing in the vigorous American branch of the Catholic Church. Clearly, it is the urgent task of more Protestants to move into the middle ground of Critical Pluralism. . . ." He located "the main body of culturally alert prophetic Judaism" in the position of critical pluralism also.

While George Williams was the first to spot Protestant, Catholic, Jewish interrelationships as an emerging pattern of religious pluralism in the United States, he was by no means the first advocate of the pattern. A small group of Roman Catholic thinkers of whom Father John Courtney Murray of Woodstock College was and is the leader may claim a "first" here as Williams said. As early as 1948 Father Murray was saying, "I am not minimizing Catholic truth when I identify in the Bull Unam Sanctam certain affirmations that savor of a certain time-conditioned conception of papal [power]. The power of the Church in the temporal order is permanent. Its method of asserting that power, changes in accordance with the times. Catholics are not now stuck with medieval doctrines of supremacy and persecution of heretics."

"The Church stepped into a political vacuum," he concluded in another paper written in the same year, "when it asserted authority over the state." It is the thrust of his argument that that was a new power exercised by the church at that time, a power which it need not and should not exercise now.

Developing his thesis in subsequent articles appearing almost yearly thereafter, Father Murray increasingly articulated his belief that pluralism was and ought to be the American way and that it was wholly congenial to the position of the Roman Catholic Church. "It is through the freedom of the citizen (in the modern sense)," he said, "that the freedom of the Church (in the medieval sense) is effectively assured—her right to exercise her spiritual sovereignty over her subjects and to reach those elements of human affairs which are 'quoquo modo sacrum'."

His position attained full statement in 1954 when he asserted that the doctrine of pluralism makes two assumptions:

1. There are several divergent inconsistent points of view with regard to religion present in society.
2. Nevertheless there is a consensus by which these divergent elements agree to get along with each other. Meanwhile, they co-operate toward a common good.

The First Amendment clauses of no-establishment and the free exercise of religion, he argued, are not articles of faith but articles of peace. They offer a method by which divergent elements in religion propose to get along with each other. Because of the wide variety of immigrants to this country, this pattern was, he said, politically inevitable. In short, Father Murray supported the American thesis of separation of church and state because it is a disclaimer on the part of the state of any competence in matters religious.

Meanwhile, the de facto recognition of pluralism continues to mount in the standard inclusion of Protestant, Catholic, and Jewish clergymen on state occasions, at public dinners, and affairs of every sort. Protestant, Catholic, and Jewish chapels and chaplains in the armed forces, at schools and colleges—all these are further evidence of what is transpiring in fact. Whether by design or as an inevitable concomitant of the American doctrine of tolerance, religious pluralism has become our way of life and those thinkers who argue for it and defend it are but providing a theoretical and rational basis for a widely accepted and increasingly pervasive point of view and practice.

This is another way of saying that American Protestants on the whole have practiced the tolerance they have preached and are now confronted with its practical result. They wrote the principle of disestablishment into the Constitution and have kept to it. They believed in religious freedom, and while they did not always practice it, they wrote it into their state constitutions as well and have since increasingly made the principle more explicit both in theory and in practice. The decisions of the United States Supreme Court first in the Regents Prayer case and the next year on Bible reading and the recitation of the Lord's Prayer in the public schools are contemporary examples of the continued application of a now firmly established principle.

The Jewish and Catholic minorities did not always have an easy time of it to be sure, but if the record of tolerance since the founding of the colonies is compared with religious attitudes and practices that prevailed elsewhere during the same period, it will be seen that they enjoyed a religious freedom that was virtually unique in human history. That freedom alone can explain the enormous growth and prosperity of Judaism and Catholicism in the United States. The tripartite faith of which both now speak could have come into existence in no other way.

The result is by no means to be attributed to Protestant virtue alone. Necessity played its part as well. American religious tolerance, like most political institutions, is a result of the welding of high principle and hard necessity. The principle was the demand for religious liberty which drove many of our immigrants out of their comfortable homes in Europe into the American wilderness, and its articulation is to be found in successive political documents from Roger Williams' *Bloudy Tenent of Persecution for Cause of Conscience* to the First Amendment to the Constitution. It is not possible now to say which or how many of the religious groups in this country, given the chance, would have established itself as official. But we can say with ample evidence to back us up that since none was in a position to do so, all were glad to support the principle of tolerance which is now the religious mood as well as the law of the land. It was the genius of American statecraft to make law of a high principle which had emancipated so many of its immigrants and to declare that all religions stood alike in the eyes of the state, that none, regardless of any claims to divine origin or authority, should ever be acknowledged to be superior to the rest, and that therefore, none should ever be aided or supported by the state in any way.

Roman Catholic writers acknowledge that their church has been freer to pursue its own ends under Protestant tolerance in America than in European countries where the church is the established religion of the land. In a volume by a group of Roman Catholic writers, replete with evidence of the indebtedness of Rome to the American way, Edward A. Ryan said: "Rome's surveillance of the American church has, perhaps, been closer and more effective than was the case of other national churches." Charles Donahue, professor of English at Fordham, wrote: "The Protestant majority [during the great immigration of Roman Catholics to this country] abided by [the principle of American] constitutional pluralism and permitted it to come into complete act." John Courtney Murray wrote: "The Church in the United States, even in the absence of public legal status, enjoys a freedom that she never had under their most Catholic or most Christian majesties."

Undoubtedly, what we have achieved is a working compromise. Each of the three religious groups fears dominance by one of the other two. None at the moment can look forward to becoming the state religion, although many Roman Catholic writers still argue that Rome can never logically claim anything less. But the growth pattern of Rome over the last two generations, during which time the Roman Church has made the greatest surge forward, does not justify such ambitions. Protestant growth has at least kept pace with it. There is no evidence that the Protestants want to depart from the doctrine of tolerance which they made part of the law of the land at its founding, and the Jews are too few to make anything but pluralism a practicable philosophy. Some in fact do not agree with Herberg's analysis. They find the ghetto still very real in this country. One study, covering ten American cities, concludes emphatically that there is not a tripartite faith in this country but rather a triple ghetto, at least in our larger cities.

The point of view crystallized by Will Herberg, and others who have been concerned with American postwar religiosity, is, however, gaining increasingly wide acceptance. And it is undergirded by a shrewd observation of the American scene made over a century ago. In the 1830's Alexis de Tocqueville wrote: "In France I had almost always seen the spirit of religion and the spirit of freedom marching in opposite directions. But in America I found they were intimately united and that they reigned in common over the same country." He sought an explanation of this unexpected state of affairs in his talks with people in all walks of life, but especially among the clergy. "I found that they differed upon matters of detail alone," he continued, "and that they all attributed the peaceful dominion of religion in their country mainly to the separation of church and state. I do not hesitate to affirm that during my stay in America I did not meet a single individual, of the clergy or the laity, who was not of the same opinion on this point."

3. Secularism

Politics makes strange bedfellows, it is often said. In any conflict, unlikely parties may become allies for no better reason than that they face a common enemy. As a result, different as these allies may be from each other, they discover an unexpected common ground which both unites them and distinguishes them from the common enemy. This was the factor that brought about Will Herberg's statement of the tripartite aspect of our American faith. He began with the threat of "secularism" to organized religion. He ended with the fact of American religious pluralism.

What was new, as we have seen, was the emerging pattern of religious pluralism in American life. "Secularism" so-called was an old and familiar enemy of religion. In retrospect the whole movement known as the enlightenment is now seen to have been secularist in character. In those days, however, the word still meant what it had meant in its ecclesiastical Latin form and in Middle English, namely, "the world" as against the church. Secular clergy were those not under religious orders; the secular arm was the government of the state as contrasted with that of the church.

In the nineteenth century the word began to take on its present meaning. It began to be used to designate not merely the nonecclesiastical, but a movement with religious pretensions either outside or within the church, which was deemed to threaten the church.

Rufus Jones has been given the credit for introducing the word into common parlance in the sense in which we use it today. At an ecumenical gathering in Jerusalem in 1928, Jones said that the world manifests a discontinuity between the divine and the human. The sociohistorical process is discontinuous with the divine plan of salvation, he said. But there is a special thread that runs through history which is controlled by God's direct intervention. Accordingly, the history of the church has a reference beyond history, namely, the biblical perspective. The church rejects as false all utopian accounts of progress. But secular movements contradict the Christian faith, he said. They endanger salvation because they believe progress results from the interaction of reason and intrahistorical forces. Therefore, he concluded, the church must extirpate all secular tendencies.

Here was a clear conjoining of the word "secularism" and the thought patterns associated with the enlightenment. By way of clarifying his concept, he said: "I am using 'secular' here to mean a way of life and an interpretation of life that include only the natural order of things and that do not find God, or a realm of

spiritual reality, essential for life or thought." Like the true scholar
that he was, he traced back to science and rationalism the origins
of the movement he was describing.

Christianity was at first slow to identify "secularism" as the enemy.
As late as 1937, at the Second World Conference on Faith and
Order held at Edinburgh, it was felt that the problem of secularism
fell outside the main concerns of the gathering. A decade later,
however, in the Evanston Conference of 1947, secularism had become a central concern. It was declared to be "an evasive, often
unconscious philosophy which does not deny, but ignores the presence and ethical influence of a living God." The emphasis of the
lectures was declared to have been upon the Christian witness in
a world where civilization is beset by the "sickness" or "malady" of
secularism.

Here the epithet quality the term had meanwhile acquired becomes apparent. First, secularism is denounced as a "sickness." Then
it is disqualified as "evasive." Next it is called a "philosophy" which
is by way of saying that it is not a religion. It is then castigated
because it "ignores" the central aspect of human experience, "the
living God." Finally, the editor of the lectures declares that secularism "depends upon education, science, personal aggressiveness, and
organized power, while ignoring the spiritual and ethical forces
of Jesus Christ." Here the forensic character of his concept becomes
clear. If "secularism" relies upon education, science, aggressiveness,
and organized power, so, too, do the churches. In fact, in the next
paragraph the editor calls for "the aggressive proclamation of the
Christian philosophy," apparently having overlooked the fact that
he has just denounced aggressiveness and organized power as characteristics of secularism.

"Jesus Christ" is of course the key concept in this definition of
secularism. To ignore "the spiritual and ethical forces of Jesus Christ"
means to ignore the demands of the churches organized around this
theological concept. In the fifth section of the Evanston Conference
Lectures which deals with "Christianity's Witness in a Secular
World," the specifically Christian church-centered nature of the
concept becomes clear. There secularism turns out to be any philosophy of life that does not acknowledge the central authority in
ethical and religious matters of the Christian church. This, of course,

leaves out Judaism, and you get the feeling that it is Protestant Christianity primarily that the writers have in mind.

One study, for example, entitled "How Christianity Challenges Secularism" defines it as "believing and behaving as though man were an end in himself; as though humanity existed in its own right and for the sole purpose of its own power and glory." But we soon discover that the author is not prepared to stand by his own definition. "The present age with all its engagements," he continues, "is regarded [by the secularist] as the whole of reality instead of but a part of a larger, richer, more intricately related whole." But the argument is carried no further than these assertions and the author seems not to be aware that his implicit definition of secularism includes all those who are unable to accept the Christian dogmas with which he thinks secularism is to be contrasted.

The fact that we have here a kind of dignified name-calling appears from the large number of areas within which secularism is thought to be found. The *Christian Faith and Secularism* includes, in addition to the chapter from which the above quotation comes, topics ranging from the most crass kind of materialism to the most high-minded ethical ideals; from the most amoral kind of self-seeking to the noblest spiritual principles. All these aspects of secularism have in common only the fact that they are not derived from the teaching and practice of a doctrinally centered Christian church. The authors find "secularism" in everything from education to politics, from the church to organized crime.

Following Will Herberg, it is very much the vogue just now to speak of secularism *within* the churches. People are said to look upon the church as a status symbol. It is thought of as a pleasant place to go, quite apart from one's personal faith; an opportune place for making friends and business contacts and a proper setting for weddings and funerals. Such "secularism" is deplored, and is identified with the tolerant attitude of most Protestants and many Catholics and Jews toward one another, whereby denominational differences are not looked upon as very important. Herberg is in part proclaiming the victory of Judaism and Catholicism in gaining the recognition of equal status with a formerly dominant Protestantism in American religion and cultural life. "American-ness today," he says, "entails religious identification as Protestant, Catholic or Jew in a way and to a degree quite unprecedented in our history. To be a Protestant, a Catholic, or a Jew are today alternative ways of being an American." But all three lie over against secularism. "As a result," he says, "American religiousness has been growing increasingly vacuous—a religiousness of belonging, without religious commitment, religious concern or religious passion."

The secular world itself, meaning the nonecclesiastical, has also taken up the refrain. In 1955 a popular magazine published a feature article in which it was stated: "Secularism . . . asserts that man, science and altruism can, by combined effort, turn the globe into a material near-Eden. It backs this assertion with the evidence of success, notably in America." The article does not take issue with the "secularist" position but merely sets over against it what it deems to be the Christian position. Christianity, it concludes, is "dedicated by its own doctrine to a world beyond this world. The Christian's very value to our civilization is his detachment from it. . . . Neither war nor peace, civilization nor catastrophe, prosperity nor adversity are for him the end of life or hope or responsibility."

Meanwhile, the concept "secularism" has been expanded to include an extraordinary number of movements. Just how hazy the thinking in this area has become, we can see in a volume entitled *The Church Faces the Isms.* Here, secularism is included as a threat to the church, along with Fundamentalism, Adventism, Dispensationalism, and Perfectionism; Judaism, Roman Catholicism, Denominationalism, Ecumenism, Totalitarianism, Fascism, Communism, Racism, Naturalism, Scientism, and Modernism. Is any comment needed on such a potpourri of opponents? This is a more diffuse echo perhaps of an earlier work which lists but a half a dozen of these as *Modern Rivals to the Christian Faith,* and lumps them all under the title "secularism." Walter Nigg thinks secularism is the latest of the Christian heresies.

Nevertheless, the word "secular" has slowly taken on a meaning all its own. It is not positive but negative like "Gentile" or "non-Catholic." It is a catch-all for widely divergent points of view that do not conform to those of a religious in-group. It is defined by what it stands over against or that which stands over against it. Will Herberg writes: "The secularism dominating the American consciousness is not an overt philosophy; it is an underlying, often unconscious orientation of life and thought." What Herberg means by the term is not so clear because he takes it for granted. We discover, however, that with him secularism is a failure to stress the importance of facts and modes of thought that come out of a particular religious tradition, coupled with a tendency to use religion to support the supreme values of the American way of life.

It was probably inevitable that "secularism" as a fourth faith would soon be added to the first three. In spite of Will Herberg's neat classification, there are many religious groups in this country which are unwilling to be classified as Protestant, Catholic, or Jewish, as Herberg himself acknowledges. He was thinking primarily in terms of Catholic and Jewish resurgence and seems not to be aware of the complexity of the third division, Protestantism, which for him becomes a kind of catchall for whatever is neither Roman Catholic nor Jewish.

As a direct result of his description of the tripartite patterns of American faith, however, and its deep involvement in "secularism," this aspect of the American faith pattern is now coming to be acknowledged as a fourth faith. We owe the concept to the fertile mind of John Courtney Murray. At a fund for the Republic seminar held in 1958, Murray spoke of four "conspiracies" in American religious life. His selection of vocabulary was unfortunate. Protestantism, Catholicism, and Judaism are hardly conspiracies. Neither is the fourth, whatever else it may be said to be. Murray hastened to add that he meant nothing invidious by his use of the word "conspiracy" —after all, had he not included his own church among the four? He defended his usage on the ground of Latin etymology. But his word choice was unfortunate nevertheless. In the English language "conspiracy" means in the minds of most people what the dictionary says it does, "a combination of persons for an evil end." A second definition omits the word "evil," but the notion of a secret plot for an evil end, which the dictionary duly notes, is inescapable. Father Murray's attempt to redefine the word only serves to introduce ambiguity and confusion where our concepts are for the moment clear.

In the same vein Father Murray wrote: "Among us civility . . . is a thing of the surface. . . . Our pluralist society has received its structure through wars, and the wars are still going on beneath a fragile surface of more or less forced urbanity. . . . There is not simply an exchange of arguments but of verbal blows. You do not have to probe deeply beneath the surface of civic amity to uncover the structure of passion and war. . . . There is finally the secularist. . . . Historically his first chosen enemy was the Catholic Church, and it still must be the enemy of his choice. . . . The pluralist society, honestly viewed, . . . is a pattern of inter-acting conspiracies. . . ."

Happily, few writers have as yet followed his lead. One of the exceptions is Martin Marty. His writings, like Murray's, give the impression that at least a part of his motivation for the use of the word "conspiracy" derives from his distaste for the "fourth faith." Marty warns that the movement "is going to have to be countered by an alert self-purifying pluralism in which committed Protestantism can play a significant part."

Both Murray and Marty are clear, however, that the "fourth faith" or "conspiracy," if you think the term apt, must be identified in order that the threat it offers to the other three faiths may be seen and prepared for. Pointing out that the movement is as yet unorganized, although very powerful, Marty says: "It has no pope or president or formal dogma. It lacks a name; the moment one names it, one limits it. It includes elements of secularism, naturalism, nationalism, and humanism." But Marty is emphatic as to the importance of identifying the fourth faith. He continues: "It is necessary to revise the time-honored terminology and to speak of a new religious establishment in America. It is a gradual growth that supplants the simple separation of church and state and the resultant religious voluntaryism that was the United States' outstanding institutional contribution to religious history. Custom and the compulsion of social pressures and national security have combined to forge this new establishment." In a later work, Marty uses the term "secularity" but it is hardly more sharply defined.

Thus Herberg's concept of American pluralism, characterized by a Protestant-Catholic-Jew pattern which stands over against secularism, is yielding to another in which a fourth faith has been added, called for lack of a better name, secularism. Actually, Herberg himself said this by implication if not directly when he described the degree to which American secular life is affected by the structures of organized religion, and the degree to which organized religion has itself been secularized. When Robert McAfee Brown became professor of religion at Stanford University in the Fall of 1962, he, too, spoke of a new fourth faith which he called "secularism." He said it was the fastest growing of the American religious groups and did not hesitate to call it a "faith." Brown had already established himself as an exponent of the idea of American pluralism by publishing with Gustav Weigel, S.J., *An American Dialogue* in which he as a Protestant and Weigel as a Catholic undertook to say how the religion of each looked to the other.

What then is the fourth American faith? What is this movement which without pope or president, dogma or institution, can yet be called the fastest growing faith in America? It has been called "secularism" more often than anything else. But this does not help us for we have seen that "secularism" is only a great basket in which the proponents of official religion sweep up all the movements and philosophies which do not make use of acknowledged traditional religious concepts and language. We shall now attempt to answer that question.

4. THE FOURTH FAITH

Those who have identified a fourth faith in American culture appear to be right. The fourth faith is at present largely unorganized, but it has a vast number of adherents both within and without the other three. It involves the kind of commitment that religion customarily requires. It is quite as capable of supporting "The American Way" as is any of the other three if that is thought to be desirable. On the other hand, it is quite as capable of criticizing the American way as any of the other three. Like them, the fourth faith makes heavy demands upon the faithful, and in the light of its principles, puts them under judgment. Few, if any, can bring their conduct into conformity with the ideals the fourth faith sets before men.

What are these ideals? What is the essence of the fourth faith? What does it stand for, and what does it stand against? We have seen that "secularism" will not do as a name for it. Even the designation "fourth" is misleading since it implies that the fourth faith is apposite to the other three. But it is not. Its central characteristic, as all the writers upon the subject have observed, is that it stands over against the other three, not severally but taken together.

If, then, we are to number our faiths, the so-called "fourth" is really a second faith which stands in contrast to the tripartite American faith Herberg and others have described. The other three have in common their acceptance of the Judeo-Christian tradition in its many forms. The fourth faith rejects the claims to priority, pre-eminence, divine authority, truth, and revelation the other three faiths are accustomed to make. It goes further. It not merely rejects these claims severally as unjustified, it rejects on principle the claim of any religion to priority, pre-eminence, divine authority, truth, and revelation.

To number our several forms of faith is a poor way to distinguish them, but if we are going to do it, the designation "second" faith is hardly better than that of "fourth." Such numbering suggests priority or primacy, whether it is intended to or not. Both psychology and anthropology testify to the fact that antecedent to the particular faiths into which the religions of man have proliferated, there were simpler, more generalized faiths that sustained him. Moreover, each of the later faiths, as they became articulate in idea and practice, stiffened and became increasingly impervious to change. As time went on, each became increasingly archaic and increasingly worldly at the same time. Thus each generated one or more rebellions in the name of its own highest teachings. These rebellions were always based upon a supposed return to the basic principles and practices which had characterized the religion at the outset but which had since been obscured or forgotten. This was the basis of the Christian rebellion against Judaism and of the Protestant rebellion against Rome.

The fourth faith as it expresses itself historically in our time is just such a rebellion. It is directed against the archaic modes of expression in which the official religious faiths of our time are couched. It is directed also against the ecclesiasticism to which all religious institutions are subject. The fourth faith as we know it today is an aspect of the eternal protest which man must always make against his religions.

In this sense the fourth faith is primordial. It is not confined to any one place or time. It is not a historical faith, but finds expression in many times and places, under varying conditions and within historical faiths. The fourth faith, taken in this sense, does not derive from, and is not fastened to, any particular historical tradition. It often expresses itself as an attempt to return to an earlier supposedly purer form of a prevailing tradition, but the judgment as to whether or not it does so is in the end personal and relies upon nothing more substantial than the authority of the man who makes the attempt. And so, what is today often called "secularism" and the "fourth faith" would in fact, be the first, if we were to arrange the faiths of men in numerical order. It is first in the sense that it belongs to the nature of man and was his long before any of the present historic faiths made their appearance. Indeed, each of the historic faiths is but a particularization of the faith that is a part of man's native endowment.

This faith as it has taken form in our time, so that for us it becomes a fourth to be added to three that already exist, is most easily understood in terms of its own history. It may be seen in figures like Xenophanes and Socrates in ancient Greece, Akhenaton in Egypt, and in certain of the prophets of Israel like Amos and Isaiah. It may be seen in Jesus of Nazareth, and among a host of Christian thinkers beginning in the Middle Ages and continuing down into the present day. These might include: Pelagius, Abélard, Wycliffe, Hus, Servetus, Socinus, the deists, and many others including Averroës, the Arab thinker of the twelfth century of whom we have spoken at some length.

One of the clearest expressions of this faith in the Renaissance-Reformation period comes to us from the pen of the virtually forgotten Italian, Sebastian Castellio, who stood against both church and state in sixteenth-century Switzerland, and against both Protestants and Catholics in declaring that it is truth, not coercion, that persuades the minds and hearts of men. This is the essence of the fourth faith as it expresses itself historically in our place and time.

It is a faith Western culture has recognized and put into practice with incredible results. Witness our science, our economy, and our political institutions. But it is a faith the religions of Western culture have not recognized. Protestant, Catholic, Jew, all three believe that ultimate truth does not emerge from the open encounter of mind with mind. They hold that in the most important area of life, namely, in religion, the truth is already in hand because God has revealed it through his "Word," the Torah, the Bible, through Jesus Christ, through the Church which He founded, the Cross, the Resurrection, the Holy Spirit, and so on—the details vary but the basic point of view remains the same.

The fourth faith, on the contrary, places no reliance whatever on the doctrine of revelation. It does not dogmatically reject the idea as impossible: it maintains the same "let's examine the evidence" point of view it adopts toward every aspect of life. We shall examine some of this evidence in subsequent chapters. But such a position does not make the fourth faith "secular." On the contrary, the fourth faith insists that any attempt to distinguish between the sacred and the secular produces a false dichotomy. To the members of the fourth faith the sacred-secular division boils down to nothing more than a device by which to distinguish orthodoxy from unorthodoxy. The distinction breaks down in practice because so many things that are declared to be sacred by one religion are not held sacred by another.

Neither is the fourth faith merely humanistic, although its devotees would argue that all experience is human experience and all knowledge human knowledge. The fourth faith, therefore, begins with what men know, not with "knowledge" some men believe to have been handed down by a celestial being. It does not deny the possibility that celestial knowledge can be given to men from a celestial realm. It says only that the means by which we determine the truth of such an allegation must be human. The fourth faith is not merely scientific although it believes no method for eliciting truth about the nature of things is superior to the scientific method. Its devotees do not worship science or the findings of science. They worship that which presents itself in human experience as being most worthy of worship.

Finally, the fourth faith seeks truth as all religions do, but with a fundamental difference as to what the word "truth" is taken to mean, how you reach it and what you do with it after you get it. The fourth faith centers in questions while traditional religion centers in answers. It centers in movement toward truth rather than in the teaching of truth which is already established. It holds every "truth" subject to continuous questioning and the world subject to continuous inquiry, while traditional religion tries to persuade the faithful to accept the truth it already holds. For the fourth faith there are no questions that may not be asked, no principle that may not be doubted, no doctrine that ought not to be examined.

The men of the fourth faith are first of all men of *faith*. They start with the implicit assumption that religion is important. They seek to modify or change it only because they think it worth the effort. They are religious men. They are believers. Their problem is the inadequacies they find in the religions of their time. They are found inside the church and outside of it; they are both for the church and against it. They both build it and destroy it, but always in the name of the highest principles of the churches and temples they attack. They believe in the ends toward which religion is directed—worship and service, justice and morality.

The fourth faith is the basic faith-mood of man which flows in his conscience like a great underground stream of water. Ever and anon it emerges in history in the form of particular faiths, each designed to improve or correct an earlier mode of expression. Each then hardens into a particular tradition, assuming itself to be the final expression of all faith. Judaism, Catholicism, Protestantism, each in succession, attempted to correct the earlier form.

The fourth faith is not necessarily a rival of any established faith. It is not the opposite of orthodoxy. The two are more alike than different. Both are expressions of the religion of man. Each believes itself to be in possession of truth it must expound and protect. The devotees of both are believers. The difference is that one holds its truth inviolate and adapts it to changing circumstance by interpretation. The other holds its truth tentatively, and is thus more adaptable to changing circumstance.

Man's primordial faith, which knows neither time nor place, neither a particular church nor a particular religion, is the faith of inquiry, the faith of exploration, the faith of hope and expectation. This is why it is also the faith of rebellion, for whoever would go exploring in religion is, as we shall see, invited to be cautious; whoever would inquire, as we shall see, is told not to push his questions too far. Accordingly, whoever would explore and inquire in religion must do so against the admonitions of the religious leaders of his time. Thus, man's primordial faith is also the faith of the reformer because the reformer is never satisfied with the faith of his fathers.

Always he must improve it if he can, and against the opposition of those who think things are better left as they are.

For the same reason the opponents of the fourth faith are most frequently the priests of the prevailing religion of the day. They quite properly fear the surging uncontrolled power of the fourth faith, and well they may, for while their own writings are filled with calls to a renewal of faith, and with elaborate explanations and defenses of the faith they espouse, the writings of the men of the fourth faith contain no such summons. While the supporters of the three great faiths continually remind the faithful, as we shall see, that you can still believe if you want to and that such belief is fundamental to our civilization, the writings of men of the fourth faith are wholly lacking in such exhortations. For them the problem is to guide into useful channels, to control, to discipline, and to contain the élan of man's primordial faith so that it may be directed toward the welfare of men. The people of the fourth faith are not urged to try to believe what they find unbelievable. With them it is the other way. They believe because they are incapable of disbelieving that to which they hold.

There is a point at which it is difficult to tell whether you are adapting old truth to new circumstances, or stating new truth. For this reason, the fourth faith participates in the other three far more than either supposes. The three official faiths, on the other hand, constantly move toward the forms of expression congenial to the fourth. The fourth faith asks for a frank recognition by the established religions that this is so. Can not the religions of man be released from the necessity of expressing themselves in the old forms? Will not religion serve man in his need much better if its forms, practices, and beliefs are designed first to fit man's needs and only secondarily if at all to conform to past modes of expression.

In short, the fourth faith asks for the same provision for growth and development in religion that the West and increasingly the East is accustomed to make in theoretical science, in technology, art, literature, medicine, law, education—in fact, in every area of human endeavor except religion—yet the major effort of Christian and Jewish theology is still given to an attempt to make sense out of traditional beliefs and practices. The fourth faith holds that these efforts should now be given to designing the best possible beliefs and practices, whether or not they are to be found in the traditions of our religion.

Two of the principles which characterize the fourth faith as it has achieved expression in the culture of the West are: the assertion of the integrity and authority of the independent mind and spirit, and the assertion of the principle of self-government and democratic polity in ecclesiastical organization. They stand over against two older and opposite principles of organized religion: that of revelation on the one hand and that of hierarchical government by the elect on the other. The two former principles place authority ultimately in the individual; the two latter place authority in the ecclesiastical institution.

The nature of the relationship between faith and polity has never been understood. Faith is what religious men believe—the principles to which they hold, the metaphysics by which they answer fundamental questions, the standards by which they live. Polity is the social structure by which they organize themselves into continuing religious groups. It is the manner in which they maintain order in any given group, hold it together, govern it, and assure its continuation. The dependence of the one upon the other is very close, far more so than we have ever realized.

The fourth faith would give explicit recognition to the interrelatedness of these two concepts. It would make that interrelatedness a part of the structure of organized religion.

The fourth faith holds that how you organize and govern a church is as important as any other aspect of man's religious expression. The correlation between authoritarian structure and codified belief required of the worshiper is almost complete. Likewise, those churches which place the integrity of the individual at the center as far as religious belief is concerned also govern their churches democratically. Those with modified belief structures within which wide variation is permitted almost invariably have a correspondingly fluid governmental structure and permit wide and significant lay participation.

In Protestantism and Judaism there has been a temporary retrogression from the doctrinal variation that prevailed a generation ago. Correspondingly, increased centralization resulting from continuing mergers have served to reduce lay participation. But this is probably more apparent than real. And now today, the movement toward liberalizing doctrine seems to have set in again. Meanwhile, lay influence and participation in church affairs appears to be increasing.

The shift that has taken place in the attitude toward religious dogma and in the organization and government of the various churches since the Protestant Reformation corresponds to a similar shift that has taken place in the universities and in civil government during the same period. In education today authority lies with the independent mind able to prove its case in open combat with other minds. Our civil government likewise is today based upon the consent of the governed. As education and government have slowly revealed this tendency, so have the churches and temples of men. As in education and government, so in religion the integrity of the individual mind and spirit has slowly asserted itself.

The fourth faith does not desire separate existence. It does not stand over against the other three. It is an aspect of the religion of man which finds its spirit crushed by ancient doctrines and practices the established religions are unwilling or powerless to give up. Like Laocoön and his two sons of old, man's independent spirit in religion cannot throw off the tightening bands of ancient doctrine and practice in the established religions. The fourth faith exists in America today, if it can be said to have a separate existence at all, only because of the resistance to change that marks the other three.

CHAPTER III

The Faith of Stability

Whoever would claim the fourth faith as his own has an important question to answer. With the abundance of historical faiths available to him, in the wide variety of forms in which they exist today, what need has he of a new one? Is there not in Judaism, Catholicism, or Protestantism a faith suitable to his needs? Each has attempted to meet the challenge of modern thought. No little effort and ingenuity have been expended in the attempt. Is none satisfactory? If not, why not?

The answer is easily given, although it is offered with a heavy heart. None of the three great religions that now make up America's tripartite faith has undertaken to answer the questions the fourth faith is asking. All three, deeply rooted in the past as they are, have, as we shall see, given their energy to maintaining this tradition and to making it real and vital in the present. One of the most famous of the parables of Jesus illustrates what the members of the fourth faith see as they turn to the other three to meet their religious needs. It is known as the parable of the talents.

A man about to take a long journey, so the story goes, called to-gether his three servants. To one he gave five talents, to another two, and to the last one. Those who received five and two each, invested theirs and doubled their holdings, but the third servant hid his single talent in the ground. When the master returned he commended the two servants who had doubled his money for him and condemned the man who had hidden his in the ground and returned it to the master without interest.

One could hardly hope to find a clearer exposition of the difference between the faith of adventure and the faith of stability. Christianity, and religion generally, like the servant who hid his talent in the earth, has stored its message in the ground of history. It has striven to keep intact what it already has, not to risk any new departures from the faith of the fathers. But the man Christianity claims as its founder, and to whom it has boldly ascribed the status of divinity, co-existent and co-eternal with Deity, did not preach or practice the faith of stability. His was the faith of adventure. He broke with the traditions of his own religious heritage to the point where those who heard him asked: "What new teaching is this?" Christianity could do well to remember his parable and the practice with which he backed it up.

On the basis of the parable of the talents, the fault we should fear is not that of inquiry or adventure, but that of holding the line. We should be wary of those who bid us not to question our faith, and should follow those who do. We should search out the stars and the atoms, the wonders of the world and our own nature. We should recognize the responsibility that goes with increased knowledge, but having done so, should pursue it to the uttermost. Religious truth, yet more than money, is not designed to be held unused. It is not to be kept buried in the ground of history. It is to be kept in circulation, made to grow, develop, and expand as new conditions arise and new knowledge is attained. In the three following chapters we shall see how, for the people of the fourth faith, the other three have kept their faith buried in the ground of history. We shall see why the attempt of the faith of stability to hold to the ancient theological line made the emergence of the faith of adventure inevitable and necessary.

1. JUDAISM

Why is not Judaism an answer to the questions the fourth faith is asking? Many Jews think it is. They believe it is universal in scope and open and searching in its method. Yet to the non-Jew, the universal aspects of Judaism are not so apparent. The following statement from a book on *Judaism* edited by Arthur Hertzberg is a statement of the "universal" aspect of Judaism:

"God exists in the world and cares for all men, for are not the children of Israel, as Amos said, no more to Him than the Ethiopians? It was out of His love for mankind as a whole that He taught all men His way of redemption, the Torah, in His revelation in the desert of Sinai, to show that, like the desert, the Law belongs to anyone who dares to claim it. God does not speak to man only in the Holy Land, for He addressed Noah in the land between the rivers, Abraham in Ur, Moses in Midian, and He spoke even to Balaam, who came to curse the Jews in the desert of Sinai. The Talmud contains a vision of the end of days, in which the holiness that is particular to the land of Israel will 'spread out' to encompass all the lands."

Why does not a religion like that meet the needs of the people of the fourth faith? Because they would begin asking questions after reading the first sentence. How does Rabbi Hertzberg know that "God exists in the world," they would ask. How does he know that, supposing God does exist in the world, he cares for all men? If it be replied that this is the Jewish faith, that this is where we begin, then those who can accept that article of faith would still have questions to ask. How about the second statement: "It was out of His love for mankind as a whole that He taught all men His way of redemption." Granting that God loves not merely the Jews but all mankind, how do we know what his redemption is or that he taught it to men? Such a statement involves a vast assumption.

More difficult still is the next sentence in Hertzberg's statement: that God's way of redemption is the Torah, the law, as set forth in the Pentateuch. How does he know this? Furthermore, for the Jews to claim that their Torah is God's way of redemption for all men is to claim something that few outside of the Jewish ranks would grant. Christian, Moslem, Buddhist, skeptic alike would see the Torah as but one among many claimants to be "God's way." The analysis of this Hertzberg statement need not be carried further. The difficulties that such claims lay before the open mind are all of a similar character.

While Hertzberg stresses what he regards as the universal aspect of Judaism, he reminds us that it has a second aspect which is not universal but particular. He states it as follows: "God made covenant with a particular people that it should be His priesthood. To this people, the seed of Abraham, the slaves He had just redeemed from Egypt, He revealed the Torah, the Law which they were to obey, as the particular burden of the Jews and as the sign of their unique destiny in the world. He chose the land of Canaan as His inheritance and that of His people, the Holy Land which would forever remain the place in which He would most clearly be manifest."

Both these expressions, says Rabbi Hertzberg, the "universal" and the "particular," are true of Judaism, for "Jewish faith addresses itself not only to the Jews; it prescribes the law and the way of salvation for all mankind." Even the member of the fourth faith who is able to accept the main tenets of such a faith could not go so far. He could never claim that what seems to be true to him must then be true for all mankind. The member of the fourth faith would press for and support his own beliefs, but he would never with any sense of finality assert that those beliefs were right. He would always be ready to concede that someone else might be shown to be yet nearer to the truth.

Rabbi Hertzberg leaves no loophole for those who would claim universality for Judaism as against particularity. Turning to the doctrine of the chosen people, he says: "The truest key to understanding Judaism in its own terms, is to be found in its concept of the 'chosen people.' This doctrine of 'chosenness' is a mystery—and a scandal . . . to the Gentiles—and even to some Jews. . . . It is nonetheless my view that Judaism is inconceivable without it."

He derives his doctrine of God from his doctrine of chosenness, and concludes with an assertion that removes him forever from the possibility of offering, through Judaism, an answer to the questions the fourth faith is asking. "Classical Judaism is therefore a *revealed* religion," he writes and the italics are his. "Judaism, the religion of the Bible, is the classical paradigm of a God-made religion. It is the assertion—not the philosophical proof—that God exists and that He has spoken and speaks to man." In this Judaism takes its place with Protestantism and Catholicism. Its premises are the same. Each claims its beliefs to be eternally true because they came into man's possession as a revelation from God.

Judaism is well aware of the difficulty of maintaining such a position in the face of the Christians' faith that *their* revelation is absolute and final truth. Hertzberg offers a typical resolution of this conflict. He acknowledges that what the divine revelation contains has been at issue between Judaism and both Christianity and Islam for many centuries. But his only answer to the question: Which is *the* divine revelation? is a simple, if veiled, affirmation that the Jews believe theirs to be. "Throughout the ages, all Israel has stood fast in the faith that the Torah is the inheritance of the congregation of Jacob," he writes, which, as we shall see, is precisely the position taken by Catholicism and Protestantism with regard to their particular articles of faith.

Arthur Hertzberg's introduction to an anthology of Jewish sacred writings from which the foregoing statements have been taken is not the only authority on modern Judaism. There is in fact no single authority. His statement is, however, the most useful précis of the Jewish position to which we could turn for a swift summary of fundamental points, such as we have undertaken here. Corroboration for what he says can easily be found in a wide variety of writings, most typically perhaps in Arthur A. Cohen's *The Natural and Supernatural Jew.* The language is somewhat different, but the issues with which he deals and the concepts within which he discusses them are the same. In a preliminary set of assumptions which he says are not necessarily valid for all time but which are "existential dogmas" he is perfectly clear that the Jewish community believes itself to be "the one to whom God has opened himself. . . . God has covenanted with the Jewish people," he continues, "that it shall transcend nature and history to him alone."

Cohen, like Hertzberg, attempts to universalize the Jewish faith, but as with Hertzberg the faith he delineates never achieves universality. It remains particular. Cohen believes the Jewish consciousness of having a special vocation under God ("chosenness" for Hertzberg) is re-emphasized by the fact that the Jew is an exile, not in the physical but the spiritual sense. He is an exile because he is unredeemed. Because the Jew is unredeemed, he knows that there is no redemption for him until all men are redeemed because they too are exiles in that sense. The Jews are to achieve redemption in community with all peoples, says Cohen, and yet there is with him as with Hertzberg a sense in which the Jews as Jews have a special role to play in the process. "God elects, not the single Jew, but the Jewish people," he says. "The obligation to engage in concert in the work of redemption joins the people of Israel to the fortunes of all peoples. The Jewish people has not itself alone to redeem."

In spite of his noble words, in the end Cohen remains a particularist. He declares, for example, that Will Herberg is an unsatisfactory Jewish thinker because his *Judaism and Modern Man* is a history of providence, not a history of the Jews. That is, Herberg occasionally moves beyond Jewish particularism to a point which encompasses other movements as well. Herberg's aim is to "broaden the terms of discussion and to enter into communication with Christians more freely . . . to address himself to the common dilemmas of religion in America," says Cohen. But he says Herberg has not suffered any apparent anguish because of the high price he has paid for his universality. "He is not dismayed," Cohen continues, "as are his Jewish admirers, by the loss of the particularity and concreteness of the Jewish people and Jewish history which his general cultural concerns have required." Cohen chides Herberg for his attempt "to justify that questionable phenomenon 'the Judeo-Christian tradition.'"

Cohen's criticism of Herberg suggests something of the spectrum of Jewish theological thought which it is not our purpose to explore here. It is our purpose only to grasp if we can the essence of the Jewish position generally in its relation to the kind of question the fourth faith asks. In spite of surface differences we find broad general agreement that Judaism is based upon the claim to a unique revelation which virtually all of the official religious community holds and which some stress to an extreme degree. The Orthodox Jews are the most dogmatic and uncompromising; Reform Jews the least so while the Conservative group lies somewhere in between. Will Herberg, too, leaves no doubt as to where he stands on this issue even though to the distress of Cohen and others, he places Judaism in the Judeo-Christian tradition. "Jewish-Christian faith is God-centered," he writes, and as we have seen, he contrasts this faith with the secularism which he believes stands over against it.

Jewish particularism rises from a long and noble history. If we are to understand it we have to go back at least to the time of Elijah.

In his contest with the prophets of Baal on Mt. Carmel, we are given a vivid picture of a struggle for supremacy between two forms of religious expression that took place in Palestine about twenty-eight hundred years ago. Elijah lived in the ninth century before the Christian era, but that was four hundred years after the first invasions by the Israelites of the fertile valleys of Canaan. By Elijah's time the culture and religion of Israel and that of the Canaanites, whom she conquered, had confronted each other for many generations.

People do not readily give up the worship of the gods to whom they are accustomed. They do not easily surrender beliefs and practices to which they have long held, and this was particularly true of the Israelites. But it was also true of the Canaanites. Although the religion of Israel became dominant in the land occupied by the Twelve Tribes, the older inhabitants never gave up the worship of Baal. Furthermore, in this period the worship of Baal continued to flourish beyond Israel's borders.

The contrast between the religion of Canaan and the religion of the invaders was very great. Canaan's was a typical fertility cult, with all its accompanying rites and ceremonies, myths, idols and sacrifices, barbarities and frenzies. Its general form and expression was duplicated in innumerable instances among the early civilizations that grew up in the Near East.

The religion of Israel, on the other hand, was of quite a different sort. Originally derived from an agricultural people perhaps, it had become the religion of a pastoral people, nomads, tent dwellers who lived in the open. As a result, it developed certain unique characteristics. First, it centered in human rights. In tribal life the individual was able to be more independent than were the citizens of the larger and more complex agrarian societies of the time. He was also valued more highly as a person. Human life was more precious in the desert, simply because mere survival there was so difficult. For Israel the individual had a value we rarely find in ancient civilizations where life was held very cheap.

Secondly, and for the same reason, the religion of Israel was stern and hard. It was both Spartan and Puritan. The desert exacted these requirements of whoever proposed to live there. The rituals, the robes of office, the temple setting, the feasting, the orgies: none of

these practices, which were commonplace among the agrarian people of the time, were possible for nomads for whom mere subsistence
was difficult. With them it was the Spartan virtues that counted and
Puritan rites and ceremonies that made the most sense.

Thirdly, and again for the same reason, the family unit was central
in Israel. Tribal loyalty was strong. Among the foremost of the rules
by which this cultural pattern was maintained we find the familiar
commandment from the Decalogue, "Honor thy father and mother."
Co-operative relationships enforced by mutual agreement between
the members of the family group were one of the aspects of survival.
Desert life required that individuals in the family unit assist and
sustain each other, as a result of which the family became exceed-
ingly close-knit.

A fourth aspect of the religion of Israel that was unique is also
found in the Decalogue, "Thou shalt not have any other gods before
me." On this Israel was adamant. For the followers of Moses there
was no god but Yahweh, and he was a jealous God. He brooked no
rivals. Hence all the Baals of Canaan were false gods and must be
cast out. The altars erected for Baal worship must be thrown down.
The high places—the hilltops of Canaan—where the altars to Baal
were built must be reassigned to the worship of Yahweh, or given
up as places of worship altogether.

Fierce undeviating loyalty to Yahweh as the one and only God of
Israel might not at first seem to rise from the desert environment
which in other respects so easily explains Israel's unique character.
Yet this aspect of her religion also fits very neatly into the total
picture. The life of the nomad is lonely. He is not in constant contact
with other cultures and other views of life which are different from
his own. We might say that as a result he becomes narrow in his
outlook, and perhaps he does. But he also becomes intensely loyal
to what he believes. It was so with Israel. As the Twelve Tribes
developed a fierce family and tribal loyalty, so they also developed
a virtually fanatical loyalty to Yahweh, their God.

After Israel had conquered the land of Canaan and settled there,
her people began to accept the agricultural gods of the land where
they dwelt. Some synthesis always results when two cultures attempt
to live in the same place at the same time. No matter how devoted
to the traditions of their ancestors a people may be, they uncon-

sciously absorb elements of the culture in the midst of which they live. Each successive generation yields a little further to the impact of other cultures upon it.

In Elijah's time the syncretism of the religion of Israel with that of Canaan had proceeded far and the process was accelerating. Under Ahab, who was then king, a conscious policy of toleration and assimilation was established. Israel was enjoying great commercial prosperity at the time. Trade was particularly brisk with the city-state of Tyre. To cement the relationship, Ahab took a Tyrian bride named Jezebel, daughter of one of the high priests of Baal. Under Ahab's rule, urged on by Jezebel, altars for the worship of Baal were again set up on the high places of the land, houses for his worship were erected, a priesthood of Baal was organized, and the old agricultural cultic festivals were reintroduced.

The reaction was almost immediate, however, and it came at the hands of Elijah, not surprisingly himself a man of the desert. He demanded that Israel abandon the worship of Baal and all that it meant, and he won out. The priests of Baal were put to the sword. King Ahab died in battle and Jezebel, his queen, was thrown to the dogs.

It is interesting to speculate as to how different the history of the West might have been had Elijah lost the contest on Mt. Carmel. Suppose that Baalism had prevailed. Then the unique elements in Israel's religion would have been swallowed up. The inhabitants of Palestine would have been like those of any of the areas of the Near East at that time—worshipers of many gods and the victims of despotic kings, whose sense of selfhood and whose moral standards were no better or worse than those of anyone else. It was the victory of Yahwism at this early period in Israel's history that made the difference.

The victory won by Elijah had to be won over and over again during subsequent generations. There is a sense in which we may say that the entire Old Testament is the story of the struggle between Israel's tendency to lapse into the syncretism that characterized the other people of the ancient world and the determination of her prophets to maintain her loyalty to the ancient faith. It is the story of a constant succession of victories on the part of those who held Israel to her ancient vision. And it is this constant succession of victories that gives both Judaism and Christianity their essential character today.

Reform movements which are prophetic, even revolutionary at their inception, do not remain that way, however. They have to be regularized, stated in precise terms, and reduced to definable beliefs, rituals, and modes of conduct if they are to be sustained. Prophetic zeal is more of a mood than a practice. When the zeal is gone, cult practice must take its place and continue, in ever more standardized patterns, the reform that the prophets brought about. Otherwise the reform fails altogether.

To this general rule Israel was no exception. As she caught the vision of her prophets and sought to follow the Law of the Lord, she became a people of the Book where the utterances of her prophets had been recorded. Ever-increasing attention was given to the Scriptures, for there God's Law was presumed to be found. Ever-increasing interpretation of it became necessary as patterns of life changed and as new currents of thought flowed in. As a result, ever-increasing rules of what was right and what was not right, what God wanted and what he did not want, began to develop.

And yet there are two ways in which we may estimate the significance of Elijah's victory. We may see it as the ancients saw it— as a victory of the God of Israel over the gods of Canaan. We may also see it as the victory of a man who saw the superior moral and spiritual quality of Yahweh worship as against the baseness of Baal worship. Elijah was not important because he called the Jews back to their ancient desert faith. Had the prophets of Baal won the contest on Mt. Carmel and called their people back to the ancient worship of Baal, they would also have rescued an ancient faith from possible oblivion. If there is virtue in keeping a tradition just because it is a tradition, or of continuing a practice merely because it exists and is old, then there was nothing to commend Yahwism over Baalism. Both were old. In fact, Baalism was much the older. It was a very ancient faith, as the many barbarous elements contained within it amply show.

The fourth faith would claim Elijah as its prophet if he may be thought of as a religious revolutionary who led his people to a higher conception of deity than they had known before, or if he may be thought of as a religious leader who restored to his people a noble faith from which they had fallen away. But Elijah cannot be a prophet of the fourth faith if to any degree he is to be seen as the agent of chosenness for Jews or if in any sense he is thought of as the defender of a faith which belongs first to Jews and secondarily to others, to Jews in any sense in which it does not belong to all who would claim it as their own because of its own intrinsic worth.

As in Protestantism, and in Catholicism seen in men like Pierre Teilhard de Chardin, so in Judaism there are occasional voices that rise above the particularism that characterizes religion generally as a whole. Such a man is Rabbi Roland B. Gittelsohn. He believes that there is no reason for a division between religion and science. In his *Man's Best Hope* he quotes frequently and with approval from the books of N. J. Berrill, the great marine biologist. In fact, the main structure of his thought seems to rest on contemporary science. He rejects miracle in the usual meaning of the word and admits that in doing so he is "on the brink of heresy." As he develops his theme, it becomes clear that he has passed from Judaism to a religion that transcends place and time and sect. He answers many questions the fourth faith is asking. Even his language has lost its sectarian character. Anyone except a true believer of the Catholic, Protestant, or Jewish persuasion could read this prophet. The latter would find Gittelsohn's forthright rejection of revelation unacceptable.

2. ROMAN CATHOLIC FAITH

The faith of Rome, far more than that of Judaism or Protestantism, is a faith of stability. The Church of Rome begins with the claim to divine origin. An official publication of the church states: "The [Roman Catholic] Church is . . . a society different from all others because it was formed by God." All else flows from this initial assertion. If it be true, then the Catholic can rightfully claim, as he does, that his church is "the divinely established and only means of grace in the world." Then, too, the Roman Church may claim as it does that because of its divine origin it knows the Truth. Accordingly, men have not to debate that either, but only to believe it.

If the Roman Church was formed by God, then it may also claim as it does that "the Catholic has certainty on vital matters [pertaining to religion] because God has revealed them to him." It may claim as it does that "By revelation we [Roman Catholics] receive something of the inner radiance of God's glory; by faith we learn divine truths of which humanly we should never have dreamed." If the Roman Church was "formed by God" then it may also claim as it does "there is an order of reality above that of nature, an order of reality which is beyond the reach of the human mind: the supernatural order" and that this supernatural order may be known to man, not through his own efforts or through any endowment that is his, but because "God speaks to man, making a statement to the truth of which he testifies." This is revelation. If the Roman Catholic Church was favored by God, as the Roman Church claims to have been, then it may properly assert that "faith is a virtue whereby we [Roman Catholics] believe that the things [God] has revealed are true . . . because of the authority of God himself, who reveals them, and who can neither be deceived nor deceive." Then may the Roman Church assert too that men are helpless to know the truth, that "left to their own resources, very few would gain adequate knowledge even of the truths of natural religion . . . on this subject, above all, man needs an omniscient and infallible teacher."

These are claims of a most extraordinary character. If we were not so familiar with them, we would more readily see how extraordinary they are. Accordingly, the fourth faith would ask, Are these claims justified? Is it true that God formed the Catholic Church? Ronald Knox, an Anglican convert to Catholicism, admitted one of the central objections to the central assertion of the Roman Church when he observed that it is circular. "To say that yours is the one true church because you, who belong in it, say that it is, proves nothing," he observed. "All churches make this circular claim." Then he asked: "How do you choose between them?"

His answer was: "If you ask a Catholic 'What is the Catholic Faith?' you are told, as in all churches, it is that held by the Catholic Church. However, if you persevere," continued Knox, "and ask what is the Catholic Church, you are no longer met with the irritatingly circular definition 'the church which holds the Catholic Faith'; you are told it is the church which is in communion with the Bishop of Rome." Here is as simple and direct a statement of the Roman Catholic position as one might hope to find. It is the principle of institutional authority in religion. The Catholic believes first of all in the authority of the Bishop of Rome—the lineal descendant of Peter, who received his authority from Christ who was God.

But there is still no answer here to the question Is it true? On what does Ronald Knox base his assertion that the claims made by the church which is in communion with the Bishop of Rome are true. Why should Catholic, Protestant, Jew, or infidel believe that they are? Who is to say that the Bishop of Rome possesses the authority the Roman Church claims for him? Again, the Roman Catholic answer is plain if not convincing. The Roman Church, basing its thought on the philosophy of Aristotle, has long held that the mind of man can know about things with the finality all men desire. Hence, in Christian thought, "truth" can be known by men; not partial truth; not approximate truth, but the final Truth which God himself knows.

"Truth is eternal because it is identical with Eternal Deity," says the Church of Rome. "Finite minds participate in Truth in the same manner in which they participate in being." Here we have no doctrine of the progressive discovery of truth. According to Catholic teachings, the truth may be known now through man's participation in the being of God. "God's apprehension of contingent things is the act which originates them," says the Roman Church. "Thus in knowing them we share in his manifestations. There is no other adequate explanation of the ultimate origin of truth."

The propaganda literature of the Roman Church designed for popular consumption is not always written at so high a level, but it asserts the same position and deals with these issues with a clarity that leaves no room for misunderstanding. *Our Sunday Visitor,* the national Catholic Action weekly newspaper, addressed itself to this question in a feature article under the title, "Are All Churches Equally Good?" "We Catholics believe that ours is the one true Church founded by Jesus Christ," the author replies to his own question, "and we believe that every Protestant is bound to say that his own is the only Church founded by Jesus Christ. Now, if he's right, we're wrong, and if we're right, then he's wrong. But for heaven's sake, let's not be so stupid ('broad-minded' I believe they call it) as to say that both the Catholic Church and the Protestant Churches are right, that each is the only true Church founded by Jesus Christ."

The question "Are All Churches Equally Good?" is a favorite with Roman Catholic polemicists, as is the either-or form of argument. A Paulist Press publication asks the same question and the argument runs as follows: "One who really holds that all religions are equally good, places the various pagan religions on a par with Christianity. They are all forms of religion, and one religion, in his opinion, is just as good as any other. The Catholic Church holds that Jesus Christ is true God as well as true man; that He is a Divine person; eternal, all-wise, all-powerful, all-good. She commands her children to adore Him. The Unitarian Church regards Christ as a mere man, and refuses Him divine worship. If Christ is not God, then the Catholic Church stands guilty of idolatry. She has forgotten, ignored, and insulted the true God by putting a creature in His place. If Christ is God, then Unitarianism is a blasphemy, for she has denied Him His rights, and has tried to drag Him down from His throne. Clearly, then, one who says that these two churches are equally good, implicitly asserts either that idolatry does no harm, or that blasphemy is a good and profitable thing."

If you grant the polemicist's premises, then you are readily hung on the horns of his dilemma. You are for blasphemy or idolatry. But if you do not grant his premises, then there is no problem. For those who do not hold "that Jesus Christ is true God," the argument must begin further back. Jews, members of the fourth faith, Hindus, Moslems, and the nonreligious all would say, "We need something more on which to go than your affirmation of your own belief, if we are to be persuaded of the truth of what you say." Many would not even grant the Roman Catholic assumption that truth of the kind it claims to possess can be known at all. And none but Roman Catholics would grant their exclusive claim to know what that truth might be, supposing it were knowable.

Perhaps the most succinct defense of the Roman Catholic position is to be found in our history books. When Martin Luther in 1517 challenged the Church of Rome with his Ninety-five Theses, he was taken before the Diet of Worms and asked to give an account of himself. He did so as best he was able. Then Johann Eck, a leading theologian of the day, assigned to answer him, rose and said:

"Your plea to be heard from Scripture is the one always made by heretics. You do nothing but renew the errors of Wyclif and Hus. How will the Jews, how will the Turks exult to hear Christians discussing whether they have been wrong all these years! Martin, how can you assume that you are the only one to understand the sense of Scripture? Would you put your judgment above that of so many famous men and claim that you know more than they all? You have no right to call into question the most holy orthodox faith, instituted by Christ, the perfect lawgiver, proclaimed throughout the world by the apostles, sealed by the red blood of the martyrs, confirmed by the sacred councils, defined by the Church in which all our fathers believed until death and gave to us an inheritance, and which now we are forbidden by the Pope and the Emperor to discuss lest there be no end of debate. I ask you, Martin—answer candidly and without horns—do you not repudiate your books and the errors which they contain?"

These remain the basic arguments of the Church of Rome. What answer would the fourth faith offer? Oddly enough, it would respond much as Luther did. Standing alone before the Emperor, the assembled nobility and the churchmen, he replied:

"Since then your Majesty and your Lordships desire a simple reply, I will answer without horns and without teeth. Unless I am convicted by Scripture and plain reason—I do not accept the authority of popes and councils, for they have contradicted each other —my conscience is captive to the Word of God. I cannot and I will not recant anything, for to go against conscience is neither right nor safe. God help me. Here I stand. I cannot do otherwise."

That Luther later retreated from this position both in theory and in practice is not so important here as the clarity and boldness of his first statement made under the duress of the circumstances under which he spoke. "I cannot go against conscience," he declared in essence. His point of departure was not the authority of a church but the authority of a man who trusts his own judgment.

We can best grasp the essential points of the Roman Catholic position if we take Eck's points seriatim, and observe to what degree if any they meet the questions the fourth faith would ask.

1. "All heretics base their argument on Scripture." It is true that Luther and all subsequent dissenters from the Roman position based their arguments on Scripture. But so also did Rome as we have seen. Luther and Rome did not disagree on the authority of Scripture. They divided on the manner in which Scripture was to be interpreted. Eck was right when he said that all dissenters argue from the Bible. Those who accept it as the Word of God, as all Catholics and most Protestants do, must begin their argument there. What higher authority can there be than God's word? In consequence, the only force in this point lay in Eck's attempt to convict Luther through guilt by association. As Luther, like all the condemned heretics, based his dissent on Scripture, so he, like them, was guilty of the gravest offense with which a man at that time might be charged.

2. "There is nothing original in what you say." This is the familiar "old stuff" argument, still one of the most popular weapons in the armory of theological debate. It is the argument of the half-suppressed yet openly condescending yawn, "We've heard all that before," "I thought we had passed beyond all that." Essentially, it is an appeal to the concensus that the invalidity of the point at issue has long since been settled and need not be argued again. Its use, however, now as in Luther's time, belies the strength of the point to which it is addressed. There would be no need to meet the arguments of the Luthers or anyone else if the error in their position had in fact already been established.

3. "Our enemies will rejoice at the dissension in our ranks." This has always been true and it is inescapable. But such an argument, posing as the way of wisdom, easily becomes an instrument of tyranny. Every challenge to authority, every controversy, leads to temporary weakness in the organization challenged. For this reason, whoever would question the established order should do so only out of the profound conviction that in the long run he can strengthen and improve what he criticizes. But there comes a time when silence is not golden, but venal. Then, though one's enemies may rejoice, the criticism must be made and the improvement sought at the risk of the temporary disruption that accompanies it, for the sake of the long-term gain that will follow.

4. "If you are right, Christianity has been wrong these fifteen

hundred years." This argument has great power still. How is it possible that Christianity could have been wrong all this time? Just as possible as that men were wrong for an even longer time in their belief that the earth was the center of the universe merely because it was central for them.

5. "Who do you think you are? Why do you think that you alone can understand Scripture? Would you put your judgment ahead of so many famous men?" Every man who has ever had an idea that differed from the prevailing thought and practice of his time has had to ask himself this question. Who would dare set himself up against divine revelation? And yet, have not all advances in human thought come at the hands of those who have dared to stand against all their contemporaries? Was that not what Copernicus and Galileo, Darwin and Einstein, did? The problem faced by Luther is the problem every dissenter must face. Each must decide whether he or the world is right. It is no easy decision to make, for the chances are very great that in any given instance, you are wrong, and the world is right.

6. "Christ himself instituted the Roman Catholic faith." The fourth faith would simply point out that this is the question at issue. To assert it is by no means to establish the fact.

7. "The faith has been proclaimed by uncounted people." As an assertion is not a demonstration, so increasing the number of people who believe it to be true does not establish the fact any more securely. The millions upon millions of people who lived and died, believing that the world was flat, did not make it so.

8. "Our fathers believed in this church." All human progress has been based upon a willingness to depart from the beliefs of one's fathers.

9. "We are forbidden to discuss these matters." The world has long since demonstrated that truth emerges where questioning is encouraged and discussion is free. The Roman Church itself no longer takes the attitude that these matters are not to be discussed. The Index Expurgatoris itself is now under question.

The issue as between the Roman Catholic position and all others is plain. In the words of Cardinal Newman, those outside the church make "the mistake of subjecting to human judgment those revealed doctrines which are in their nature beyond and independent of it, and of claiming to determine on intrinsic grounds the truth and value of propositions which rest for their reception on the external authority of the Divine Word." But he overlooked the fact that the external authority of which he spoke is really internal because it is asserted by the church which in turn claims to be unique because of what the "Divine Word" says. And it is that same church which holds the "Word" to be divine.

An Anglican, William P. Witcutt, who was converted to Catholicism and later left the church, said he was attracted in the first instance by the system of belief taught by the Roman Church. "Here was an intellectual scheme," he wrote, "moulded and shaped to include every detail. One had only to make an act of faith, and one was settled intellectually for life. No more questions need be asked."

But the convert discovered that there was more to religion than intellectual symmetry and that even the symmetry itself was insufficient. "The God of Scholasticism was unworshipable," he wrote on returning to the Church of England. "Nor do Roman Catholics worship Him. They cannot. They worship the Sacred Heart, the Virgin and the Saints." And he discovered, too, that his initial act of faith did not set him free. It locked him in an intellectual prison. "Roman Catholicism," he wrote, "does not allow for any advance in philosophy made since the 13th century," or for any in physical science or history. Cardinal Newman corroborated this observation when he said in describing his progress toward Catholicism: "From the time that I became a Catholic, of course I have no further history of my religious opinions to narrate." Willard Sperry, late Dean of the Harvard Divinity School, remarked after quoting this passage: "This has always seemed to me one of the most melancholy bits of religious autobiography on record."

Rome is, of course, not the monolith she sometimes seems to be. There are deep divisions among her leaders as to the position the church ought to take on matters of doctrine and dogma as well as on policy in the social and political sphere. We have spoken of John Courtney Murray and his attempt to find a place for the Roman Catholic Church in American society consistent with the age-old principles of the church. We have seen that he has repudiated as a late medieval development in Roman thought the doctrine that the church must, where it has the power, suppress all rivals. The church accommodated itself to these views when it was necessary for it to do so. But this was a passing phase in the development of church-state relationships, he insists, and must not be projected into the present, as in Franco Spain, for example, where Protestantism is very strictly limited *on principle*.

Father Murray goes back to Pope Gelasius XIII and John of Paris for authority for his point of view. In their thinking he finds support for the American doctrine of the separation of church and state. By this doctrine the state disclaims competence in matters religious. But, he argues, the Roman Catholic Church failed to see that this peculiarly American political doctrine was in fact an implementation of a much older Catholic teaching. This was due, he thinks, to the attempts of the Church to meet continental liberalism which it failed to distinguish from American political democracy. "It is the present task of Catholics," he argues, "to work toward the purification of the liberal tradition (which is their own real tradition) and of the democratic form of state in which it finds expression, by restoring both the idea and the institutions of democracy to their proper Christian foundations."

We have seen that the thinking of John Courtney Murray has become the basis for new rapprochement between American Catholics and their fellow religionists. Here we shall examine the validity of Father Murray's argument. On the surface his views offer the promise of religious harmony on the pattern of pluralism. But questions soon begin to arise. If the claim of the Roman Catholic Church to the right of official recognition can now be dismissed as an accommodation to the particular historical situation that developed in the late Middle Ages and continued on into the nineteenth century, cannot Father Murray's view be interpreted in the same way? Is it not also accommodational? Might not it too be dismissed at a later date?

Father Murray has been widely praised for interpreting Roman Catholic theology in such a manner that through it the Roman Church can find a place for itself in the contemporary American scene. But he has also been widely criticized by his fellow Catholics and he has been factually contradicted by the Holy See. In 1953 one of Rome's experts in ecclesiastical law, Cardinal Ottaviani, made a speech backing the suppression of Protestants in Spain. It was at first thought by the supporters of Father Murray that the Cardinal might have spoken out of turn. But they were soon disabused of any such hope. A Vatican official pronounced Cardinal Ottaviani's speech "unexceptionable" and as if to underscore the authority and ancient lineage of the view, he added: "Certainly there was nothing new in it." Said the Cardinal: "Now if there is any certain and indisputable truth to be found among the general principles of public ecclesiastical law, it is the truth that the rulers in a state composed almost entirely of Catholics, and consequently and consistently governed by Catholics, have the duty to influence the legislation of that state in a Catholic sense . . . [and] to protect . . . the religious unity of a people who unanimously know themselves to be in secure possession of religious truth."

Father Murray thought the Cardinal's views "neither official nor semi-official." It was, he said, still "legitimate for Catholics to doubt or dispute whether Cardinal Ottaviani's discourse represents the full, adequate and balanced doctrine of the church." But there was no doubt left in anyone's mind where the Holy See and many other Roman Catholic leaders stood on the matter. Father Murray might think what he liked. Rome stood, not with Pope Gelasius but with Gregory VII and Innocent III.

The prophetic nature of the utterances of Father Murray have, however, been made apparent with the recent marked change in the climate at Rome itself. The determined efforts at interfaith conciliation made by Pope John XXIII, coupled with the warm world-wide reception of those overtures on the part of Catholics and non-Catholics alike, led to the election of the moderate to liberal Paul VI. This means that the mood of conciliation and co-operation is likely to be with us for a generation or more. Pope Paul continued the Vatican Council. Cardinal Ottaviani and his followers, who include two American Cardinals, are for the moment the party of the minority, in influence if not in numbers.

Yet still the questions that are foremost in the faith of adventure remain, as they remain for many Protestants and people of other religious persuasions. Father Murray may argue that the separation of church and state is a more ancient and, therefore, more authentic Catholic doctrine. But what of Rome's claims to spiritual supremacy? None of these has been relinquished. What of her claims to know the truth? What of her claims to the authority with which the possession of that truth endows her? If "accommodation" should require it, what is to prevent Rome from again asserting the view that she is morally bound to suppress error where she has the power to do so, as she does today in Spain and South America, a power she does not have in the United States. On the theory of accommodation, what assurance is there that complete freedom would continue to be the birthright of all religious groups in this country, should it ever have a Catholic majority?

There is a further ambiguity. The doctrine of freedom is central in Father Murray's thought. But we need to examine it very carefully for it is a special kind of freedom he is talking about. "The whole system of Roman Catholic attitudes on Church-state pivots on the doctrines of freedom," he writes. "There is first the free obedience of the Christian conscience to the magisterial and jurisdictional authority of the Church; there is secondly the free participation of the citizen as a Christian, in the institutions whereby all the processes of temporal life are directed to their proper ends."

We understand the "free participation of the citizen in the institutions whereby all the processes of temporal life are directed." But Father Murray speaks of the "proper ends" of the institutions of temporal life. What are they and who decides? We have noted his answer and it is very clear. "There is first the free obedience of the Christian [Roman Catholic?] conscience to the magisterial and jurisdictional authority of the Church." The word "freedom" here obviously does not mean what it means in contemporary American parlance for we are not accustomed to speak of "free obedience," and when we find these words together we do not know what they mean.

We find the answer to our question in another of Father Murray's monographs. In 1954 he wrote: "In pursuing the argument it is taken for granted that the principles of Catholic faith and morality are controlling. Religious faith and morals are not subject to judgment by the norms of any political or social system. The question sometimes raised, whether Catholicism is compatible with American democracy, is an invalid and impertinent question: for the manner of its position inverts the order of values. The question is whether American democracy . . . is compatible with Catholicism. No other manner of putting the question would be acceptable to anyone who places the imperatives of conscience which mediate the law of God above the imperatives whose origins are in human law and sentiment."

One further aspect of American religious pluralism as it relates to the Roman Catholic Church must be considered. It has nothing to do with ideas, although this confusion is sometimes present. It has only to do with power and the readiness to use it. The American community from time to time views with alarm the enormous and rapidly growing power of the Roman Catholic Church because great power in and of itself constitutes a threat, when as in the case of the Roman Church it is concentrated in the hands of a very few men.

To illustrate, a feature article in *Fortune* magazine in 1960 on Francis Cardinal Spellman reported the following facts for the Archdiocese of New York alone. Current annual outlay runs to at least fifty million dollars. Numerous Catholic charities spend another fifty million a year. Operating costs of Catholic schools probably approach twenty-two million a year. Annual reviews and collections of all Catholic institutions in the archdiocese must be around one hundred fifty million a year.

To sum up, those who find they have moved to what is now being called the fourth faith do not find an answer to the questions they are asking in all the beauty and power, the variety and symmetry, the age, the size, or the extent of the Church of Rome. In the faith of adventure, claims to truth, claims to authority, claims to divine connections are not admitted to advanced standing. Such claims may present themselves, as do all other claimants to truth. They may offer such credentials as they have. But neither the claims of Rome nor those of any other church will be weighted because of their age or their allegedly divine origin, neither because of the number of people who supposedly accept them nor because of the economic or political power the Roman Church commands. In the fourth faith all the claims of all the religions are examined by the same standard and the worth of each is assessed in the same way. In accordance with these standards, we shall now examine the claims of Protestantism.

3. PROTESTANT LIBERALISM

It has been said that the Protestant Reformation shifted religious authority from the Pope to the Bible. Like all broad generalizations, this one both illumines and obscures the truth. It is true that the Bible was the central authority for the Reformation Protestants, or so they thought. It is true that in the Roman Church which they rejected, authority lay with the Pope and the Roman Curia. But it is also true that the Bible proved to be a very uncertain source of authority for the Protestants. Far from clear in its precepts, the Bible almost at once became a source of conflict. The "plain meaning of Scripture" proved to be a chimera. Endless and furious disputation resulted from its use as the final authority for Christian teaching and practice.

Thus the real difference between the Roman Catholic Church, nearly fifteen hundred years old at the time of the Reformation, and the newly formed Protestant churches was not their respective sources of authority but their experience in dealing with contentious men. The Roman Church, in its institutional development, had long since met, and according to its own lights, solved the problems that now threatened to destroy the Protestant churches. Rome long ago had established the lines of governmental authority within the church and everyone knew what they were. Rome had also long since established what the "plain meaning of Scripture" was, and how that meaning was to be established where it was still in doubt. By the time of the Protestant Reformation Rome, as we have seen, had long since established the Inquisition, an instrument that readily induced outward acceptance of her interpretations, even when strong inward dissent was present, as in the case of Galileo.

Nevertheless, both the extent of the Inquisition and the extreme measures it employed bear witness to the fact that the mind of the West had, by the sixteenth century, begun to outrun the concepts by which Rome had established the uniformity of thought that made peace within the church possible. And while Rome might succeed for centuries more in maintaining outward, if not inward, conformity to her metaphysics, morals, and patterns of procedure, Protestantism was doomed from the start to fail in maintaining such rigidity, for her premises were different. Among Martin Luther's doctrines, "the priesthood of all believers" was one of the most central. So also was "the freedom of the Christian man." However Luther might understand these words, or Calvin or Zwingli or Henry VIII, they meant freedom of conscience to most of those who heard them. "Sufficiency of Scripture," another central Reformation doctrine, meant the same.

To men generally, these words meant what Luther meant at the

Diet of Worms: that each might read the Bible and that the truth was what the Bible meant to him, not what some learned theologian said it was supposed to mean. Furthermore, if religious freedom from a tyrannical Roman Curia was abroad, it was so only because it was part of the more general European mood of political freedom, social freedom, intellectual freedom—freedom of every kind.

From the time of the Renaissance, when the modern mood of inquiry first took form, the Protestant churches have consistently sought to modify their teachings in accordance with its demands. In fact, the Reformation itself has often been interpreted as a part of the great movement toward independency and the exploration of new areas of thought and conduct that mark the beginnings of modern Western culture. The formation of the new Protestant churches in Germany, Switzerland, France, England, and Poland did not result from, but were concomitants of, the breakdown of the medieval way of life and the emergence of the modern spirit.

Those were the days of the great voyages of exploration, when the mind of all Europe was aglow with the spirit of adventure. Those were the days of Copernicus, Kepler, and Galileo, when the horizons of the mind suddenly widened in spite of the efforts of the church to keep the ancient thought pattern intact. Those were the days of Desiderius Erasmus, author of biblical criticism, and of Francis Bacon, often called the founder of modern science.

They were also the days of two obscure men who took the spirit of nascent Protestantism more literally than most, and in contrast to Calvin and Luther, sought to implement it in the church. One was Faustus Socinus, who established in Poland, at that time the most tolerant nation in Europe, a church in which the Protestant principle of individual freedom might be practiced in a way that was not possible in any other church of the time. He did not succeed, for the controversies that wracked the Polish Minor Church, as it was called, could not be controlled. A vivid picture of the inability of the church to control the freedom it espoused is provided in a tract written by one of the defectors from the church, giving his reasons for his decision. "Dissension is rife, not only among the ministers," he wrote, "but also in the private quarrels of the ministers and the poor with the gentry; there is uncertainty and much contention as to the right form of baptism. . . ."

Eventually the Polish Minor Church was destroyed by a combination of factors: dissension within; attacks from without by the dominant Calvinist church; and in the end it was overwhelmed by the Counter-Reformation led by the Jesuits. The other man who attempted to establish a church in which the minds of men might be free was Francis David, who established a Unitarian church in Hungary at about the same time. It, too, was wracked by controversy and because of this was effective for only a short period of time.

Brief reference to these men—others might have been chosen—will serve to illustrate the expectations of doctrinal and governmental independence in the church that the Protestant Reformation generated in the minds and hearts of men. The movement was born in freedom, and it had no valid basis if freedom was not one of its central tenets. On the authoritarian basis Rome could maintain her claim to be the one true church. Unless it were held that the free minds of men might challenge the authority Rome claimed to possess, she could not be challenged.

Many writers have traced the beginnings of religious liberalism in America to these same forces surging through the Renaissance and the Reformation in Europe. Ernest Sutherland Bates summarized these views as follows: "Democracy did not arise out of eighteenth-century political and industrial conflicts, as a momentarily popular view misconceives. Its roots are to be found in the attempted revival of primitive Christianity by the radical lower-class sects of the Protestant Reformation, those peasants and yeomen who were our own ancestors, and who initiated the Reformation and eventually carried out its basic principles—especially in America—to conclusions undreamt of in the beginning. The ideal of local self-government was brought to America by the Pilgrims; the separation of church and state was derived from the Baptists; the right to free speech was a development of the right to freedom of conscience established by Roger Williams and William Penn; the equality spoken of in the Declaration of Independence was an outgrowth of the equality practiced by the Quakers; Democracy was envisaged in religious terms long before it assumed a political terminology."

Protestantism has never since escaped from the logic of its own position. Separate churches have asserted their authority over against the individual conscience as Rome had done long before, but the principle of the free mind and the individual conscience is like yeast and it has never ceased to work on the Protestant loaf. It continually possessed the minds of individual Protestants as it had Faustus Socinus and Francis David, the Anabaptists, the Puritans, the Separatists, and countless others both known and forgotten.

A second and perhaps more important influence upon American Protestantism came from the European intellectual movement we know as the Enlightenment. In the eighteenth century the deists had attempted to deal with the implications of Newton's thought for theology. But the placid calm of the church remained undisturbed by their efforts. Then in the nineteenth century biblical criticism got underway, as a result of which the extraordinarily complex and very human origins of the Bible were laid before the minds of men. In 1863 Ernest Renan published the first in what has become a steady stream of popular novel-like lives of Christ, in which he is treated as a human rather than a divine figure. Renan's "Life" still makes very good reading.

But it was not until the work of Bible scholars had long since been accepted and taught in the Unitarian churches of England and America that the impact of biblical criticism and other studies began to be faced in the church as a whole. The break came in 1891, when biblical scholarship had so changed men's thought about the Bible that the noted preacher, Washington Gladden, felt called upon to tackle the problem openly in a volume under what must have been a very startling title for the time, *Who Wrote the Bible?*

Then came the deluge. What now were Christians to believe? Copernicus and Galileo had destroyed the earth-centered universe implicit in much of Christian theology. Newtonian physics had undercut it further. Darwin's *Origin of Species* had demoted man to a place among the other creatures of the earth, while the sciences of geology and paleontology had made Genesis literally if not figuratively unbelievable.

After Darwin the issue could no longer be avoided. Nowhere is this process better illustrated than in an anthology published in 1932 depicting the religious pilgrimage of thirty leading American Protestant theologians. Almost to a man, they testify to the impact of scientific thinking upon the theological doctrines taught them in their youth. These men came to maturity about the turn of the century. It was a period of unprecedented freedom of thought and discussion within the churches themselves and was characterized by the exhilarating sense of discovery, of new fields conquered, and of old ideas cast away.

The problems which confronted the men of that time were many. The higher criticism of the Bible had shaken their faith in the infallibility of the Scriptures. Seeing the difficulties involved in the idea of a theological Christ, they joined in the search for the Jesus of history. Yet the further problem remained before them as to how the historical Jesus could play the role in Christianity the theological Christ had played heretofore. They asked why there were so many creeds; they wondered why there seemed to be so great a difference between "scientific" and "religious" truth, and they asked whether religious experience was objectively valid, or only subjective and personal.

They asked whether Christianity were really unique, as they had been taught to believe. They wanted to know in what sense Christianity was different, if it was, in fact, different from other religions. They asked whether there was any difference between philosophy and theology. If not, they demanded to know how theology was anything more than a metaphysics which included the concept of God. They wanted to know how science was possible without determinism, how religion was possible without freedom. Most of all, they wanted to know how it was possible to have the determinism of science and the freedom of religion both at the same time.

Two important results followed upon the constant yeasting of independency within Protestantism and therein lies the importance of this bit of history for us. One result was the proliferation of separate denominations. The other was the constant development and reinterpretation of Christian doctrine. With the independent mind at work in the church, no credal formulation was safe. The erosion resulting from constant questioning wore down the sturdiest of them. New interpretations of the old language flourished and one by one, treasured beliefs and ancient practices were modified until some of them disappeared altogether.

Liberalism, as it appeared in the Protestant churches in the nineteenth and early twentieth centuries, was the culmination of this yeasting process. Liberalism has been defined in many ways both by its enemies and its friends, but essentially it was an attempt on the part of churchmen to make Christian theology a part of the Western intellectual tradition. It was an attempt to face up to all that that tradition meant for Christian theology. In a very real sense the liberals undertook to bring to a close the "war between religion and science." It was not their purpose to make the one conform to the tenets of the other. They believed in both and thought it necessary only to find the common ground between them. They took Christian truth for granted. They took scientific truth for granted also. The problem, as they saw it, was to show how the new knowledge of the natural world illuminated and enhanced the older truths that had already come into their possession through the Christian religion.

There are uncounted definitions of liberalism available, most of which fail to grasp its essential quality. Most students of the movement have given their attention to the surface phenomena and have thus failed to grasp its essence. When they have described it they have done so quite naturally in terms of the orthodoxy against which it rebelled. Thus, John Herman Randall, Jr. wrote: "In the history of American religion, liberalism has had a number of very different meanings. . . . Each had its own special character . . . but all of them have shared in the common faith in the power of man . . . to work out under the will of God his own destiny." It is true that most liberals in fact held this view, but only as a counterpart of their rejection of the opposite traditional Christian doctrine, especially that of the Calvinists, which held man to be the helpless victim of God's wrath or the benefactor of His mercy.

Randall's definition fails to come to grips with the essential quality in liberalism because the characteristic it singles out—self-reliance—is by no means confined to the liberals. The difference is theoretical rather than practical; it is theological rather than actual. The "man from Mars" who happened to stop in on our planet and knew nothing about the beliefs of liberals and nonliberals could not tell the difference between them unless he saw them at prayer. Watching what they did afterward, he would find no difference in the energy with which each of them applied himself to whatever task he had in hand. The one might be said to be relying upon himself; the other to be acting with God's help for which he had prayed and which he supposed himself to be receiving. But except for this theological difference, it would be impossible to distinguish between them. What the "man from Mars" could not understand in all probability would be the fact that frequently the man who did not pray succeeded, while the man who did, failed.

There has always been a strong tendency to define liberalism in terms of the theological position held by those who professed to be liberal. In 1932 when the movement had reached its highest point of development, A. C. McGiffert, Jr. described it as "the reinterpretation of Christian theological traditions in order to give validity to those aspects of culture which may in general be called humanistic." However, most such writing is confined to the latter-day critics and analysts of the movement. Typical is Kenneth Cauthen, who has recently completed a thoroughgoing study of twentieth-century liberalism in America. Characteristically, he defines liberalism as a movement tending toward Monism, believing in the immanence of God, the knowability of God, the Bible as a record of the religious pilgrimage of Israel, and the world as a place where the victory of the spirit over nature may be won by man. To sum up, he thinks liberalism believed in "a dynamic unitary world in which Spirit is gradually permeating nature with meaning and value is fundamental to the modern understanding of reality."

Liberalism was in some sense all of these things. That is to say, liberals generally espoused these views. But to assert that this particular set of beliefs is the essence of liberalism is to confuse the accident with the essence. Perhaps the clearest evidence of this is to be found in a comment made by a reviewer of Cauthen's book. Snorted he: "The real weakness of Christian liberalism is not (as seems to be here indicated) that it loves to regard the natural world, and human life in it, as a continuous process. Nor is it the characteristic doctrine that God is immanent in the process. Both these propositions are a part of the Christian truth. The radical failure of liberal theology, and of some prominent schools of postliberal thought likewise, is that they cannot fully join with historic Christianity, Catholic and Evangelical, in singing:

> 'Let the water and the blood,
> From Thy riven side which flowed,
> Be of sin the double cure,
> Cleanse me from its guilt and power.'

"That which has made essential Christianity," continued Cauthen's reviewer, "is the clear apostolic witness that in the person of the divine Son made man, crucified and risen, the sovereign God has performed an objective act upon the plane of history, which has conquered the enslaving power of sin, and has so dissolved the bonds of guilt that sinful man dare come to the holy God in order to receive the effect of that historic victory."

The vehemence of this man's reaction bespeaks not only his own dogmatism, but a total failure to grasp the essence of the liberal movement through Cauthen's presentation. Had the reviewer been made to see the liberal indictment of his own position, he would not have presented the kind of refutation he offers. He would have felt compelled to answer the question the liberal would ask him: How do you know the truth of those things you so dogmatically declare? Cauthen fails to see what the liberals were really attempting to do, but he does accurately present their failure to achieve their own goal. Accordingly, he does not see why they failed. He does not see that they were working at cross purposes with themselves. They entered upon the faith of adventure with high hopes, and for a time their achievements were impressive. But having gone only a short way in some cases, a longer way in others, they grew afraid. Most of them really did not want to leave the faith of stability. In their minds they were merely refurbishing it. Few if any of them were prepared to take their departure from the faith of their fathers—to give up their particular historic faith for a more general set of principles that transcended both time and place.

In theological circles liberalism is still thought of in the same way. As I write, a periodical comes to my desk containing several articles gathered under the general head, "Liberalism: a Re-evaluation," But the editor obviously had in mind not the liberal approach to the religion of man but liberal Christianity. In an editorial that introduces their several feature articles, he wrote: "The five papers in this symposium illustrate how differently two Methodist and two Anglican theologians to say nothing of a Baptist-preacher-theologian are inclined to analyze the liberal tendency of nineteenth- and twentieth-century theology." But he also makes it clear that whatever it was that made the fires of liberalism burn so brightly in the nineteenth and early twentieth centuries has not yet died out. "There is in all of these papers . . . a clue to a strong undercurrent of uneasiness and discontent on the part of a considerable sector of the theological community."

John Herman Randall, Jr., came closer to the generic idea of liberalism when he wrote: "Any liberal tradition must insist on the right of the individual to oppose and attack the opinions of the majority." If those who undertake to describe the movement would remember its name and the etymology of that name, they would have less difficulty understanding its essential character. As William Ernest Hocking said, "Liberalism is dissent from finality. It is a doctrine of growth."

One of the most perceptive descriptions of liberalism was made by Henry E. Kolbe. The spirit of liberalism, he said, is characterized by open-mindedness toward truth, by humility and tolerance toward those whose views differ. It is nondogmatic and refuses to close accounts permanently; it is inquisitive and sets no limits to the ranging of the mind; it is generous, optimistic, reforming, progressive, and is charitable, like that of I Corinthians 13. Liberalism has, said Kolbe, a close affinity with the Christian spirit and the democratic spirit as well.

In its method, he continues, liberalism is closely akin to scientific empiricism, to idealistic philosophy and to rationalistic philosophy. It depends upon reason to solve its problems, is skeptical toward authority as a source or criterion for truth, and is skeptical of revelation in the same way. Liberalism emphasized experiment and observation as a means of learning. It has a predilection for "nature" and questions those things that cannot be apprehended in these categories. It prefers the historical, psychological, sociological approach to religion and seeks the significance of its doctrines in human experience. It is open-ended as opposed to the closed systems of orthodoxy.

Liberalism in principle is identical with the fourth faith, but for the present at least, the two terms cannot be used interchangeably. Liberalism was a movement in nineteenth- and twentieth-century Christianity which rose to a pre-eminent position in Protestantism and in Judaism during the 1920's. In theological circles the liberal has now fallen upon such evil times that "liberal" is often considered to be a dirty word. Kenneth Cauthen's study indicates the growing tendency to think of liberalism not generically but historically. Liberalism in the eyes of most scholars today is the name for a movement in American Protestantism that reached its high-water mark in the 1920's when it was known as "Modernism" and abruptly died out in the early 1930's.

4. MODERNISM

Did liberalism succeed in answering the questions the modern mind increasingly put to theology? The showdown on that question came with the phase of liberalism known as "Modernism." By the time of the conclusion of World War I, the liberal movement in theology had spread into most of the Protestant denominations. The postwar decade found them attempting to draw the mass of knowledge accumulating in all fields of endeavor into some kind of consistency with the ancient traditions of the Christian church. Because of the Protestant character of the movement and because Protestantism has traditionally been centered in the Bible, most, if not all, of the issues with which they dealt came back in the end to the Bible. How was it to be understood?

Within this larger question a more specific one proved to be pivotal. How were the Gospels to be understood? What did they say about Jesus Christ, and what did they not say? Back in the obscure times the Bible recorded, what had happened and what had not happened? Was it possible to get at the historical facts, it was asked. Aware as men now were of the role of ritual and myth in ancient times, aware as they now were of the credulity of ancient men, particularly in religious matters, they undertook a sorting process in an attempt to distinguish between the imaginary, the bizarre, mistakes of judgment and what had *really* happened in Bible times.

Shirley Jackson Case, for example, undertook to prove that Christianity did not introduce any supernaturalism into religion. Supernaturalism was not central in Christianity at the beginning, Case assured the faithful, but it was at the heart of Christianity's rivals. Christianity had to adopt this way of thinking in order to compete, he said. The real true original Christianity was a moral and spiritual way of life. This was gradually laid over with other worldly imagery because of the influence of the other pagan religions and so the true nature of Christianity was obscured.

This was a fairly novel, not to say basic, thesis in the light of the biblical account of the part supernaturalism played in the minds of the first Christians and still plays in the minds of most of them. It was a well-documented presentation and wholly congenial to the mind of the 1920's, but few have been persuaded to his point of view. Now, with the benefit of over thirty years of hindsight, his study looks like but one more futile effort to draw Christianity and modern thought together. Case was simply in error. A moral and spiritual, nonsupernatural religion might be wholly congenial to the mind of the 1920's, but it was not the Christianity of the Apostolic Age. Had Case been able to show that Christianity in reality had been such a religion at the outset, then the gap would have been closed and modern knowledge and ancient faith could have joined hands in a common enterprise. But Case did not succeed because he forced the facts to support his thesis, rather than letting the facts determine what his thesis ought to be.

Case's effort to rid Christianity of supernaturalism was part of a more general attempt on the part of Modernist Bible scholars to sift their way back through the many disparate elements which are to be found in it, particularly in the Gospels, to the true story of Jesus' life. None of these men was consciously distorting history. Each began with the assumption that history, as it was to be found in the Bible, had been corrupted by well-intentioned but ignorant men. Each thought that beneath the overlay of adulation and miracle and beneath the purposeful writing of the Gospel authors, the true man could be revealed. J. Estlin Carpenter, in a volume entitled *The Historical Jesus and the Theological Christ,* cast the issue in a phrase. The liberals concluded that the gentle Galilean had been completely obscured and transformed by the theology of Paul and later Christian thinkers. They proposed to restore the simple unadorned man of Nazareth who walked the earth even as you and I, who, without the use of miracles, transformed men by the power of his spirit and the depth of his insight. For them, Jesus was not so much the Second Person of the Trinity, coequal and coexistent with God, as he was the divine Son of God through whom God was revealed to man and whose teachings and patterns of life men were to follow.

It was the *person* of Jesus they found commanding. Cried Kirby Page at the close of a typical book entitled *Jesus or Christianity:* "No greater tragedy has ever occurred than the obscuration of that matchless character by the wrangling of the theologians. The followers of Jesus, in their eagerness to do him homage, have all but destroyed his reality." The book is an outline of Christian history from its beginnings. In it the author attempts to show the difference that always prevailed between Christian teaching and practice. It is an indictment of the evils perpetrated in the name of Christianity.

Harry Emerson Fosdick, the leader of the Modernist movement in the United States, still holds to the position he reached forty years ago. In his autobiography he writes: "For me the essence of Christianty is incarnate in the personality of the Master, and it means basic faith in God, in the divinity revealed in Christ, in personality's sacredness and possibilities, and in the fundamental principles of life's conduct which Jesus of Nazareth exhibited. I am sure that the world today desperately needs his faith and his way of life, and that without them, there is no hope."

The Modernist movement reached its apex perhaps when in 1924 Fosdick was invited to give the Lyman Beecher Lectures at Yale. He took the opportunity to set forth the Modernist position with unmistakable clarity. Choosing as his topic "The Modern Use of the Bible," he moved to the center of the controversy with the Fundamentalists. The lectures, subsequently published in book form, went through edition after edition. In paperback they are still widely read today. For a great many people he successfully resolved the conflict between an authoritative Bible written in ancient times and the thought of a day nineteen centuries later, the concepts of which are fundamentally different.

He first pays his compliments to the accomplishments of the Higher Criticism. He spells these words with capitals as if to canonize them. What are the accomplishments of the Higher Criticism? he asks. First, it has shown that the Bible contains the story of the religious development of Israel. This explains the barbarity of much of the Old Testament. Thus it all leads to the New Testament by religious development. Thus the Bible is, after all, a progressive revelation. He then lists the advantages which are obvious to any contemporary who has ever tried to reconcile the various inconsistencies in Holy Writ. The Higher Criticism enables us to see the events related in their own time; and thus their bizarre character can be explained. We must learn to distinguish between man's abiding experiences and their contemporary expressions.

Oddly enough, Fosdick does not acknowledge that he is treading a well-worn path. Nearly a hundred years before Theodore Parker, the Unitarian, had said the same thing to the men of his time and was ostracized by his fellow liberals because of his "attack" upon Christianity. Fosdick's words are reminiscent of the earlier prophet: "If there are new ways of approaching men's minds, new methods of argument and apologetic, let us have them. . . . If there are new powers disclosed by science, let us have them and put them at the disposal of the Lord of life to make our service more efficient!"

He rejects the ancient solution of allegory, insisting again that "a man must be able to recognize the abiding messages" of the Bible, even though they be "in a transient setting": the concepts and language of Theodore Parker again. Then he goes on to ask whether we must continue to think in the old categories, or whether we cannot discard them while holding to the essential truth they originally contained. Why, for example, can we not continue to believe in immortality without continuing to believe in the resurrection of the body.

There follow other examples of the old category rejected but the new truth retained: "I believe in the victory of righteousness upon this earth, in the coming Kingdom of God, whereon Christ looking shall see the travail of his soul and be satisfied, but I do not believe in the physical return of Jesus." And later: "So we surrender the old category of demonology . . . but . . . the age-long eclipse of man's life in sin and misery is as much of a fact and as terrible a fact as ever it was." "Having frankly recognized . . . the outgrown nature of the category we . . . should seek to understand . . . the abiding experience." "An important part of the modern preacher's responsibility is thus to decode the abiding meanings of Scripture from outgrown phraseology." The last example in his chapter on "Abiding Experiences" concerns angels. He says of them: "Angels represent our fathers' profound and practical consciousness of the reality, friendliness and availability of the spiritual world." He resolves the problem of miracles through the same formula.

Fosdick sums up the process which he has been describing in words which are not merely reminiscent of Theodore Parker but which were central in his religious vocabulary. He says: "In every case we have found that the category which at first seemed outgrown was in fact the transient phrasing of a permanent experience," and thus he aligns Modernism with German thought in the mid-nineteenth century from which Theodore Parker derived both his ideas and vocabulary. Parker had borrowed the title of his famous sermon on the "Transient and Permanent in Christianity" from an essay by David Friedrich Strauss of the same title.

The culminating point of the volume is Fosdick's application of the "old category-new meaning" formula to the figure of Jesus Christ. He states his conviction that a preacher "will find that what he wishes most to say about Jesus to his people now is at heart the same message which in the mental categories of their own time New Testament Christians were expressing when they called him Messiah and Logos." He concludes with the standard liberal doctrine of the immanence of God, in Christ and in all men.

What was the "Modern" solution of the religious problem at which Fosdick aimed? It was the kind of reinterpretation of orthodoxy Cauthen so well describes. Fosdick's lectures were in fact a repudiation of the liberal objective. His *Modern Use of the Bible* marks the beginning of the return to orthodoxy. The old categories will remain, he asserts in effect, but they will be interpreted in a new way so that they may be kept and used. The old faith remains. This is the "permanent" that continues on through successive expressions in the "transient" thought of men. "I, for one, return from trying to see [Jesus] as he actually lived and died in Palestine," he says. "Therefore I call him Christ indeed." "I am," he says, "convinced that he was divinely appointed to be the world's Savior and that he plays an indispensable part in establishing God's kingdom in the earth." Although no one seems to have realized it at the time, this utterance marked the end of Modernism. Its central figure had sounded the retreat to orthodoxy.

A decade later Fosdick made his return explicit in a sermon at the

Riverside Church entitled "The Church Must Go Beyond Modern-ism." "If ever I needed something deeper to go on than . . . senti-mental humanism about man as the master of things, it is now," he cried, "a philosophy, namely a profound philosophy about what is ultimately and eternally real in this universe." He paid proper trib-ute to the accomplishments of Modernism, but concluded, "We can-not harmonize Christ himself with modern culture. What Christ does to modern culture is to challenge it."

Actually the difficulty with the Modernist movement was not that its leaders lost heart and returned to a more comfortable and sophis-ticated orthodoxy. Modernism failed because it never left orthodoxy. The Modernists were believers. They were men who accepted the Christian faith and never questioned it, but who were troubled by the inconsistencies with modern thought the acceptance of that faith involved. It was the purpose of the Modernists to keep the faith and to understand it in the light of modern knowledge.

Modernism, however, did not fall at the hands of Harry Emerson Fosdick, its chief exponent. It fell before it was born at the hands of one of the patron saints of liberalism, Albert Schweitzer. It is a curi-ous fact of Christian history that the search for the historical Jesus, at least in this country, continued on for a generation after Albert Schweitzer as a young man of thirty had administered the *coup de grâce* to the effort. His *Von Reimarus Zu Wrede,* published in Eng-lish as *The Quest of the Historical Jesus,* after reviewing all the nineteenth-century attempts to rescue the historical Jesus from the theology of the Gospels, showed conclusively that the goal could not be reached.

After a protracted study of all the sources, Schweitzer concluded: "The study of the Life of Jesus has had a curious history. It set out in quest of the historical Jesus, believing that when it had found Him it could bring Him straight into our time as a Teacher and Saviour. It loosed the bands by which He had been riveted for centuries to the stony rocks of ecclesiastical doctrine, and rejoiced to see life and movement coming into the figure once more, and the historical Jesus advancing, as it seemed, to meet it. But He does not stay; He passes by our time and returns to His own. What surprised and dismayed the theology of the last forty years was that despite all forced and arbitrary interpretations, it could not keep Him in our time, but had to let Him go. He returned to His own time, not owing to the application of any historical ingenuity, but by the same inevitable necessity by which the liberated pendulum returns to its original position."

In point of fact, as Schweitzer himself observed, "each individual creates Jesus in accordance with his own character." "No vital force comes into the figure unless a man breathes into it all the hate or all the love of which he is capable," said Schweitzer. The Modernists, coming at the culmination of more than a century of effort to depict the true figure of Jesus, poured into him all the idealisms they possessed. As a result, Jesus the man of history was not restored—a new personage was created who was in reality the prototype of each man's ideal. As the Modernists saw Jesus, he was all they believed a man ought to be. This method of interpretation provided a religious as well as a historical base for the social gospel crystallized by the thought of Walter Rauschenbusch. Out of it also came the pacifism of the First World War and two decades after it, the Second.

Only slowly did the truth of Schweitzer's conclusion come to be understood and accepted by the Modernists. They accepted it when they found in their own experience that the historical Jesus receded from them as they reached toward him, precisely as Schweitzer had said a generation before. The Modernists, in short, like most of the liberals of whom they were a particular expression, found that there was no answer but only increasing problems in their pursuit. They were working by a dual set of purposes that were contrary to each other. One perceptive writer warned at the beginning of the movement in 1922 that to accept Modernist principles might even result in letting Unitarians and agnostics into the Christian church! He was right. But his fears were unfounded because Modernism did not pursue its principles to the complete independency of the mind to which they led. Neither did it reject them. In the end Modernism simply turned its back upon the faith of adventure from which it took its rise.

As a result the movement which began as a crusade became a retreat. The liberals set out to reconcile the Western intellectual tradition with the Christian tradition, but in the process they too became what Christendom had been since the eighteenth century—a salvage society. They took their place with their predecessors and they, too, began reluctantly to yield to science areas the church once had claimed for itself. Meanwhile, they continued to hold on to the remainder which skeptics and scoffers might deny, but could not disprove.

Yet liberalism and Modernism were unique in Christendom. They represent a movement within the church which sought to do directly and by choice what had long been going on indirectly and as a matter of necessity. Heretofore, the attempt to bring Christian thought into harmony with the Western intellectual tradition had been made by individuals or by groups like the deists, who were outside the church or who belonged to relatively small churches like the Unitarian. The liberals derive their importance from the fact that they took this effort into the church for a while. It was their misfortune that what they began in a prophetic mood ended first as a retreat, then a rout. It was their glory that the church will never be the same again. But the contribution of the liberals to the ongoing stream of Christian thought was not to receive recognition until forty years after its influence had begun to ebb. Meanwhile, neo-orthodoxy took the center of the stage.

CHAPTER IV

The Return to Orthodoxy

The concept of orthodoxy is very congenial to the mind of man. He easily accepts it, not only because it saves him the trouble of determining for himself what is right, but also because he knows the value of informed experienced experts. As he turns to his doctor for authoritative direction regarding his bodily health, to the music master to teach him to play or to sing, and to the astronomer to tell him about the stars, so he turns to his clergyman to answer his questions about God, man, and the meaning of life.

The faith of stability is organized on this principle. It is a faith about which the experts know and the faithful do not. The experts articulate and defend it. The ordinary worshiper usually cannot, but this does not trouble him. He no more feels called upon to expound Christian theology than to understand modern medicine or to write music. All these things he is glad to leave to the theologians. For this reason heresy troubles him greatly. It raises profound questions he cannot answer and it creates for him the same kind of dilemma as when two doctors give him conflicting advice or when the scientific world divides on the steady-state, big-bang theory of the origin of the universe. Such disputes leave him helpless because he has not the means to resolve them. He feels no less helpless when theological experts cannot agree as to whether the Bible is God's Word, whether the Apostles' Creed may be said or sung or neither, or whether God is "up there," "out there," "over there," "in here," or nowhere at all. And, theologically speaking, he is never so desolate as when his clergyman tells him, as sometimes happens, that there are no final answers to fundamental theological questions, that what he wants to know, no one knows, and probably no one can know, at least in our time.

It was here that the inherent weakness in nineteenth- and early twentieth-century liberalism became apparent. It moved increasingly from certainty to uncertainty, from answers to questions, from faith to doubt. In the relative peace and security of western Europe and America, in the late Victorian era, men might express their doubts about fundamental matters and live contentedly with them. But engulfed in the suffering and tragedy of World War I, they found they could not. This is the explanation of the new orthodoxy that appeared in Europe after World War I and in America a decade later. The new orthodoxy offered men answers where liberalism had only questions, hopes, and guesses. It backed its assertions with the authority of the Bible which the liberals themselves still considered to be God's Word. It backed its assertions with the authority of nearly two thousand years of Christian history, Christian thought, Christian tradition, and Christian life. Faced by a liberalism that had first doubted Christian dogma and ended by doubting itself, neo-orthodoxy very quickly moved to the center of the theological stage. It made no attempt to answer the kind of questions liberalism had asked. It began with answers, and rejected liberalism's questions as irrelevant. How adequate were the answers neo-orthodoxy offered? That is the question to which we turn in this chapter.

1. KARL BARTH AND THE RETURN TO ORTHODOXY IN EUROPE

The mood of moral idealism and religious optimism that characterized the first decade of the twentieth century continued strong in the United States after World War I. In Europe, however, it came to an abrupt end. It vanished amid the slaughter of Europe's young manhood on the western front. There the optimism which had been felt in the first decade of the twentieth century gave way to a deep pessimism which expressed itself in every aspect of Europe's thought and culture. Christianity, its liberal expression included, was not exempt. In fact, liberalism suffered most because it had been optimistic and also because it had been the bequest of German thought to Europe. Now the war and its attendant desolation was Germany's legacy also. No one moved to take up the work of her great prewar thinkers, Adolf Harnack and Albrecht Ritschl, either in Germany or outside.

Scarcely had the war been concluded when Karl Barth, the Swiss theologian, published his now famous *Epistle to the Romans*. Barth's own life story provides us with the clearest understanding of his religious philosophy. During the war he had been preaching a kind of liberal Christianity stemming from the thought of Ritschl, and in general of the continental liberalism of the late nineteenth century. It was marked by piety and a deep social concern. But to his dismay, his message seemed to have no real meaning for his parishioners. Confronted by the maelstrom of war that whirled fiercely around them, they found Barth's piety and his plans for social reform irrelevant to their own personal needs and to the situation they faced in their daily lives.

In the light of this experience Karl Barth began a re-examination of his own faith. He concluded that the trouble lay with himself, not with his parishioners. He concluded that his approach to religious questions was wrong. He had thought to save the world by applying Christian principles to the economic and social order. But this, he now came to see, was not enough. Something larger, more certain, and more imperative was required. The result was the theology of crisis, which his study of Paul's Epistle to the Romans revealed to him.

"We have once more to recognize God as God," he wrote in 1916. "If we do a childlike joyfulness will come to us. The humility and joy we then experience are called faith by the Bible," he went on. "This is the way of Christ." Of Paul he wrote in the preface to the first edition of his *Romans:* Men "could not remain unmoved spectators in his presence," and he suggested that we too are entering upon such a time. Then in the preface to the second edition he joyfully exclaimed: "What I hardly dared to hope has been fulfilled. The book [Epistle to the Romans] brought Paul and the Bible to the notice of some who had thought little about them."

Barth's first principle was that the Bible is the Word of God. His second was that that Word is spoken to man today as it was in ancient times. His third was that that Word can save man now. These principles were opposite to the liberalism in which Barth had been reared. He had been taught to start with man, and through the use of reason, natural theology, and mystical experience to reach toward God. But God can never be found in such a manner, said Barth. Whatever we find as a result of such a method is only a projection of ourselves. Men are helpless in these matters, he insisted, although they proceed as if they were omnipotent. Hence, he concluded, it is folly to preach to men that they should rise up in their strength and reform the social order or that they should piously seek God in their inner experience. They cannot do it. They can only wait until God in his strength comes to them. They can only fling themselves upon his mercy. They can only await his gift of grace.

How did Barth establish the validity of his position? It was very simple. God, the infinite and eternal, the omnipotent and omniscient, he said, is by definition unknowable. He is what Rudolf Otto called "Wholly Other." As a result, man cannot express his relationship to God in the rational way in which he is accustomed to express everything else. To explain how it was possible to say anything about God at all, Barth seized upon the idea of the paradox. Only through the paradox, he said, can man attempt to describe God. He is both hidden and revealed—both known and unknown. The final paradox is, of course, Jesus Christ, who was both God and man.

With man there is no paradox. He is plainly and simply a creature of sin, helpless to save himself. No amount of righteous living can gain for man the reward of God's favor. It comes, when it comes, through grace and then not through any merit of any kind. It is God's free gift.

For Barth the Bible was the answer. There God spoke directly to man through his Word. For Barth the Bible was the record of how God had spoken of old and it was also the vehicle through which God still speaks today. But Barth was no literalist. What he meant by the "Word of God" was not the Scriptures themselves. The Word, he said, came to men *through* the Scriptures as a result of reading them. Bible words, Bible stories, and Bible characters are merely "tokens" of the eternal truth that the Bible speaks, Barth held. Thus the true Word of God is always spoken to man in a particular place and time. That means it is spoken to us in our time.

It will be seen that Barth was a true Protestant in his approach. It was on the doctrine of the sufficiency of Scripture that Luther and Zwingli, Calvin and Melanchthon, took their departure from the medieval church. It will also be seen why the Barthian message gained such wide and rapid acceptance. Here was the answer to the question liberalism could not answer. Here was the certainty religious men crave. For the liberals the Bible was a record of the religious pilgrimage of Israel. At their hands it had become a source of inspiration more than a source of authority. The neo-orthodox restored it to its former pre-eminent position as a revelation of God's will and way. The liberal question mark had been replaced with a neo-orthodox exclamation point. The liberal search was brought to a close with the neo-orthodox answer.

Liberalism, Karl Barth concluded, in attempting to slough off what it considered to be the errors accumulated during nineteen hundred years of Christian theology, had sloughed off essential Christianity at the same time. The baby had been poured out with the bath. The silver spoon had been dissolved in the cleaning fluid. Liberalism, in its search for the true Christianity, had destroyed it and naught but the dry husk remained. The essence, said Barth, in sharp contrast with Adolf Harnack, was the Word that was not to be found in history or in particular Bible texts. It was transmitted in the Bible and not once, long ago, but then, and now, and always.

Barth did not attempt to demonstrate his thesis. He declared it and invited others to accept it. The demonstration came, he said, not in proof and evidence and rational argument, but in experience. Thus the central characteristic of his theology lay in the reassertion of the truth of the old orthodoxy. Barth argued a great deal, but the argument was always incidental. The heart of his Gospel was a declaration.

In this he stands close to the original. It was so with Jesus. He, too, was ready to argue his case, and did so with telling effect, but he, too, essentially declared the truths he uttered. He came preaching the good news that the time was come; the kingdom of God was at hand. He did not try to prove it. He proclaimed it, urged men to repent, and to believe that what he said was true. The similarity in the two approaches did not pass unnoticed among the readers of Barth.

Neo-orthodoxy, as the Barthian movement came to be called, derived its name from the fact that it was not a new development in the religious thought of man. It was a reversion to an older pattern of thinking. Characterized in general terms, neo-orthodoxy was a return to the Reformation theology of Martin Luther and John Calvin. This theology in its turn was also not new. Its roots go far back in the thought of the church, many of its aspects reaching back through Augustine to the Apostle Paul. It was no accident that the thought of Paul was central with the neo-orthodox. And it was perhaps poetic justice that the Apostle whom the liberals had made a villain because he obscured the figure of Jesus should have become at the hands of the neo-orthodox the fountainhead of Christian thought.

The contrast between the faith of stability and the faith of adventure is here as sharp as one could wish. For the neo-orthodox the truth is already in hand although it is constantly restated. It is not progressively discovered, it has already been revealed and has only to be accepted and believed. Barth simply declares that what Christianity has taught is true, specifically Christianity as stated by Paul, interpreted by Augustine and Luther.

2. REINHOLD NIEBUHR AND AMERICAN NEO-ORTHODOXY

As Fosdick was the spokesman for Modernism in the United States and Barth was the spokesman for neo-orthodoxy in Europe, Reinhold Niebuhr was the spokesman for neo-orthodoxy in America. All the leading themes of the movement are treated at length in his writings, and since it is not our purpose to attempt a historical survey we shall confine ourselves largely to his work, and to those parts of his voluminous writings which concern the central issue with basic liberalism.

It is perhaps no coincidence that Reinhold Niebuhr abandoned the liberalism in which he had been reared and returned to orthodoxy out of the same sense of need that animated Karl Barth. The particular circumstances were different. The pattern was the same. Niebuhr faced a congregation of working men in Detroit each Sunday, while the Great Depression that beset the United States in 1929 steadily deepened. Finding, as Barth had found a generation before, that his message of piety and social reform did not reach his people, he too rethought his position, and he too returned to a biblical faith of the sort that had been worked out during the Reformation and had its roots in the thought of St. Augustine and the Apostle Paul.

It nowhere appears that Reinhold Niebuhr's change in position was directly due to the work of the Swiss theologian. But it is clear that the latter's work was making a broad impact upon American thinkers several years before Niebuhr in 1932 published his blistering attack upon American religious liberalism, *Moral Man and Immoral Society.* Five years before, a young Congregational minister was idly fingering the "new books" on a special shelf provided for them at nearby Harvard Divinity School. He picked up Barth's *The Word of God and the Word of Man* and began to read.

Douglas Horton at once began a translation of Barth's work. It was published the following year and was widely read and discussed. Horton turned to Emerson to find words in which to describe the importance he attributed to Barth. He wrote: " 'Beware,' warns Emerson, 'when the great God lets loose a thinker in this planet. Then all things are at risk. It is when a conflagration has broken out in a great city, and no man knows what is safe or when it will end.' Nothing less than conflagration appears to have broken out in the religious thought of Europe. Many incendiaries may be pointed to, but there is one whose torch seems to have burned more brightly than any of the others." The years have proven Horton right. Barth eventually made no less an impact on the religious thought of America than he had Europe.

One of Barth's deepest criticisms of liberalism was that for all its allegiance to "facts" and for all its determination to search out the "truth," no matter where that search might lead, liberalism itself was factually in error and consequently wide of the truth at a very crucial point, namely, in its estimate of man. Liberalism believed in man's perfectability through his own efforts. It believed that man could change the social order so that the kingdom of God might eventually be built on earth. Some liberals had in fact taught a doctrine of inevitable progress based on the social theory of evolution whereby society would continue to evolve to increasingly higher levels of development.

Reinhold Niebuhr's opening blast was leveled against this particular aspect of liberal thought. In *Moral Man and Immoral Society* he took as his thesis the sharp distinction between the moral behavior of individuals and that of groups. There are elements in man's nature, he argued, that neither rationality nor good will can bring under control. These elements belong to the order of nature. Neither reason nor conscience can control them. The real cause of our social ills is our predatory self-interest. Therefore, any optimism as to our ability to improve man or the social order through reason and conscience is hopeless sentimentality, he insisted.

"We developed a type of religious idealism which is saturated with sentimentality," he wrote. "In spite of the disillusionment of the World War, the average liberal Protestant Christian is still convinced that the kingdom of God is gradually approaching, that the League of Nations is its partial fulfillment and the Kellogg Pact its covenant, that the wealthy will be persuaded by the Church to dedicate their power and privilege to the common good, and that they are doing so in increasing numbers, that the conversion of individuals is the only safe method of solving the social problem, and that such ethical weaknesses as religion still betrays are due to its theological obscurantism, which will be sloughed off by the progress of enlightenment."

This statement is, of course, a caricature of what most liberals believed and taught. Nevertheless, the exaggerations of Niebuhr backed by the polemics of Karl Barth carried the day. No answer came from the liberals to meet the acclaim with which Niebuhr's words were received. In fact, the acclaim came from those who were still classed as liberals at the time, not from the Fundamentalists who might have been expected to rejoice at this first breach in the liberal position.

The new orthodoxy continued the development of this more somber doctrine of man in contrast to the teaching of the liberals. Man, they said, is fallen and condemned to sin. He is weak and cannot help himself. No utopia will save him. Only God can do that.

This, they insisted, is the fact about man. Liberalism never became a living religion because it failed to see that this is so.

"All the difficult Christian theological dogmas of Atonement and justification," wrote Niebuhr, "are efforts to explicate the ultimate mystery of divine wrath and mercy in its relation to man. The good news of the gospel is that God takes the sinfulness of man into Himself; and overcomes in his own Heart what cannot be overcome in human life, since human life remains within the vicious circle of sinful self-glorification on every level of moral advance. This is rightly regarded as the final revelation of the personality of God." Or, as he said more directly, "The message of the cross is love triumphant in its own integrity, not triumphant in the world and in society. The triumph of love in the world will only come by the intervention of God."

Another aspect of liberalism's error, as Niebuhr and the new orthodox saw it, was their man-centered approach to ultimate problems. "Glory to man in the highest, for man is the master of things," they repeated derisively, asserting that this was the battlecry of liberalism. Here too, they maintained, liberalism was factually in error. The center of the universe and the center of life is not man but God. All these misconceptions were made possible, Niebuhr argued, by another fact about man the liberals had forgotten, namely, his ability to deceive himself. Self-deception, he argued, is but an aspect of the sin of pride. Pride closes the eyes to any honest self-appraisal. Only by admitting that man is a victim of his own pride can he hope to penetrate through his erroneous self-estimate and see himself as he really is. "The question of biblical theology," he wrote, "is not How can Man know God, but How can sinful man be reconciled to God?"

These passages illustrate another aspect of Niebuhr's thought which is characteristic of neo-orthodoxy as a whole. He does not say that the Christian dogmas of atonement and justification are true in the literal sense. Thus he avoids inviting belief in an ancient and unbelievable teaching of the Christian church. And yet he saves these dogmas and makes them usable to the faithful on the ground that they reach *toward* a truth that is important, namely, the fact of God's divine wrath and mercy considered in the light of man's sin.

Much of Niebuhr's polemic against liberalism was directed against a vapid and extreme form of the movement that was rarely to be found. Liberalism was not unaware of the evil and sin in man, and Niebuhr's insistence that to try to improve society does no good has never been substantiated. In fact, Niebuhr's own participation in social movements throughout his life belies his own argument. He did, however, see the central defect in the liberalism or Modernism against which he reacted. Liberalism, he wrote in his Gifford Lectures in 1941, "is no more than an alternated form of the orthodox faith. . . . The effort is made to maintain some contact with the traditional faith by affirming simply that Jesus was a very, very, very good man, but that of course, a better man might appear, at a future date, in which case the loyalty of the faithful would be transferred to him."

While Niebuhr made it plain that he thought the liberals held much too high an opinion of human nature, he did not go to the other extreme and condemn man for the blundering stupid venal oaf he often is. Niebuhr spared no rhetoric in denouncing man for his sin and his ability to hide his sin from himself, but he did not revile him. Some of the neo-orthodox, however, did. Among them was Bernard Iddings Bell, an acid-tongued churchman, who said men were too stupid to be educated as the liberals would like to educate them. Like Niebuhr, he thought that the liberals shut their eyes to man's fundamental moral defect, the original sin that is in them, and he also denounced the liberals for believing that a change in environment could change a person. Characteristically, he accused liberalism of creating God in its own image. It is arrogant and prideful, he charged, because it believes man can know all he needs to know.

Bell, however, carried his argument far beyond anything attempted by Niebuhr, and in doing so asked a question any liberal must answer. The arrogance of the liberals in presuming to question the Christian faith, he charged, led to the arrogance of the Nazis who questioned all faith and all wisdom but their own. The Nazi philosophy was a direct outgrowth of liberalism, Bell said. As Nazism attacked Christianity, he argued, so had liberalism before it, and in so doing created the climate in which Nazism prospered. Others found Nazi rootage in liberalism in the fact that both were man-made religions contrasted with the worship of a transcendent God. Both were secular, individualistic, inward, emotional, enthusiastic, broadly tolerant, stemming from the Renaissance and the Enlightenment, these men argued. Since liberalism was a man-made religion, it could be adapted to any purposes to which men might wish, they said.

But the argument from history is a dangerous one and can be run either way. To prove their point, men like Bell would have had to show that liberalism was a causative factor in the Nazis' coming to power. Obviously they could not do it. A great many evangelical Christians succumbed to the Nazis without protest, although many also stood firm. On the other hand, liberals stood firm against the Nazis and many also succumbed. Whatever the causes of Nazism may have been, if liberalism is to be included among them, a better case will have to be made than in the superficialities pointed to by Bell and others of the same mind. To make their case they will have first to explain how a philosophy that centers in the freedom of the mind and will and in the dignity of the individual could have brought into being a philosophy that centered in the denial of both.

Barbara Ward has said that "totalitarian government in its extremest form has returned where the waning of religion left the altars of the soul empty and turned men back to the oldest gods of all, the idols of the tribe." This also is regarded as an implied if not overt challenge to liberalism. But she forgets, as Bell forgot, that the gods of a people are not always what they are supposed to be. A national god, as with Israel in Old Testament times, may be of the most exalted character. He may demand of his people an ethic which is universal in its scope and total in its concept of humanity. On the other hand, the god of a religion with universal claims may in fact be quite nationalistic in character. The God of Christianity has too often been a God of national dictatorships and the excuse for the oppression of subject peoples. The difficulty with the God of liberalism was not that he lacked a high moral imperative, or that the philosophy that gave him birth was rationalistic. The difficulty, as Niebuhr saw, was that liberalism led back to the God of New Testament theology whom it supposed itself to have abandoned, and left the true liberal with a choice between that and no God at all.

American neo-orthodoxy under the leadership of Niebuhr has had an insistent social gospel as Barth's in Europe did not. This is an aspect of Niebuhr's earlier liberalism that he never abandoned. For this reason I omit all reference to it as I did in the discussion of liberalism. It must be observed, however, that the social gospel was a logical concomitant of liberalism in a way that it was not for neo-orthodoxy. The liberal centered his interest and activity in this world and took upon himself the responsibility of changing conditions he thought evil. This approach exactly fitted his theology, but it in no way fitted the crisis theology of Niebuhr. Here, the thinker who found paradox at the heart of his world bequeathed a paradox to his followers, whom he admonished at once to seek God's mercy and grace and also to be up and doing to mend the world's evils. However, there was ample precedent for his position. The Calvinists for four hundred years had faced the same theological dilemma without its materially impeding their notable achievements in the world of material things.

Does Reinhold Niebuhr answer the questions the members of the fourth faith are asking? Often he comes extraordinarily close, for no matter how high flown or sinuous his theology, he keeps his eyes fixed upon the contemporary scene where all men, orthodox and liberal, Protestant, Catholic, and secular, dwell. As ably as one can, perhaps, he has stated and defended the biblical view of this earthly life. Sin, redemption, God, history, salvation—all are gathered up and explained in his voluminous writings.

Will Herberg said of Reinhold Niebuhr that it is his purpose "to restate, assess and vindicate the essential Augustinian-Reformation teaching on man." The fourth faith would ask, To what end? Why attempt to restate Augustine, Calvin, or Luther? Why try to vindicate their teachings? Why not accept the validity of the work they did in their time and proceed to state our problem for our time, not in ancient concepts twisted into contemporary form, but in modern concepts designed to meet contemporary needs?

When Reinhold Niebuhr is finished, the man of independent mind still has a question to ask that has not been answered. Is Niebuhr's the clearest and most forceful way to lay before mid-twentieth-century man the need for him to recognize his weakness, his involvement in contradiction, his self-serving and self-seeking in spite of his high aims, and his colossal capacity to deceive himself while he is about it? Granting for the sake of argument that Niebuhr has

succeeded in stating many truths about man through his reinterpretation of Bible myths and orthodox theology, is this the best way
to draw men toward virtue? Is this the most illuminating way to
explain man's place in the cosmos and his destiny in eternity?
Granted that Niebuhr has succeeded in making a respectable case
for Christian theology and for the use of the Bible as God's Word,
might not his basic message have been better laid before a world
in today's language and imagery rather than in the trappings of an
ancient religion reinterpreted for modern use?

3. The Neo-orthodox Debt to Fundamentalism

It was an early twentieth-century Fundamentalist, John Gresham
Machen, who pointed out the weakness in the liberal doctrine of
tolerance. It means, said Machen, believing that differences in doctrine are not important. This in turn means believing that the
doctrines themselves are not important. That is a point of view
anyone may adopt and defend if he wishes to, said Machen. But
the Fundamentalists emphatically disagreed. Doctrine was important
to them, so important that they believed any deviation from it was
not to be tolerated.

If the liberal were truly broad-minded, argued Machen, he would
not insist upon the Fundamentalist's adopting his doctrine of tolerance. He would try to understand what the Fundamentalist is saying. And he would see that to ask the Fundamentalist to become
tolerant is to ask him to give up his own faith and to adopt the
liberal faith in its place.

The attitude of the new orthodoxy toward liberalism is almost
identical to that of Machen toward the liberals of the 1920's. The
new orthodox argue, as did he, that certain doctrines are fundamental to Christianity. If these are given up, Christianity itself is
lost. They hold, as did Machen, that it makes a difference whether
one's doctrines are accepted or rejected. They hold, as did Machen,
that you can tell which doctrines are fundamental by a simple reference to the history of Christianity. And like him they hold that
on the keeping or rejecting of these doctrines there can be no tolerance.

The neo-orthodox attack upon liberalism was but an adaptation, in more sophisticated form, of the Fundamentalist attack upon liberalism. The Fundamentalists lost the battle, in the sense that Protestantism never conceded the victory to them. But they won the war, in the sense that main-line Protestantism, as it abandoned liberalism, made use of the Fundamentalist arguments in their attempt to destroy the liberalism they were giving up.

There were differences, of course, but in the perspective of time we can now see to how great a degree the new orthodoxy was the old Fundamentalism intellectually refurbished. Both made the Bible central in their theology. For the Fundamentalist the Bible is the *literal* Word of God. The neo-orthodox accords the Bible a place of no less importance, but he is not literalistic in his approach. Like the liberal he accepts all the findings of archaeology and many if not all the results of the higher criticism. Yet at the same time he holds with the Fundamentalists that the Bible is God's Word, that it contains God's revelation to man, and that it is a Book set apart and is not to be confused with any other.

The real difference between the new orthodox and the old Fundamentalist position is not the interpretation of the Bible over which the Fundamentalists and the liberals argued so fiercely, but the manner in which theological teaching is to be applied to the living of life. The Fundamentalists, continuing the tradition of revivalism which had been strong in the United States from colonial times, sought conversion in a personal experience of commitment to Christ. The new orthodox concerned themselves with the structure of society. In this they continued the liberal tradition, in particular that aspect associated with Walter Rauschenbusch and the movement that came to be known as the social gospel.

The neo-orthodox were strong advocates of social action of various types. Reinhold Niebuhr has been greatly concerned with the philosophy of power in politics and the practical methods by which man's predatory instincts may be held in check. He has played an active part in a number of movements leading toward the strengthening of democracy. "Theologically to the right, socially to the left" was the watchword of neo-orthodoxy during the 1930's when it was taking hold in this country, and this philosophy still holds for them.

And yet the neo-orthodox did not see that in their social philosophy they were still carrying the banner of the liberal movement.

Under the leadership of Reinhold Neibuhr, they launched a bitter attack upon the social philosophy of the liberals, no less bitter than their attack upon liberal theology. Niebuhr, like the Fundamentalists, and unlike the liberals, found the cause of man's plight, not so much in the evils of society, as in man's own evil nature. Like the Fundamentalists, he found the explanation of man's sin in the story of his fall in the Garden of Eden. Again, the only difference between the two was in the sophistication with which they handled their material.

For the Fundamentalists the story of Adam and Eve—the serpent, the eating of the forbidden fruit contrary to God's express decree, and the expulsion from Paradise—was literally true. They thought those things had actually happened. They believed men today live by the sweat of their brow and women bear children in pain because the first man and the first woman disobeyed God's command.

For the neo-orthodox, on the other hand, the Genesis story, while not thought to be literally true, was held to convey a fundamental truth about man. It was held to be the vehicle by which we understand man's present plight. It points, said the neo-orthodox, to the fact that man achieves salvation, not through social reform, but through God's grace—through the redemption from sin which has been made available to him by the death and resurrection of Jesus Christ. Thus the neo-orthodox and the Fundamentalists reached the same result, even though they began with different premises. Both accepted and treasured the Garden of Eden story as a means of understanding man's fallen sinful state. The only difference between them lay in the fact that the one relied upon a biblical literalism the other eschewed.

If we go down the line of the neo-orthodox attack on liberalism point for point, we can readily see how it is the old Fundamentalist argument in new form. Both movements centered their thought in God's majesty, man's sin, and his helplessness to save himself. Both center in grace, the fact that it is free, and that man cannot earn it, although he may choose to reject it. Both believe that the doctrine of the Incarnation is central—and that without it there can be no Christianity. Both hold that to believe God was in Christ *is* Christianity. Both believe in the importance of the resurrection, and both emphasize the importance of eschatology. With both the doctrine of revelation constitutes the heart of religion and of Christianity. God did reveal himself in Christ, both hold, and this is something you do not prove. It is a matter of faith and its truth comes to you as a kind of personal revelation.

The Fundamentalist divided with the liberal over the supernatural. The liberal was trying to explain things in a naturalistic manner, such things, for example, as the miracles in the Bible. The Fundamentalist simply said emphatically that he thought this was the wrong way to go about it. He began with the assumption, derived from his faith, that the supernatural was real and that one should expect to find evidences of the fact in God's Word. Today's orthodoxy wholly concurs. Its first premise is the acceptance of the supernatural.

This contrast is emphasized in Kenneth Cauthen's recent study of the subject to which we have already referred. "Theology today, in varying degrees, affirms the discontinuity of faith and reason," he wrote. "No longer is the accent on moral and spiritual intuition . . . but rather on a daring leap of faith which affirms that God has uniquely disclosed himself in Jesus Christ. . . . The emphasis is shifted from reason to revelation, but revelation is now thought of, not in terms of propositions of doctrine . . . but in terms of a personal encounter with God which elicits an affirmative response of trust and commitment."

Perhaps the clearest evidence of the close but unacknowledged relationship between Fundamentalism and neo-orthodoxy is the rising concern among main-line Protestants over present-day Fundamentalist growth. "The narrow and divisive creed which the churches rejected a generation ago is staging a comeback," warned the *Christian Century* in 1957. "Fundamentalistic forces are now in a position aggressively to exploit the churches." Why is this so? "Through skillful manipulation," said the *Century*. The remainder of the editorial revealed the fact that the writer was concerned with a specific activity of the Fundamentalists, namely, the use of Protestant churches in enlisting support for the "crusades" of Billy Graham the evangelist. He attacked "the acquiescence of evangelical churchmen to high pressure mass evangelism, even though they do not believe in it. At worst," he concluded, "they co-operate because they lack courage to stand up against the powerful coercions of conformity applied in behalf of religion. . . ."

The editor's method of presenting his case well illustrates the affinity between the two approaches to Christianity. Fundamentalism is a "narrow and divisive creed," he said. Yet it was just such a "narrow" creed for which neo-orthodoxy called in its attack on liberalism. The precision of orthodoxy has often been urged against the broad formlessness of liberalism very much as the Fundamentalists had done a decade before.

Another writer, seeking to distinguish between the new Protestant orthodoxy and the Fundamentalism of Billy Graham, wrote: "Faith is more than a plunge into the unknown or an acceptance of true dogmas; it is a total God-initiated and Spirit-created act of trust in the forgiving mercy of God in Jesus Christ." These words sound very fine. But if this represents main-line Protestantism, then main-line Protestantism has to explain how its views and those of the Fundamentalists are to be distinguished. Do not both believe their faith to be based upon "a total God-initiated and Spirit-created act of trust in the forgiving mercy of God in Jesus Christ?"

The heyday of neo-orthodoxy is already past. On the one hand we now see increasing emphasis on the values that were to be found in the older liberalism and on the other, there is an ever-lessening emphasis upon the biblicism and dogmatism that characterized the early phase of the movement. It is already being suggested that the term be given up altogether. Even those who stand to praise Karl Barth stress the importance of his thought more than its validity. Barth's significance is increasingly seen to have been that he bore witness to the power and majesty of God in an age to which God had become remote, rather than that he was right in his biblicism and dogmatics.

But the Fundamentalists, too, bear witness to the truth as they see it: and their truth, except for its biblicism, is the truth of the neo-orthodox; that God was in Christ, redeeming sinful man and reconciling him to himself; that he summons us and judges us. We have only to obey. All this is to be known only through faith. Barth declared that the Bible contained divine thoughts about men, not human thoughts about God, the same thing the Fundamentalists had said to the liberals. The Bible was not, as the liberals had said, the story of man's religious experience; it was, said Barth, and all the neo-orthodox after him, God's Word to man, as the Fundamentalists had insisted all along. The emphasis on evangelism grows apace in Protestant Christianity. It is in part the legacy of the neo-orthodox movement. It is also the legacy of the Fundamentalists, for it is the position they held at the beginning and from which they have never departed.

Perhaps the chief reason the new orthodoxy has never been able to see its debt to Fundamentalism is that it has so long been accustomed to think of liberalism rather than of itself as similar to Fundamentalism. Liberalism and Fundamentalism are alike, it is said, in that both take a literalistic view of facts, and both rely upon them as a basis for their religious faith. The Fundamentalist rested his faith upon a nineteenth-century view of history, so the argument runs, and believed that if the factual stories in the Bible were given up, then the faith derived from them would have to be given up also. The liberal view was essentially the same, it was held. It, too, in line with nineteenth-century thinking, rested its faith upon the "facts" that history, biblical or of any other kind, set forth.

No doubt some liberals did just that. But liberalism as a movement did not. True, it sought to learn what a study of the Bible might reveal about history as it sought man's life story in every possible source from geology to paleography. But the last thing any true liberal would do would be to rest his faith upon the alleged "facts" of history, for he would be the first to assert that nothing could be more uncertain, and he would be the first to assert also that whether "facts" are certain or uncertain has nothing to do with faith. It was precisely because the liberal did not wish to rest his faith upon any of the alleged facts of history that he abandoned the use of creeds which required him to say he believed certain supposed historical facts, such, for example, as that Christ was born of a virgin, or that he rose from the dead. It was the liberal position that men did not and could not know whether such events took place, and it was also his position that should such knowledge become available, or should he learn that no such events took place, his religion would not be affected in either case because it did not rest upon those events or any others.

The Fundamentalists are now quite properly asking the new orthodox as they once asked the liberals: "If you are interested in the meaning of a Bible story rather than in its truth, in what sense can you be said to believe it?" They are asking: "What do you mean when you call the Book that contains the story 'God's Word'? In what sense is the Bible authoritative if its meaning is something which does not appear upon its surface, but which you read out of it? How do you decide who is to read those meanings out, and when you have done so, how do you decide whose is right if they differ?"

These are the same questions present-day liberalism would ask the new orthodox, but for quite different reasons. All of which shows that liberalism owes perhaps as much to Fundamentalism as does neo-orthodoxy. But the greatest debt is that of neo-orthodoxy to liberalism. It has been estimated that as much as 85 per cent of present-day Protestant Christian orthodox teaching is derived from liberalism's initial accomplishments.

4. PAUL TILLICH

Paul Tillich is not usually classed with the neo-orthodox, although one occasionally finds his name among them. But neo-orthodox or not, there is no doubt about his influence as a theologian on the contemporary mind. Where does he stand as between the faith of stability and the faith of adventure? Paul Tillich is supremely the apostle of the faith of stability. His mind is so keen, he offers us so many profound insights, and he often comes so close to the faith of adventure, it is tempting to try to put him in that category. But we cannot. He has given his life to defending the existing theological order. He has had to invent a whole new terminology to do it, and to reinterpret almost everything Christianity has said as well. But he has given himself to this task with single-minded purpose. If he has not succeeded, it is only because he has attempted the impossible.

Tillich thinks of himself as a mediator between the two opposing points of view. He wrote in 1949: "It is possible to avoid two contradictory errors in theology, the supernaturalistic and the naturalistic . . . the method of correlation shows a way out of the blind alley in which the discussion between fundamentalism or neo-orthodoxy on the one hand, and theological humanism or liberalism on the other, is caught." By correlation he means the relating of "existential questions to theological answers." Again he said: "The human situation is interpreted in existential philosophy and the psychology and sociology related to it posits the question; the divine revelation as interpreted in the symbols of classical theology, gives the answer." In this comment, Tillich gives the answer to the question we are asking of him, and thereby places himself squarely in the faith of stability.

For what is "the divine revelation as interpreted in the symbols of classical theology"? It is the Christian revelation, the same starting point that marks the point of departure for all the defenders of the faith. True, Tillich understands revelation differently than do some. It is not, he says, like a stone cast down from heaven into history. Yet neither is it essentially different from revelation as we have always understood it, and it is this revelation which provides the necessary authority for the symbols of classical theology.

Tillich comes very close to the faith of adventure in his concept of the "Protestant principle." Protestantism, he says, is a special historical embodiment of a universal principle, the Protestant principle. It is effective in all periods of human history, and in all religions. We see it in the prophets, in Jesus, and in the Reformation. But then he says that the task of theology is mediation between the eternal criterion of truth which is Jesus Christ and the changing experiences of individuals.

The Protestant principle, says Tillich, is the proper relationship between the conditioned (man) and the unconditioned (God), between the creature and the Creator. This requires us to single out and denounce idolatry wherever we find it. Idolatry consists in taking something that is finite and looking upon it as if it were infinite. It means worshiping something as if it were holy that is not holy. The Protestant principle requires a criticism of Protestantism when it sets itself up as having final authority. To do this is again to make the infinite finite. Since this cannot be done, it is idolatry to try.

Protestantism is the criticism of all idolatries. But it is also a recognition of emerging novelty coming from the creative principle. Evil and good go together. Man idolizes what he finds good. But as a result, these things become demonic. He worships the finite. It then becomes a destructive evil as a result of being idolized. This is why most destructive evils also have a creative element in them. Judgment and fulfillment go together. We do not have one without the other.

For this reason man is always insecure in his search for truth. He can never reach it for he can never know the absolute. The only possible ultimate faith or commitment is in God, who is the ground of being. Anything else is idolatry. The uniqueness of the church is due to the fact that it bears witness to the Protestant principle. The Protestant church is a special historical embodiment of a universal principle.

If Paul Tillich were willing to stop there his sweeping and majestic theological system would be more than acceptable to the proponents of the faith of adventure. True he is clear that we must not have an unexamined faith. "The statement that Jesus is the Christ and therefore the incarnation of the universal Logos of God is a matter of continuous testing," he once said, "not only in view of secular culture [i.e., the fourth faith] but also in view of the other world religions." He believes the test should be made both theoretically, through theology, but practically also by missions. "In the depths of faith doubt is always hidden," he reminds us. But the faith of adventure would start from the other end. It would not begin with the claims of the historic faiths and test them to see whether they are valid. It would start in the opposite direction, from the experience of men, and reach such conclusions as those experiences might seem to require.

From the point of view of the fourth faith, perhaps the most trenchant criticism of Tillich's thought has been made not by his liberal critics but by those who are orthodox. Perhaps this is true because, starting with the same set of premises as he does, and moving toward the same conclusions as he (viz., that Jesus Christ is the incarnation of the universal Logos of God), they are the more eager that he shall succeed, and in their eagerness they are more searching in their criticism. Such critics, liberal or orthodox, are few in number just now, but among them one of the clearest, because the most outspoken, is Nels F. S. Ferré.

"Tillich's chief difficulty becomes most clearly apparent," he writes, "where he presupposes that the problem of being versus not being is ultimate."

Ferré like many another Christian theologian does not think the problem of being vs. not being is the ultimate problem. He believes Being-itself can be contained within a historical experience, specifically the Incarnation. He dissents from Tillich because Tillich makes of Christ, not a historical person, but an entity in which the universal and the concrete are united. But, remarks Ferré pointedly, if Tillich "had started with Christ as the Agape of God instead of with a mathematical-metaphysical idea of Being-itself, that cannot be incarnated as such in history. . . . if he would begin with the concrete Christ as *Agape,* he could find as ultimate through him the God who is personal Spirit, an uncreated Reality, supernatural but not supranatural. . . . He need, for the most part," Ferré concludes, "only accept as true what he describes as Christian."

Ferré openly embraces the Christian supernaturalism Tillich rejects. "[I believe in] a *really* existent personal God," he declares, "who *really* controls the world [and who] will *really* raise us to a new life after death." Then he declares: "I must not only acknowledge but proclaim that in my opinion there is no more dangerous theological leader alive than Dr. Tillich. Choose we must! . . . Dr. Tillich is a prophet of a new order which to him is the cleansing and clarifying of original Christianity but to me it is the destruction of it."

For the fourth faith these questions must be answered not because it is important to establish Tillich's thought either inside or outside the Christian tradition, but because it is important to know to how great a degree he answers the questions the fourth faith is asking. If Tillich's theology is acceptable to Christianity, in what sense can it be said to be the Christianity for which Nels Ferré speaks? But if it is not, it still cannot be a theology for the fourth faith because it amounts to an apologetic for the Christian faith. Ferré remarks: "Because of [Tillich's] use of symbols and traditional Christian language, some have thought him orthodox." Indeed many have. He is the leading theologian of Protestant orthodoxy today.

And indeed he should be. For as we read him, we do not get the feeling that Tillich ever will or indeed that he ever can come out with any other than the Christian answer, often as he may undertake to test it. There is no question of his sincerity, which is complete. It is a matter of the set of his mind. In all his writings he is both the philosopher and the theologian, both the critic and the apologist. In his *Dynamics of Faith,* for example, he is the philosopher examining the nature of faith, but throughout he also is the apologist explaining the nature of the Christian faith and justifying it as well, and he concludes his discussion as an apologist rather than as a philosopher. Speaking of the universal desire for a unity of faith and the desire of the several separate faiths to become the one universal faith, he reminds us that such a hope can be justified only by a religion that holds all religions to be finite and not infinite, temporal and not eternal.

If he would stop there he would have faced one of the most basic questions that trouble the people of the fourth faith. But he does not. He continues on and here the apologist appears:

"Christianity expresses this awareness [of the fact that it is finite rather that infinite] in the symbol of the 'Cross of Christ,' even if the Christian churches neglect the meaning of this symbol by attributing ultimacy to their own particular expression of ultimacy. The radical self-criticism of Christianity makes it most capable of universality— so long as it maintains this self-criticism as a power in its own life." Who but the believer in the finality of the Christian religion would not agree. And yet Tillich neither concedes that he is talking about an idealized Christianity that hardly exists, since most Christians regard their religion as final in some sense; nor does he recognize that self-criticism exists to any degree outside of Christianity, as in Judaism for example. And so his Christ becomes a dogma, or his whole argument falls to the ground in a contest over who is the most self-critical.

The picture of Tillich as the best of our contemporary Christian apologists rather than as a philosopher is confirmed not only by a study of his writings but also by the estimates made of him by his admirers. "Tillich sets our feet upon a path for the continuous exploration of God in Christ," says one. And another adds: he "is the apologist par excellence for our time"; to which the men of the fourth faith can only reply: "Then there is the end of it." Christianity, to sustain itself, undoubtedly needs apologists, but is survival Christianity's purpose? Tillich is a superb apologist for Christianity. Doubtless he has made the best case possible. But insofar as he is an apologist he is not a philosopher. He remains a theologian whose system of thought, while heavy with metaphysics and ontology, is theological in its final analysis. In short, Tillich stands in the tradition of Augustine and Aquinas, of Calvin and Barth, not that of Plato and Descartes, Kant and Whitehead.

Of whom else should we speak? Søren Kierkegaard, the spiritual father of neo-orthodoxy? Surely his emphatic demand that we come to terms with the assertions of Christianity provides as clear an example of the faith of stability as one could ask. Kierkegaard thought that faith in Christ was the only way a man could escape from the subjectivity in which all of us are inevitably involved. He believed that only through such a leap of faith could he escape from the dread and the guilt that beset him. How close is the religionist Kierkegaard to the philosopher Tillich and the theologian Niebuhr! Faith in Christ is the norm, the standard from which we take our departure, and through which we reach truth and understanding.

Shall we perchance find the faith of adventure in the writings of Rudolf Bultmann who undertook to demythologize the Bible? But to what purpose did he do it? That the old familiar faith might be re-established: that the faithful might not be troubled in their faith by the ancient myths with which the Bible is replete. With Dietrich Bonhoeffer and Emil Brunner it is the same.

Shall we find the answer in the writings of H. Richard Niebuhr? We might, had he followed the direction in which he was moving in his brilliant study *The Social Sources of Denominationalism,* published in 1929. But he himself was later severely critical of that work. By 1935, he was saying that the need of the church was to emancipate itself from "modernism," "humanism," and "liberalism" and to return to the Gospel. Niebuhr was wise enough to see that the church of modernism had actually been in retreat when people thought it was on the advance. He did not see that he aided and abetted the retreat when he advocated drawing it back to the arms of orthodoxy again. We might expect to find the faith of adventure in a thinker like Karl Jaspers, who used to talk about the "philosophy of existence," but who is now beginning to talk about the "philosophy of reason." He does not do it in connection with his religion, however, but rather in connection with his political faith.

In point of fact we find the principles of the fourth faith laid down with clarity in the early writings of many of the liberals. Perhaps the most notable example is Douglas Clyde Macintosh of Yale

University. In 1919 he published his *Theology as an Empirical Science* and in the introduction laid down the principles by which he proposed to be guided. Religion, he said, is devotion to the fundamental values worth living for, and theology is its intellectual expression. Theology is the attempt to systematize our knowledge of the divine. It is not satisfactory, he said, for religion to retreat behind a dogma inaccessible to scientific inquiry. We must begin with what we can be certain of, and add to it as we are able. This is our method in contrast to that of the conservative who begins with the dogmas he inherits and is then forced to delete those the thought of his age proves unacceptable. If theology is to be truly scientific, he said, it must take the experimental road; it must make observations and generalize from them. This puts him squarely in the faith of adventure.

Macintosh then examines the thought of Schleiermacher, Ritschl, Troeltsch, and Wobbermin and finds they each fall short of a truly objective approach to religious truth. He then undertakes the construction of his own scientific theology. He does not succeed in meeting his own standards: but no matter. Neither does any of the other theologians who make the attempt, and most do not succeed nearly as well as he. What is important in the thought of Macintosh is that he set the standard for a religion which has freed itself from commitments to the past. He set the standard the faith of adventure sets for itself.

What thinker then can be said truly to express the position of the fourth faith? Perhaps the best choice is not a theologian at all, but a mathematician turned philosopher, Alfred North Whitehead. Not only does he reject all preconceptions as he begins his thinking, he more than most is aware that this is the chief problem in all conceptual thinking, religion included. The religions consciously declare their preconceptions to be valid. Any such notion he summarily rejects. But he also insists that the unstated premises of science operate in the same fashion and that these must be exposed and examined also. In his *Science and the Modern World*, for example, he pointed out how science had been unaware of its assumption that there is a fundamental order in nature.

Whitehead called for a clearer understanding of the idea of certainty. There are no final indubitable truths, he declared. Any formulation must hold itself subject to later and more adequate re-formulation. Our progress in knowledge is not in finding more things that are certain, it is from composition to the ingredients of composition. Clarity and vagueness are much more relevant concepts than certainty and probability. Analysis is our primary weapon of insight. We evoke insight by the formulation of hypotheses, he said, and thought in its turn is evoked by insight. These generalizations apply as well to religion as to any other aspect of man's experience. My personal debt to Whitehead will be clear when it is seen that the phrase "faith of adventure" was suggested by the title of his book, *Adventures of Ideas,* where these concepts are spelled out in great detail.

And yet it must be clear that we are not attempting here a re-statement of the thought of Whitehead in contemporary dress. Such an effort would neither do justice to his thought nor serve the purpose toward which this discussion is directed. We are not saying as Charles Hartshorne said in a volume of essays on Tillich's philosophy that we think "process-itself" a better starting point than "being-itself." Who knows which is better, or whether a third alternative might not be best of all. We have been examining the religious scene of our day. We shall continue that examination in the next chapter. Within the contemporary scene we have sought our answer to the questions religious men and women are now asking. We have examined the answers that are offered today in an attempt to see to what degree they may be answers for the men and women of the fourth faith. We conclude this all too cursory glance with the observation that the mathematician-philosopher Whitehead, not the theologians of the present day, is asking the kind of questions which we, in our religious need, must answer. We have said that the theologians to a great degree are not asking these questions and that, therefore, helpful and illuminating as their writings are in many respects, they do not go to the root of the issue that has brought the fourth faith into existence in our time.

CHAPTER V

The House Built Upon the Sand

Arthur Lovejoy once remarked: "Students are repelled when called upon to study some writer whose work *as* literature, is now dead . . . why not stick to the masterpieces, such students complain. . . . But the minor writer may be more important than the authors of what are now regarded as masterpieces. Professor [George Herbert] Palmer has said with truth and felicity, 'The tendencies of our age appear more distinctly in its writers of inferior rank than in those of commanding genius.'" His observation is no less true for theology than for literature. Our task would be much easier, and the fourth faith less necessary, if thoughtful men had only to think of religion as the best minds, Catholic, Protestant, and Jewish, present it. The opposite is the case. Most men never get to see the writings of Tillich and Niebuhr, Murray and Weigel, Herberg and Herzberg. Most would not have the ability or the knowledge, even the mental stamina, to read the writings of these men.

The fourth faith exists and derives its vitality, in no small part, as a reaction against the writings and speeches of the religious popularizers. This literature is produced by the hundreds of tons and the appeal it makes has driven many a quiescent member of the faith of stability to look for something else or to abandon religion altogether. It serves no purpose when the defenders of the faith declare indignantly that such writing is not to be taken seriously. A vast body of consumers must take it seriously, and a resourceful body of producers must do so too, or the market would not be glutted with so much of it. The shelves of our theological libraries are lined with this literature; new volumes are issued every day, periodicals of all sorts are filled with it, and the bins of every parish church literature rack are stuffed with the same material in leaflet form.

Happily for our purposes, most of this writing can be considered under a few main headings, although its volume is such that the present work might easily have been confined to this material alone. The chief fallacy in most of this writing is that of the circular argument. Theologians as a group seem to be happily oblivious to its basic flaw. We shall omit any extended reference to Protestantism as it is represented by Norman Vincent Peale and Billy Graham, as their shortcomings have been dealt with at length in the writings of main-line Protestantism. For the same reason we shall also omit the Fundamentalist tract literature.

1. BIBLICAL THEOLOGY

One of the developments growing out of the thought of Karl Barth was a resurgence of theology centered in the Bible. Indeed, we may say that what is called biblical theology now lies at the center of Protestant thought. It is much wider in scope than the thought of any single man or any group of men. Accordingly, we consider it as a topic, rather than as an aspect of the thought of any of our contemporaries.

Biblical theology is a postliberal phenomenon. It results from the failure of the liberals to explain how the Bible could be looked upon in natural human terms, and remain at the same time the fountain-head of faith, Jewish or Christian. Biblical theology is intended to solve that problem. It begins with the dual assumption first that the Bible, as Karl Barth insisted, is God's Word in a very special sense, but in the second place, that all the techniques employed by the liberals to illumine the Bible should be retained. Accordingly, biblical theology makes use of the higher criticism, archaeology, history, anthropology, in short all the disciplines the liberals developed.

The claims for the divine authorship of the Bible to which the neo-orthodox reverted vary from church to church, but in one sense or another, virtually all assert the ancient Christian conviction that it is God's Word. As a matter of fact, perhaps the majority of Protestants never departed from this position, even in the heydey of liberalism.

The most extreme of these were the Fundamentalists who insisted that every word in the Bible is literally true—i.e., that a real whale swallowed a real Jonah, a real Noah built a real ark and gathered real animals two by two into its cavernous inside, and a real man, Jesus of Nazareth, was conceived by a virgin and performed real miracles during his lifetime, and rose bodily from the dead after he was crucified. Even with the Fundamentalists, however, "interpretation" is now beginning to appear as they attempt to bridge the gap between such biblical literalism and contemporary knowledge.

As with Barth, so with all these groups, the Bible is the center. It is the starting point for almost every writer. For example, one sets forth *Basic Christian Beliefs* for laymen and students. All of his "basic beliefs" are derived from the Bible. Another defends the proposition that the Bible may be used. He holds that *The Unity of the Bible* makes it possible to use it as a sourcebook for contemporary theology. Another says simply in a series of published sermons, *I Believe in the Bible.*

The basis for such writing is always the same simple affirmation: the Bible, if not the record of God's own spoken Word as the Fundamentalists claim, is at least a kind of open door to the nature of God. "It is not necessary to believe in the literal inerrancy and infallibility of the Bible," runs a typical affirmation. "But you must believe that the Bible is the record of God's uniquely significant self-revelation to a particular people, culminating in Jesus Christ." No doubt there is a distinction in the author's mind between "literal inerrancy" and the "record of God's uniquely significant self-revelation," but it is hardly important. At best it becomes a device by which to explain away the anomalies, the inconsistencies, and the barbarities of the

Bible. The record might be in error. It might be subject to human passions and our limited human understanding. But that which the record attempted to state could not, namely, the work of God among men.

W. F. Albright attempts to sustain the dogma of the divine status of the Bible through a reference to history: "Climaxing and transcending all ancient religious literatures [the Bible] represents God's culminating revelation to man at the latter's coming to the age of maturity. At least a hundred thousand years had elapsed since man first learned to make artifacts—less than two thousand years have passed since the close of the Canon."

Albright implies, but does not attempt to demonstrate, the idea that man's rapid development since biblical times proves the divine nature of that record. It would be interesting to see what evidence might be gathered to support the opposite view; namely, that modern civilization came about in spite of the attempts of the biblicists to contain religious thought in an older pattern. It might well be possible to show that contrary to Albright's thesis, the development of Western culture has been due, not to the belief that the Bible is God's Word, but to the spread of the moral and spiritual ideals the Bible contains. And even then, in part only.

What is the basis upon which these broad claims on behalf of the Bible are made? Perhaps the best answer is to be found in the introduction to *The Interpreter's Bible*, a large twelve-volume work which undertakes to analyze, explain, and give the meaning of the Bible. The introduction, written by a leading Anglican, H. H. Farmer, tackles this question head-on. He writes: "I accept as a datum, the uniquely normative status which the church has always assigned to the Bible. . . . In other words, the question of the Bible is here considered as a theological question; the answering of it involves raising the question as to what the Christian faith essentially is, for only on that basis can we determine the essential significance and authority of the Bible."

We need to be clear as to what Farmer is and is not saying here. He nowhere says the Bible is an historically accurate record. This is the error the Fundamentalists made, which closed for them the door of biblical criticism and attendant disciplines. He nowhere says a careful study of the Bible and related subjects (history, archaeology, etc.) will bring us to the true historical events the Bible refers to, even in a garbled, poetic, miraculous, or archaic form. This was the mistake the liberals made. What he does say is that he accepts as his point of departure, without argument and without proof, the fact that the Bible is what Christianity has always said it is, the human record of the Word of God. For Farmer the Bible is unique. He looks upon it in a manner different from the manner in which he looks upon any other book.

But he still has not answered our question. *Why* does he accept "the uniquely normative status the church has always assigned to the Bible"? He finds his answer by shifting the question. For him what the Bible is becomes not a factual but a theological question. There is no deception here. The reader is set straight at the outset. *The Interpreter's Bible* is not an interpretation of the Bible as one might interpret Aeschylus or the Bhagavad-Gita. It is an interpretation of what Christianity *says* the Bible is. Farmer is telling us that *The Interpreter's Bible* presents the reader with a picture of what Protestant Christianity *thinks* the Bible is, what it says and what it means. The material presented is not what H. H. Farmer and the other writers thinking independently might suppose it to be. It is what the church and churchmen have said and are still saying it is. "Only on the basis of what the Christian faith essentially is," says Farmer, "can we determine the essential significance and authority of the Bible."

He concedes that if we choose we may look at the Bible as we might look at any other book. But *The Interpreter's Bible* does not propose to do so. "It is, of course, possible to approach the Bible from other angles, in relation to other interests and beliefs," he writes. "The books of the Bible provide material for the historian, the archeologist, the anthropologist and many others. . . . Such different approaches may provide important material for the Christian theologian . . . [but] . . . we raise the question of the significance and authority of the Bible as part of the wider theological question of the essence of the Christian faith which the Church is commissioned to proclaim to the world."

Yet still our question is not answered. Who is to say that the church is right? Who knows whether Christian claims on behalf of the Bible are true or false? Farmer acknowledges that he has been reasoning in a circle here. He has said that the Christian faith is derived from the Bible, and that the Bible is to be understood in the light of Christian faith. He thinks to escape from his circular position by comparing Christianity to a living organism which has "an indwelling normative principle." But has he so escaped? If he has, then a circular argument is as valid as any other. In fact, it is better. Its presence establishes "an indwelling normative principle" or "spirit of the whole" so that as the entity supported by the argument grows, it "preserves its distinctive character."

Does not Farmer and do not the theologians who edit *The Interpreter's Bible* see that by an indwelling normative principle we can also validate Islam, Buddhism, or Voodoo? Had Farmer been living in ancient times, he could by the same principle have validated the worship of Ahura-Mazda, Mithra, or Osiris, not to speak of the Bacchanalia or the Taurobolium. Each had a normative principle that determined its character. He fails to see apparently the weakness of such an argument. It does not provide any means by which to judge between the various indwelling principles a movement may claim. When he says his argument is circular, he is right. The fact that Christianity has a normative principle does not save him. He can escape his circularity only by stating the basis upon which he thinks the normative principle of Christianity—whatever it may be —is superior to the normative principles that may be discerned in other religions or in other social movements.

The manner in which *The Interpreter's Bible* is edited exhibits some of the further problems of biblical theology. The editors have printed the text, an exposition, and an exegesis, all three on each of the pages of these volumes. Thus the student may easily refer from his Bible text to its exposition and exegesis, and back to the text again. It is instructive to see how the editors have handled some of the more archaic and accordingly distasteful passages in the Old Testament. Take, for example, the fearful tale in the Book of Joshua which relates how God, over Joshua's protest, demanded that he slaughter the people of Ai. The biblical text is printed in full as one would expect. But whereas throughout the twelve volumes the text is accompanied with extensive exposition, there is almost none here.

Immediately following this passage, there comes another containing the curses that God pronounces upon Israel should Joshua not carry out the dire command. That Bible text, too, is of course printed in full. Not one jot or tittle is omitted. But again there is almost no exposition and in neither case is there any exegesis at all. We may commend the taste of the editors in passing over these two sections in merciful silence. And yet where is the ordinary Bible reader more in need of an explanation of the meaning of "God's Word." Since both exegesis and exposition are extensive throughout the twelve volumes, their diminution or total absence are more than noticeable at this point.

Biblical theology, however, is not accustomed to explain the Bible through silence. Usually its proponents take familiar and difficult passages and attempt to show how they can make sense to modern-minded men. Again to illustrate, Alan Richardson, an exponent of this point of view, has undertaken to explain Genesis 1-11, surely difficult material for anyone conversant with modern knowledge. These chapters, says Richardson, were not written as history as they purport to have been. They were written as parables. It was not the purpose of the author or authors, he argues, as we have erroneously supposed, to explain how things began. It was their purpose only to illustrate, through these tales, man's awareness of his existence in the presence of God, his dependency upon God, and his responsibility toward God.

If Richardson is right, he has at least saved God's Word the humiliation of human error, since few educated men now try to argue that the Genesis creation stories, those of Cain and Abel, the Flood, Babel, Sodom and Gomorrah, and the rest, were true in any but a legendary or mythical sense. But Richardson has not answered a more fundamental question. He devotes all his strength to showing how Genesis 1-11 can be made meaningful if looked upon as a set of parables. But he gives no time at all to the real question he raises: Is there any evidence to show that the authors of Genesis themselves thought they were constructing parables rather than writing history.

No one questions the ability of Alan Richardson or anyone else to make splendid modern parables out of ancient Bible tales. It is done in ten thousand pulpits and ten times the number of church-school classes every Sunday morning. Presumably the process has value or it would not be so often repeated. But biblical theology will persuade no one until it addresses its energy, not to the exposition of the parables it is able to contrive out of Bible texts, but rather to demonstrating why we ought now to believe that this is what the Bible authors themselves had in mind.

In the light of such efforts, many people today find themselves saying with Galileo: "The fact that something is logically possible is no evidence that it is true." And all too many are not even convinced that such interpretations as Richardson's are even logically possible. The passages with which he deals are often stretched so far out of their original meaning, in order to be made to conform to the theological position from which Richardson starts, one begins to wonder as he reads whether Homer or *Alice in Wonderland* might not have served his purpose as well or possibly much better.

Contemporary Bible scholars might have learned a lesson in this regard from a group of their colleagues in ancient Israel, the Essenes. Any Bible scholar is aware of the lengths to which these precursors of Christianity went in their effort to "interpret" Scripture. They seemed to be able to read into or out of the Bible what they wished almost at will. They, like today's neo-orthodox, believed that the Bible (our Old Testament) was God's Word. To that they added the belief that hidden meanings lay embedded in it. They believed that those hidden meanings could be read out of the text by the initiated who were wise enough to know how.

Among the hidden meanings of Scripture the Essenes found were prophecies of things to come. Specifically, they believed that the events of their own time had been predicted centuries before in the writings of Israel's prophets. Accordingly, they searched the Scriptures for these prophecies and recorded what they found. In the perspective of two thousand years of human history two characteristics of their interpretative readings stand out. Their writings are so hazy that only the most thoroughgoing scholarship has enabled us to learn what period they are writing about. If we make our writing hazy enough we can readily move the events of one period to another because people have a way of doing the same kinds of things in the same way in different ages. This is particularly true where the general conditions remain the same and exactly this has happened in the case of the Essene writings. They had no trouble finding in the writings of several hundred years before, descriptions of the events of their own times.

It was one thing for this little Jewish sect to search the ancient Scriptures of their people for prophecies of events through which they themselves had recently passed. It was quite another matter when they attempted by the same method to predict events which had not as yet occurred. Here their failure was complete. In fact, the author of one of their commentaries, that on Habakkuk, reveals his hand. He successfully (from his own point of view) reads the immediate past out of Habakkuk's first chapter. Then at Habakkuk 2:1-2 when he reaches his own times he writes, "And God told Habakkuk to write the things that were to come upon the last generation"—meaning the Essene commentator's own time—"but," he adds, "the consummation of the period"—meaning the future immediately before the Essene commentator—"he did not make known to him."

Perhaps the Essene commentator had been made cautious by the difficulty into which the author of the Book of Daniel had fallen in trying to predict the future. The book can be dated almost precisely to the year 165 B.C., because its prophecies of the future, supposedly written long before, are accurate down to that date. After that date the events the author records show an amazing lack of knowledge of what he might be expected to know.

The New Testament authors, generally speaking, also seem to have believed that secret prophecies lay hidden in Old Testament texts. This was particularly true of the authors of the Book of Matthew. It now appears that an entire school systematically scoured the Old Testament in an effort to find hidden references to the events of Jesus' life. The results of their work are recorded in Matthew's Gospel. But as with the Essenes, such writing, seen in the perspective of history, is not an effort to discern the meanings an ancient author had in mind which do not appear upon the surface of his writing. It is an exercise rather in reading back into a writing meanings of our own which the original author never had in mind at all.

The penchant for seeking in the writings of men, meanings other than those that appear on the surface, is not confined to the Bible or to religion. Perhaps the most persistent such effort in Western culture has been the attempt to prove from the works of William Shakespeare that he was not their author. Here the pattern is the same as with the Essenes, with the early Christians, and many contemporary Bible scholars. We assume, let us say, that Francis Bacon or Christopher Marlowe wrote Shakespeare. By contriving hidden signatures out of the printed text of the first edition, we attempt to prove it. Bible scholars rightly laugh at such mental gymnastics. But if we force out of a Bible text a meaning that was not present in the author's mind, what is the real difference?

Again, biblical theology, except that of the most sophisticated sort, constantly falls into the trap of affirming that the Bible is true because such and such new evidence proves its truth. Therefore, all skeptics are now routed, and all believers are confirmed in their belief. An extreme example, of a kind that frequently occurs, appeared in a Sunday news magazine article. It proclaimed in a bold-faced title, "Dramatic New Evidence Confirms the Story of Jesus." "I was sent to the Holy Land," begins the author, who is no Bible scholar, "to examine these [new archaeological] finds, to assess the battle between the believers and the scoffers." He concludes, "Among the disciples of Jesus was one Thomas, the man of many doubts. There are still many Doubting Thomases in the world today. The Holy Land has yet to yield up all the secrets of its past, but enough has been unearthed to satisfy many men that the New Testament is true."

His meaning is plain, but his "evidence," when we examine it, proves little more than that there was a Jerusalem in ancient times, a ruler named Caesar Augustus, and a Sea of Galilee. The "truth" of the Communist Manifesto or the notorious "Protocols of the Elders of Zion" could in that manner be just as easily established.

Biblical theology, although often unable to see that it falls into such an error, can perceive it in previous generations. G. Ernest Wright reports that in 1827 it was said: "The Mosaic narrative of the Deluge is confirmed by the fossilized remains of animals belonging to a former world which are found in every quarter of the globe, frequently on the summits of the most lofty mountains, and it is worthy of remark that the remains of animals, belonging to *one* part of the globe, are often found in *another part very distant*." To-day we know that the presence of fossils on a mountaintop proves nothing of the sort. We can see, of course, how the desire to prove Scripture correct gave rise to such an interpretation.

Biblical theology, skilled as it is in the art of the parable, has forgotten one of the most vivid of them all—the story of the house built upon a rock and the house built upon the sand. Biblical theology at best rests upon the sand of circular reasoning. At worst it rests upon dogma. It matters not how lovely or imposing a structure Karl Barth or Reinhold Niebuhr or anyone else may build upon the Bible; that structure will be swept away unless it can be shown to rest upon the solid rock of truth. What more solid rock could we ask for than God's Word upon which to rest a theology? None. But the question to which the fourth faith wants an answer is anterior to that assertion. Let us first persuade men that the Bible is uniquely God's Word. Then all the rest will follow as a matter of course. But until we do, nothing follows. Until we do, the Bible remains what it has become to an increasing number of people, not God's Word, but the remarkable record of the religious pilgrimage of Israel, culminating in the life of Jesus and the founding of the Christian church.

2. THE PARADOX

It was Karl Barth who offered the paradox to modern Protestantism as the one ever-ready answer to the questions neo-orthodoxy could not answer. We have now to ask whether the paradox is an adequate answer to man's religious questions. Barth did not invent this solution, of course. He found it in Kierkegaard, who in turn had found it at the heart of Christian apologetics where it had lain since the time of Paul. The Apostle did not use the word "paradox" itself, but his theology is replete with paradoxical statements. The idea is developed in the opening paragraphs of his first letter to the church he founded at Corinth.

"The word of the cross is folly to those who are perishing," he wrote, "but to us who are being saved it is the power of God. . . . Where is the wise man? Has not God made foolish the wisdom of the world . . . ? Since the world did not know God through wisdom, it pleased God through the folly of what we preach to save those who believe. . . . We preach Christ crucified," he concluded, "a stumbling block to Jews and folly to Gentiles, but to those who are called, both Jews and Greeks, Christ the power of God and the wisdom of God. For the foolishness of God is wiser than men, and the weakness of God is stronger than men."

After reading this passage we can see that Karl Barth, the erstwhile liberal who reverted to an older and more orthodox Christianity, had ample grounds upon which to rest his doctrine of the paradox. If Paul, the Apostle of the Lord, preached that the wisdom of the world is foolishness and belief in Christian doctrine is the power of salvation, should he, Karl Barth, expect to do more?

One thing he might have done would have been to continue on with the First Epistle to the Corinthians. For Paul does not end with paradox. He ends with secret teachings, an idea which came from the Essenes. There presumably all paradox would be resolved.

"Yet among the mature we do impart wisdom," Paul wrote, "although it is not a wisdom of this age or of the rules of this age. . . . We impart a secret and hidden wisdom of God which God decreed before the ages." There is no paradox, said Paul, where the secrets of God are understood. Unlike Barth and contemporary theology, he did not invite men to kneel before a paradox. Paul believed he had solved the wisdom-foolishness dilemma of the first Christians by revealing to them the secret teachings of God.

Christianity, however, took the other turn. Christian theologians early began teaching that the deepest religious truths present themselves to us as a mystery. Here again they borrowed a concept of Paul. It was one he used in connection with the transformation which occurs in us at death. "Lo! I tell you a mystery," he wrote in that same letter to the Corinthians. "We shall all be changed at the last trumpet." We need not here pursue further Paul's doctrine of immortality and the judgment day. Suffice it to say that his doctrine of the mystery of Christian teaching soon afterward became central in Christian dogmatics and has remained so ever since. It is the doctrine of mystery through which the presence of paradox has been explained.

Barth, like Kierkegaard, held that the ways of God are incomprehensible to the rational mind. We can express God's nature only through the paradox, he said, as we have seen. Niebuhr found the paradox equally useful in resolving the theological problems created by his neo-orthodox position. Life is full of paradoxes for him, and not the least of them is man himself. In his definitive *Nature and Destiny of Man,* for example, he based his thought upon "a principle of comprehensions that is beyond our comprehension," which is paradox enough for anybody.

But does it solve a problem to offer a paradox as a solution of it? Is that not rather where we begin? Do we not ask our questions in religion because its teachings seem to be contradictory and we wish to know how and what to choose? If, for example, Niebuhr bases his thought on a principle beyond our comprehension, how does he know, if the principle is really beyond our understanding, that he has not based it upon an erroneous guess or a chimera? What good is such a principle? In fact, how do we know what it is? By what criterion are we to choose a principle which by definition is beyond our understanding? Says Arthur E. Murphy caustically: "Apparently Niebuhr's own thought about this principle is at least one judgment that is exempt from the limitations found in all finite thinking." Murphy is saying politely that Niebuhr is talking nonsense unless he admits that his (Niebuhr's) discussion of the incomprehensible is an exception to his own rule and may therefore be understood. We have then to ask why Niebuhr's writing should enjoy so happy a privilege. But if, on the other hand, Niebuhr denies this, as he surely would, and says that his writing is to be looked upon like any other, then he finds himself explaining the incomprehensible, which he says cannot be done.

The idea of the paradox rests easily in the realm of religion, however, for religion addresses itself to the ultimate mysteries of life. For this reason it has always seemed logical to the minds of religious men that their answers to religious questions might well be but a declaration of the fact of that mystery. Closely allied to this point of view has been the further conviction, widely popular in recent times, yet always present, that religious belief comes hard, and that we should expect it to be difficult, even incredible. We find much of this in Paul, and much of it in contemporary Christianity. The Episcopalians, for example, have a jingle, descriptive of themselves, which runs:

> Low and lazy,
> middle and hazy,
> high and crazy.

People who favor the so-called low church are thought not to be willing to exert themselves sufficiently to embrace any other. "An Episcopal Clergyman," the Roman Catholics like to say, "is a priest who has flunked his Latin," and again the point is the same: the Episcopal faith is easy; the Roman Catholic, difficult.

How often the faithful are told that they must exert themselves if they are to keep the faith. They must read. They must study. They must strive on. They must become religiously literate. Anything so important and so precious as faith cannot be expected to come without effort—even great effort. And when it comes to accepting the faith, difficulty in believing is no obstacle. It is often a prerequisite, the devotee is assured. Then Tertullian, the third-century theologian, is quoted. "I believe because it is impossible!" he cried.

You might think that such a statement had best be left to the credulity of the early third century when Christian faith was still new, and men were not bothered by modern standards of truth and demonstrability. But old Tertullian is still so often quoted with approval that we need to ask ourselves whether or not there is any force in his argument. There would seem to be if the popularity of another more recent quotation is any criterion. C. S. Lewis, redoubtable defender of the faith, recounted in his autobiography the difficulty he experienced in accepting the faith as if the fact somehow lent validity to his conversion. "I came into the church," he wrote, "the most dejected and reluctant convert in all England . . . a prodigal who is brought kicking, struggling, resentful, and darting his eyes in every direction for a chance to escape. . . . The words *compello intrare* . . . properly understood . . . plumb the depth of the divine mercy. Here too we have the paradox, although unlabeled, the paradox of God's divine mercy as men are compelled to join his church."

One further example must suffice. This one is drawn from so-called "resurrection theology." Richard Reinhold Niebuhr, son of the late Richard and nephew of Reinhold, is perhaps its foremost present exponent. Niebuhr calls for a radically independent theology, and he believes it can be found only in resurrection faith. That such faith is difficult for moderns goes without saying. But it is its very difficulty that commends it, we are told. We must, says Niebuhr, recognize that the Christians' most significant contact with reality is the resurrection of Jesus. From this, he thinks, we can develop a Christian epistemology and metaphysics, that is to say, a Christian theology.

In the uncompromising manner in which he puts his questions young Niebuhr reminds the reader of Kierkegaard. There is no theological doubletalk with him, no allegorizing, no redefining old and familiar terms. "We have to face the tension between Jesus Christ," he writes, "and the consciousness itself. This appears most markedly in the confession that Jesus has been declared Lord and Christ by his resurrection from the dead." There is no mincing of words here and no theological sleight of hand. Niebuhr supposes that the Bible means what it says, specifically Mark 16:8, where the women found the tomb empty, and Acts 26:22-25, where Paul testifies to the fact that Christ rose from the dead to proclaim light to the world. "The resurrection tradition about Jesus," he says, "is the point at which the whole Christian world view is placed under judgment." The fourth faith would most emphatically agree. "Christ and the resurrection are inseparable," says Niebuhr, and again the fourth faith would agree. "The old dichotomy of Jesus of history-Christ of faith does not solve this problem: it only dissolves Christ and the [orthodox Christian] church."

These are fourth faith questions, asked in the fourth faith manner. Niebuhr does not have an answer for us. He is saying merely that we must face up to the question. But those who offer us an answer to the problem of the resurrection tradition in Christianity have no help to offer us at all. We accept it on faith, they say, and go on to argue that our difficulty in accepting it is evidence of the profundity of the truth which of course is really beyond our power to grasp. And yet does the difficulty of accepting a body of religious faith say anything about its truth? Does the incredibility of a doctrine indicate that it is valid? Many of us suspect that our inability to understand what the theologians say does not always rise from the profundity of their statements. Sometimes, it seems to us, we are unable to grasp theological doctrines because they are actually meaningless. Others we reject because they are simply unbelievable. When this happens, it is not because we are stubborn or proud. It is because no amount of will power that we can summon enables us to believe what we find to be incredible or incomprehensible.

Modern science came into existence because men like Copernicus and Galileo, Descartes and Newton, emphatically rejected Tertullian's argument, even if they were careful not to say so. They, like all the men of science, strove to separate the believable from the unbelievable, the comprehensible from the incomprehensible, and to reject the latter while holding to the former. More accurate knowledge of our world became possible only when they ceased to try to believe the impossible. Modern civilization is the direct result of this revolution in human thinking.

Those who would take us back to the ancient Christian view must do more than quote Tertullian, for back of him lurks the figure of the White Queen in Lewis Carroll's *Through the Looking Glass*. The brief passage in which Carroll deals with belief through effort is a classic:

" 'Now I'll give *you* something to believe,' said the Queen to Alice. 'I'm just one hundred and one, five months and a day.'

" 'I can't believe *that!*' said Alice.

" 'Can't you?' the Queen said in a pitying tone. 'Try again: draw a long breath, and shut your eyes.'

"Alice laughed. 'There's no use trying,' she said: 'one *can't* believe impossible things.'

" 'I daresay you haven't had much practice,' said the Queen. 'When I was your age, I always did it for half-an-hour a day. Why, sometimes I've believed as many as six impossible things before breakfast.' "

Once we have perceived the folly in this method of believing, with the aid of Lewis Carroll's wit, it is easier to see that the principle applies equally well in theology. By shutting our eyes and trying very hard we may, like the White Queen, be able to believe almost anything. But neither the earnestness of our effort nor the success that follows upon it can have the slightest bearing upon the truth or falsity of the beliefs we then acquire.

We can take a lesson from our children on matters like this. Perhaps that is why Lewis Carroll wrote for children. Their simple wisdom is not equal to the fantastic self-deceptions and the tortuous reasonings of the adult mind. There is a time, to be sure, when the child makes no apparent distinction between his teddy bear, Winnie-the-Pooh, and the bear in the zoo. Yet we never find him doing anything which reveals the kind of confusion in his mind which adults argue with the utmost seriousness in the realm of religion. The child revels in Wonderland, Oz, and the Never-Never Land. He is happy in the Deep Deep Woods with Raggedy Ann and Raggedy Andy and joyously follows Zephir, Jack the Giant Killer or Dick Whittington and his cat through their innumerable adventures. But he never gets mixed up. He never argues that the fish in McElligot's Pool must be real because they are so outrageous. As soon as he sees that they are outrageous he also sees that they are not real. Nor does he believe the stories of Big Farmer Big or the Bowl of Porridge that was Never Empty, because they are plainly and incontrovertibly impossible.

These stories merely amuse our children, as they are intended to do. But we would hardly argue that theological teachings have such a purpose. If our inability to believe is the proof that a statement is true, are we not the most piteous of creatures? If our inability to understand a theology demonstrates its truth, man is flung back into the jungle whence he came, back into the primordial ignorance out of which he has risen through eons of time. If incredulity is evidence of truth, then is man a creature who cannot hope to understand or to control his environment, but who merely reacts to it, like the amoeba or the toad. If we are no longer to ask whether a theological doctrine is true when it is a paradox or downright unbelievable, then is religion become politics, and dogma, the supposed vehicle of divine truth, propaganda.

3. You Can Believe if You Want To

We have seen that the paradox and the difficulty of believing have become weapons in the armory of the orthodox. They are used in seeking the convert and in an attempt to sustain the faith of the believer. A closely allied argument of which very wide use is made holds simply that you *can* believe if you *want* to. Both words are intentionally italicized, for both are equally and heavily stressed. The corollary of this statement is the maddening imputation to the unbeliever that he does not believe because he has not tried hard enough, as if he were not very persistent, and after a halfhearted try, gave up.

For a number of years theological popularizers undertook to show that religious faith had not been *dis*proved, and that, therefore, faith was still possible. The earliest work of this kind was probably A. J. Balfour's *Foundations of Belief*, published in 1895. F. W. Robertson had perhaps paved the way by assuring his congregations that confidence in the all-sufficiency of Christ was enough. But the floodgates really opened in the United States in the 1920's when the Modernists were struggling with the problem of the impact of contemporary knowledge on traditional beliefs. Here are a few titles of books from that period and later which attempted to show the faithful that belief was still possible: that the faith of their fathers had not been disproved:

1926	Charles Gore,	*Can We Then Believe?*
1926	Frank M. Goodchild,	*Can We Believe?*
1927	Bruce Barton,	*What Can a Man Believe?*
1931	Elmore M. McKee, ed.,	*What Can Students Believe?*
1933	J. G. Gilkey,	*What Can We Believe?*
1941	James B. Pratt,	*Can We Keep the Faith?*
1948	Vergilius Ferm,	*What Can We Believe?*
1952	Ralph W. Sockman,	*How to Believe*
1954	Mortimer Ostow, *et al.,*	*The Need to Believe*

Few of these writers seemed to be aware that they were advocating a basic change in theology. Until recent times, theology assumed that it was its task to demonstrate the truth of the Christian religion, as science or history or any other discipline would undertake to prove its case, and as Roman Catholic theology has always done. But these men attempted to shift the burden of proof. Christian teaching, they said, some directly and some by implication, is true and may be believed since it has not as yet been *dis*proved!

Even the mass media took up the refrain. You *can* believe if you *want* to. It's up to *you. You* must make the necessary effort. An editorial entitled "The Greatest Gift" appeared in a popular national magazine at Christmastime, 1949. The subtitle ran: "Belief declines, but it is still within the grasp of men." After reviewing the familiar changes in the intellectual scene which have brought about unbelief in Christian dogma, the editorial reiterates the equally familiar fact that there is an increased yearning on the part of people for something to believe in. Then in the last paragraph, the writer asked: "What is belief?" Answering his own question, he wrote: "It is an act of the will, or at least of willingness. Modern man has it within his power to hear, and hearing, to accept the words of Christ across 20 centuries." After a Bible quote, he concluded: "There, for all who elect to receive it, is the greatest gift."

One still meets the "You-can-believe-it-if-you-want-to" argument on every hand. The clergy, of course, make constant use of it. Bishop James Pike, a popular writer on these subjects, entitled one of his books *Roadblocks to Faith*. The implication here is plainly that faith emerges readily if impediments are removed, and that is the point the book makes. A lawyer wrote a book entitled *You Can Believe, A Lawyer's Brief for Christianity*. Again, the implication is clear that the difficulties have been disposed of so now you can believe.

It was an historian, not a lawyer or a clergyman, who administered the coup de grâce to this kind of reasoning. Many years ago, J. B. Bury, the English protagonist for independent inquiry and scientific accuracy, said of such thinking: "Any number of propositions can be invented which cannot be disproved, and it is open to anyone who possesses exuberant faith to believe them; but no one will maintain that they all deserve credence so long as their falsehood is not demonstrated."

The end is not yet. A book recently published by Martin Marty concludes on the same note. You *can* believe if you *want* to. It's up to *you*. After explaining that Protestantism has a second chance to influence American culture, the author asserts that only true Christian believers can do it. "Can one *still* believe?" he asks, repeating the familiar strain. And he answers his own question. The true Christian today is "called to the vision of the glory . . . in the middle of the world. He is asked not to worry about the future of faith; faith *is* future. Faith is again possible in the midst of the very world which displaces [the true Christian]. Not easy, but possible."

Another instance, and this our last, of the you-can-believe-if-you-only-try school of thought is to be found among the barbs that the religious fling at each other in an effort to establish their own superiority. A Roman Catholic writer, for example, finds Protestantism inadequate because it does not have any doctrine of the real presence of Christ. "Protestantism," he says, "is content with mere historical memory of His Appearance in the flesh long ago. Its sacraments are mere signs; its Scriptures supposedly the sole rule of faith, actually have created a new tradition, which is not dependable; its grace is imputed and no real righteousness results."

The proponent of this view does nothing more than assert the value of believing. Does he seriously maintain that Roman Catholic insistence on more than "the mere historical memory of [Christ's] appearance in the flesh long ago" brings that doctrine any nearer the truth? As a matter of fact, Protestantism insists on much more, but does such insistence make its sacraments any better or its Scriptures any more reliable or its doctrine any more sound? If so, then he who shouts the loudest and claims the most for his faith, by the fact of his wider claims, is thereby said to have the truth.

The Roman Catholics have no monopoly on this kind of theological argument. The Protestants use it with a will upon one another. The Fundamentalists look down upon other Protestants because they are content to get along with believing so little. The churches that make the most of ancient Christian lore condescendingly speak of those that do not as "religiously illiterate," content to get along without knowledge of, or benefit from, the rich liturgical tradition of Christianity.

Churches that stress the importance of ancient theological doctrines refer slightingly to the churches that do not. W. E. Garrison, attempting to summarize the central Protestant position a decade ago, wrote: "Sin, atonement, forgiveness, redemption, grace, salvation and eternal life. . . . These are ideas, events, experiences, and hopes which distinguish religion from any *mere* system of morality." The italics are mine. Garrison here capsuled a position that has been stated in a thousand similar texts.

Here we have a quantitative measure for belief! The more we believe, if this argument holds, the better off we are, since those who are "content to get along" with less are apparently to be pitied. To see the folly of such a line of reasoning, let us turn to the cult that believes the history of the world is built into the Great Pyramid at Gizeh. They have countless charts, diagrams, and figures to prove what they allege. The rest of the world remains unconvinced, among other reasons because few think that the future is determined for us in advance, which would be necessary if the future could be predicted by the Great Pyramid or any other device. No one feels deprived because he does not hold the beliefs of the Pyramid cult, and no one thinks of himself as "content to get along" without such beliefs.

Thus, when it is alleged that certain Protestants are content to get along without believing in the risen Christ, a literal heaven, the efficacy of the sacraments, or any other doctrine, the error is the same. Those who do not accept such doctrines suffer no sense of deprivation. They enjoy a sense of freedom from dogmas that are no longer meaningful to them. They are not "getting along" without the advantage of spiritual sustenance that others enjoy. They have, instead, experienced a new birth of freedom which is exhilarating to them, in which there is neither envy of the believer nor nostalgia for the doctrines of an earlier day. They reject both the allegation and the effrontery implicit in pronouncements that their religion is "merely ethical," "merely opinion," "merely voluntary," or "merely human."

4. GOD IN HISTORY

We owe to Reinhold Niebuhr more than to anyone our contemporary emphasis upon the idea that God is in history, not outside of it. The meaning of the Incarnation, the Event, is for him that God in Christ broke into human history. "The good news of the Gospel," he says, "is that God takes the sinfulness of men into Himself, and overcomes in His own heart what cannot be overcome in human life. . . . Christian faith regards the revelation in Christ as final because this ultimate problem is solved by the assurance that God takes man's sins upon Himself. . . ." The biblical view of life affirms the meaning of history, he thinks, but the center source and fulfillment of history lie beyond history.

There is, of course, nothing new in affirming that history records "the mighty acts of God" as many a theologian is now beginning to say. This is the central theme of the Old Testament. The ancient Jews looked upon history as the scene of God's activities. He was for them Lord of history. The events recorded there are recorded as God's activities. The Song of Deborah, one of the oldest passages in the Hebrew Bible, is also one of the most explicit in attributing the events of history to the intervention of God. The opening lines of the ancient poem which celebrates Israel's great victory at the crucial battle of Megiddo illustrate Israel's philosophy of history. Here Deborah and Barak, singers of the song, give credit not so much to the brave men of Israel as to Israel's God Jahweh.

> Then sang Deborah and Barak the son of Abinoam on that day, saying:
>
> > Hear, O kings; give ear, O princes; to the Lord I will sing,
> > I will make melody to the Lord, the God of Israel.
>
> > Lord, when thou didst go forth from Seir,
> > when thou didst march from the region of Edom,
> > the earth trembled, and the heavens dropped,
> > yea, the clouds dropped water.
> > The mountains quaked before the Lord,
> > yon Sinai before the Lord, the God of Israel.

A later editor with no poetry in his soul, after rewriting the poem in prose, states flatly: "So on that day God subdued Jabin the King of Canaan before the people of Israel." Even the most casual reader of the Old Testament is familiar with the degree to which this interpretation is standard. The later editors of the early texts interpreted them all as recording the acts of God. The line with which the editor of the Song of Deborah introduces his retelling of the story is repeated over and over in the Old Testament: "And the people of Israel again did what was evil in the sight of the Lord. . . ." Virtually everything that happens is interpreted as God's punishment for wrongdoing, or his reward for fulfilling his commandments.

It is one of the characteristics of contemporary orthodoxy to view history in much the same way as the people of ancient Israel did. "What is biblical faith," asks George Ernest Wright, a leading authority in contemporary biblical archaeology, "but the knowledge of life's meaning in the light of what God did in a particular history?" Like the true scientist he is, Wright acknowledges that there may be some risk in the study of biblical archaeology. "Suppose certain events accepted on faith are discovered not to have happened?" he asks, but his answer is plain and sure. "There is an interpretation of events and of experience which is not subject to historical and archeological testing," he answers. "Israel's history was directed by God for His own righteous ends. This is an interpretation by faith which is not subject to historical testing, and this principle is the last redoubt of the Christian theologians—the last of his assertions that still cannot be rejected. All the others have fallen one by one."

No Christian theologian has made a more forthright statement than this Old Testament scholar. But consider the consequences of what he has said. Wright is correct in stating that we cannot actually refute the theory that Israel's history was "directed by God for His own righteous ends." But on what does this affirmation rest? "We must study the history of the Chosen People in exactly the same way as we do that of any people," says Wright. He lives up to his standard completely in his writings, but he never explains why, apart from Christian theology, the Bible is to be taken as a record of what God did. Here lies the stumbling block for the people of the fourth faith. They want to know why they should accept the Bible as a record of what God did any more than Homer, Thucydides, Spengler, or Toynbee. Surely no one would say that we should accept it as such a record because the Israelites of the first millennium B.C. did so. If we did, then any book which says it is a record of God's acts becomes such a record merely by making the claim—anything from the *Book of Mormon* to the *Iliad*.

Wright rests his case upon the special qualities he finds in the literature of the Bible. "It can be stated emphatically," he says, "that to those who are willing to run the risk of destroying the uniqueness of the Bible through a scientific study of its contents, the literature of Israel and of the Church appears more distinctive than ever before. . . . The Bible . . . radiates an atmosphere, a spirit, a faith far more profound and radically different than any other ancient literature." His is a respectable position, although subject to the queries of those who would readily acknowledge the outstanding moral and religious qualities of the Bible, but who find in those qualities, however outstanding, no justification for thinking that the story it tells is a record of God's doing, any more than any other writing of an elevated nature. Christian believers never seem to be quite aware of the radical nature of what they are saying, apparently because it has been said by so many people for so long a period of time. To make so astonishing a claim as to think that a particular piece of writing is a record of God's acts in some special sense or in any sense, would seem to require more support than that the ancients thought so or that as

Wright says, "Biblical writers were the religious and literary giants of ancient times."

An extreme form of the argument not only alleges that the Bible is the record of what God did in human history, but insists that in order to make things turn out as they have with men believing what they now believe, God would have done the things necessary to bring these things about. A Roman Catholic writer, J. N. Geldenhuys, seeking to show that Jesus' authority was supreme on earth, and that the church he allegedly founded is therefore supreme, first cites many Bible passages in support of his view. Then he says: "It follows logically . . . the Lord to whom all authority in heaven and on earth is given, would have regulated the history of the early church in such a way that the canon of the New Testament would be genuine and all sufficient."

This, of course, is another circular argument: the church has supreme authority because the New Testament says so. The New Testament is authoritative because Christ the supreme authority would have seen to it that only authoritative works made their way into the canon of the New Testament. But there is a second aspect of his argument we must note. Father Geldenhuys made history the tool of theology. In his hands history becomes the device by which the validity of a theological position is demonstrated. Here history is read backward in the light of theology.

The trouble is, of course, anything at all can be established by such a method, fascism or communism, Christian Science or the religion of the Bahais. Once you have established the divine truth of your teaching, then the incidents that involve its declaration become God's acts in setting it forth. Whoever will grant your premise must admit the correctness of your conclusion. But there's the rub. Who will admit the initial claim? What evidence can be found to persuade anyone that he should accept it as true? That is the question the fourth faith constantly asks.

A similar reading of history backward, this one by a Protestant scholar, is found in T. Herbert Bindley's *Oecumenical Documents of the Faith.* His view is typical and is often repeated by other writers. Seeking to relate the dogmas and creeds of Christendom to the Bible, he writes: "While the truths [of Christian dogma] were undoubtedly held from the beginning, they were often latent in the

Christian consciousness rather than verbally expressed, until the denial of them obliged the church to ponder upon her Faith, and to put it into reasoned words. The finished dogmatic results, as we now have them, were not attained without much controversy, and careful sifting of language. The Trinitarian Formula—whatever its origins, whether an actual word of the Lord or adopted by the primitive Church and based on His teaching—was, as a matter of history, recognized by the Church as the 'Hypotype,' the outline of essential credenda, which was to be filled out and enriched as necessity arose."

To weigh such an argument with a believer's compulsion is to find it valid. To weigh it in the absence of any such compulsion is to realize that in the beginning Christianity, doctrinally speaking, might have developed in any of several ways. That it developed as it did, does not prove that the hand of God guided the process or that it did not. Any such assumption merely identifies Providence with history. A penetrating Roman Catholic scholar, M. C. D'Arcy, S.J., has pointed this out. It was a mistake made by no less a person than Augustine, he reminds us, and it is one of which we must not be guilty.

If St. Augustine, generally regarded as the greatest theologian of the Christian church, could reinterpret history in order to line it up with his theology, perhaps lesser men should be pardoned for doing so. But the persistence of the habit, its widespread character, and the very low levels to which it falls, is not calculated to draw independent-minded men into the Christian faith. For example, probably no phrase commonly used by the clergy is more irritating to the laity than "God uses me." It is offensive not merely because it is presumptuous to an appalling degree, it is the more so because there is no justification for it. To say "God uses me" is again to read history backward in accordance with theology and to do so with your own personal history.

Such a comment either marks the speaker as a man of insufferable conceit who thinks that God is using him in some special sense as an instrument of the divine will; or it means that God is using us all, which is to make the statement so broad as to render it meaningless. It is to reduce life to a marionette show, with humanity dancing upon strings tugged in heaven as God uses us for this or that purpose, and it makes God in turn responsible for Dachau and the auto-da-fé, as well as for the Christian church and the good deeds of the clergy whose language implies that they think of themselves as the special instruments of his will.

We might pass all this by were it only an aberration upon the otherwise orderly and dependable thought structure of the church. But the doctrine that God is in history, and that what happened in Bible times was his doing in some special sense, permeates the entire structure of the church and is taught in virtually every church and synagogue in the land. It is seen in the persistence of another phrase currently dear to the heart of the professional clergy, "the mighty acts of God." A typical parish Christian Education bulletin states that among the aims of its education program is: "First, the church must declare the mighty acts of God's salvation. . . . This means," the bulletin explains, "that the whole community must take seriously its history as it is known in the Bible . . . so that all may come to know the actions and words of God."

We have already considered contemporary biblical theology. Here we see what it means in connection with the God-in-history doctrine. It makes God the director of the biblical drama. It makes the events recorded in the Bible, "God's mighty acts," but it leaves still to be explained why we are to believe that the events of that history are God's doing. It leaves still to be explained why the lovely and precious things in the Bible that we teach our children in Sunday School are "God's mighty acts" and why the barbarities and immoralities in the Bible which we never mention are not.

This kind of thinking is not lightly to be dismissed. It may attain a very high level in the writings of a Niebuhr, but its logical implications drawn out in the local parish church tell quite a different story. To how low a level it can sink we can see in the area of fund-raising, one of the more important aspects of contemporary church life. One of the larger professional fund-raising firms, now out of business, published a magazine which, as a part of its promotion, it distributed free to many churches. It was filled with articles by ministers who had employed this particular firm. Each article gave a glowing account of the success of the particular fund-raising effort about which the minister wrote.

The formula was the same in each case. The minister told how hard he and his people had tried to raise money working by themselves, and what little success they had had. Then he related how he called in the professional firm. In each case the firm advised the minister to set his campaign goal far above anything previously thought possible. Then the article went on to relate how the firm's know-how guided the campaign and how, as a result of that guidance, unbelievable success was achieved. In every case a seemingly impossible goal was oversubscribed by thousands of dollars.

Each of these articles was written by the minister of the fund-raising church. Each made it clear beyond the possibility of misunderstanding that the employment of the professional firm spelled the difference between success and failure. But each was also well interlaced with the Old Testament philosophy of history. A typical closing paragraph read as follows: "God's ancient promises have again been demonstrated. He has heard our prayers and has answered them in the language of our generation. In November of 1952 we were troubled and distressed. In October of 1954 our church is built, and, wonderful to relate, *our finances completely* organized. PRAISE THE LORD."

What does this minister believe in his heart? He says: "Praise the Lord." He says: "Our prayers were answered." Yet he leaves no doubt in the reader's mind that it was the professional firm, not God or prayer, that made the difference between success and failure. He could hardly say more plainly that, as he saw it, his prayers and those of his congregation were answered, not because God intervened as the Israelites believed he did at Megiddo, but because they hired the fund-raising firm.

When Reinhold Niebuhr speaks of God in human history, he means something very much more profound than such banalities as these. But is his argument at heart any different? Is he not also reading history in the light of his theology? Has he any better right to view the future of kingdoms and empires in the light of God's will than the minister and people of St. John's-by-the-Gas-Station? Is the principle said to be at work in these instances any different? And is there any more evidence in the one case than in the other that human history, or any part of it, is a record of what God did? It is such questions as these that the fourth faith is asking. It is because they have not as yet been answered that the fourth faith has emerged and offers a different answer.

As sophisticated a defender of the faith as C. S. Lewis took the same line. In his *Case for Christianity* he asked: "Why is God landing in this enemy-occupied world in disguise, and starting a sort of secret society (the Church) to undermine the devil?" This is his peroration in a short exercise in defense of Christianity. His question clearly implies that God not merely intervenes in history but that his role, as the Old Testament says, is that of field marshal directing his troops. "Christians think He's going to land in force," continued Lewis, answering his own question. "We can guess why He's delaying. He wants to give us the chance of joining His side freely."

Perhaps Lewis, if he had been challenged on this matter, would have explained urbanely that it is all a metaphor intended to help the reader grasp rather abstruse matters. But does he really intend us to take it so? "God's going to invade all right," he continued with no lack of clarity or emphasis. "But what's the good of saying you're on his side *then?* . . . It will be too late then to choose your side. . . . Now is our chance to choose the right side. God is holding back to give us that chance. It won't last forever."

Would that it were given to man—to any man—to be as sure of matters celestial as Lewis appears to be. Would that the arguments on behalf of Christian faith addressed to Lewis' large public were better than the fear of choosing the wrong side in an encounter with celestial forces. An argument such as this is not calculated to bring to the Christian banner the high-minded or the thoughtful, who before reading *The Case for Christianity* had been deeply troubled as to what that case might be.

For the fourth faith, history is not a scenario, written and directed by a supernatural agency. Neither is it the story of an armed conflict in which heaven directs the forces on one side of the battle. For the fourth faith, history is the very imperfect record of what has happened in the past insofar as man is now able to reconstruct it. The critical methods by which we do this have greatly improved. The various devices by which we can gather new knowledge, not the least of which is the science of archaeology, have also greatly improved. Meanwhile, the span of history has been extended, not only to include the two or three billion years of earth's history, but the untold billions of years that span so much of the universe as we have thus far perceived.

Man's understanding of both space and time has expanded so far in recent years that he now measures both in billions because his earlier units of measure were too small in relation to the distances they have now to encompass. History is as much the story of what happened in the farthest galaxy cluster, in the remotest time, as it is the story of the events that transpired two or three thousand years ago in Palestine or in Europe or Africa last week. History is the story of the events that happened in time, and yet even as we say this, we also say that today, with all our increased knowledge, we are less sure than we have ever been as to what time is or what the fact of history means. In all the immensity of time and space within which "events" occur, the fourth faith thinks it foolish, not to say presumptuous, to accord a special status to a volume compiled in the first millennium B.C. and the first and second centuries A.D., which purports to contain history, but which, perforce, delineates but an infinitesimal part of the whole. The fourth faith also thinks it foolish, not to say presumptuous, for any man or group of men or human institution like the church to declare that the deepest meaning of history lies in believing that the particular God they worship is directing it all from somewhere behind the scenes.

5. The Authority of Self-assertion

In ancient times a religion usually offered itself for acceptance on the simple allegation that it had been divinely revealed. Often the principle was extended to the laws of the state as well, probably because at an earlier date religious and secular laws had been indistinguishable. The Code of Hammurabi is a familiar example. His laws were found carved upon a shaft of diorite some eight feet high. The code is lettered all the way around the shaft. It is topped with a bas-relief of Hammurabi himself. To our right is depicted Shamash the sun god, seated. The god is shown in the act of handing to the king the laws which are written out on the stele below.

It is a nice touch and its meaning does not escape us. Hammurabi has not drawn up a set of rules he thinks good for the people. He has but set forth on his diorite shaft laws which he received from the hands of the sun god himself. Looking at the stele, beautifully wrought in hard black stone, dating back to 1750 B.C., we realize that Hammurabi claimed a divine revelation. Here, perhaps five centuries before Moses' time, we see that another people in another land believed, as did the children of Israel, that their laws had been divinely revealed to the leader who in turn set them down in writing.

And then a slightly shocking thought occurs to us. If our religion had descended to us from Babylonia rather than from Israel, we should believe that Hammurabi rather than Moses gave us our basic laws. In that case we should believe, too, that God's will for men was first graven on stone, not in Hebrew characters, but in cuneiform and that the divine source of our earthly wisdom was not Jahweh, God of fire and smoke on Mt. Sinai, but Shamash, god of fertility in the agricultural land of Mesopotamia. Yet the basic elements in the two traditions are the same, even to the writing on stone. It may be argued that the Pentateuch is much more elevated in its moral tone than is the Babylonian law code, but it is also true, much as we may hate to admit it, that the Babylonian system is more sophisticated and the laws, addressed as they are to an urban people in a polyglot empire, are far more complete than the rules Moses is supposed to have laid down for the desert nomads of Israel.

The laws of Hammurabi were, of course, no more original than were the laws recorded in the Pentateuch. If this was true, surely the people of Babylon knew it. If Hammurabi's laws were derived from the ancient precepts and customs of Sumer and Akkad, as we now know they were, surely the lowliest of the people who lived under them could see that the code had not come from heaven, but was derived from the ancient practices of earth. Why then surmount the stele with the image of Shamash delivering the laws to the king? Probably for the same reason that we print "In God we Trust" on our currency: for the same reason that we disrupt a rhythmic salute to the flag by inserting in it the words "under God" and for the same reason that a newly elected President of the United States, without formal religious affiliation, becomes a Presbyterian and opens his cabinet meetings with prayer.

It is not just piety, and it certainly is not the hypocrisy some have alleged. Invocation of the deity in important affairs of state is rather an attempt to give cosmic dimension to the proceedings in hand.

Students of history hold that one of the greatest achievements in the field of jurisprudence was the perception that law is not a declaration of man-made precepts, but rather a human statement of divine ordinance. Or, as we might put it in order to avoid theological questions: law is an attempt to implement in specific precepts the fundamental principles which any society must observe if it is to continue as a society and at the same time to promote the best interests of its individual citizens. It has taken the world a long time to work out the implications of this perception, and in fact, we are still at it. But this is the meaning of the two bas-relief figures at the top of Hammurabi's stele. They are intended to indicate that laws, when they are right, represent the will of God, not the whims of men. They indicate, too, that the king himself is under the law. The story of Moses on Mt. Sinai has the same meaning. It lived on among the Hebrew people because it conveyed to them the fact that their laws were not the arbitrary rules of tribal leaders, but were fundamental in character.

But for the people of the fourth faith a problem rises here which neither Judaism nor Christianity is able to solve. Why should they believe that God gave a final set of laws to Moses on Mt. Sinai rather than that he gave them to Hammurabi in Babylon. It is not an answer to say that it was God who gave the laws to Moses whereas a pagan diety Shamash was thought to have given the Babylonian precepts to Hammurabi. But we cannot escape from our dilemma merely by juggling names. Israel's God was called Yahweh, Babylon's was called Shamash. "God" is a later name for the same concept. Yahweh gains no priority over Shamash merely because our religion is descended from Palestine rather than from Babylon.

Until some element is introduced to support the belief of Jews and Christians that the one true God delivered his one true law to Moses, the affirmation remains an exercise in self-assertion, albeit a very effective one. In the present century, Selim IV and Mustapha Kemal Atatürk faced this problem in their effort to modernize Turkey. When they attempted to secularize the state, they found that their new secular laws did not enjoy the confidence of the people because they could not claim as the caliphs had that this code was rooted in Islam. As a result the task of the Turkish state in gaining acceptance for its modern law code was vastly more difficult. The

Turkish state had to ask for compliance on the ground that the new legal system was better than the old and that in any case, it was the one the state intended to enforce.

If the religions were content to express the hope that the laws they supported were the best possible embodiment of eternal law, then we should have no difficulty. What else might a legal code be. If there is any order and system in the universe, human law must somehow embody it. But the religions do not stop there. They unhesitatingly maintain that their own particular moral and spiritual teachings not merely involve the divine, but that they are, in fact, divine commands because men received them through divine intervention. But when the religions push their claims that far, they raise a fundamental question. How do they know whereof they speak? How do they know that God revealed his will to men in the manner they say he did? How can a religion establish a claim to authority without involving itself in the end in mere self-assertion?

There is perhaps no point at which the three standard American faiths and others as well more completely alienate the people of the fourth faith. Most theological literature designed for popular consumption leaves unanswered the one question the fourth faith is asking: How do you know? Either the three standard faiths assume that they already know, and that everybody knows that they know, or they meet the question by reasoning in a circle. Neither approach is calculated to win any converts among thoughtful people.

Sometimes the theologians approach the question of circular reasoning at a very high level. But sometimes their attempts to deal with it are bizarre or downright silly. It is often asserted, for example, that the authority for Christian teaching is found in Christianity itself. One man argued that just as the authority for the speed of light is found in measuring it and learning that it is 186,000 miles a second, so in like manner, we believe in God, the Incarnation and the Eternal Life, because we observe these beliefs are present in Christianity. On his logic he could also believe in palmistry, witchcraft, or divination because he can observe these beliefs in manuals written by those who have believed in such things. On the same basis he could also believe in cannibalism.

Again it is often asserted that traditional Christian teachings are self-validating. Anders Nygren finds agape (Christian love) at the heart of the New Testament. This is not, he says, man's love for God (eros) but God's love for man. This was manifest in the life of the Son of Man, and is the love of which Paul speaks in his famous thirteenth chapter of the First Epistle to the Corinthians. It is known to us in our own experience as it energizes the human heart. It is the presence of the Holy Spirit. We cannot describe or analyze this love, but we can know it, says Nygren. But he nowhere tells us how the uniquely Christian aspects of the doctrine of brotherly love are self-validating in a way that such feelings derived from another tradition are not.

A more direct and immediate instance of the same kind of reasoning was reported by Vergilius Ferm: "I once had conversation with an Episcopal minister of very high standing in his ecclesiastical circles who told me of his life-long wrestling with skepticism. It was difficult for him to believe what he thought he ought to believe. He had been a minister in a certain denomination for some years. When World War I came and he saw how little concerned his church was over the moral questions involved in that war, he became convinced that the church was just so much baggage handed down and to be handed down. The call to the life heroic seemed to come from outside the church rather than from within. He left his ministry and his church and with tongue in his cheek about ultimate questions, he took up the cause for his fellow-men who had become embroiled in what he termed a nonsensical struggle. I shall not discuss his wanderings and his utter despondency.

"One day, he said, he happened to go into an Episcopal church. He picked up a hymn book and with the congregation singing, he joined in with mumbling the words. Of a sudden, he said, it came to him that the words themselves did not mean much nor did the particular minister nor the particular choir nor the particular people who were present; but he felt the presence of a tradition, a host of those who, throughout the ages, had knelt and sung and sat together. It was as if a huge wave had swept in from the deep and lifted him above all his petty skepticism. He felt he belonged to the ages, that he was no different from the countless, the great throng, who once had hoped and aspired, though they had floundered and failed."

Rich as the experience of that minister may have been, it answers none of the questions the fourth faith is asking. To associate oneself with the traditions of the ages proves nothing whatever about their validity. The rediscovery that the church was very old did not make the traditions it handed down either more or less "baggage." Was the church any more concerned about moral questions after he dropped into that Episcopal church than before? Why did his singing and kneeling with the congregation bring his lifelong wrestling with skepticism to an end? Did that experience prove the truth of doctrines he once doubted? Did it not rather prove only that he was content now to accept the church's teachings which heretofore he had rejected?

Much has been made of the argument that religious truth can be known only when we enter its disciplines and accept its teachings. Said one writer apparently without his tongue in his cheek: "The data of religion can be no more effectively evaluated without entering into the disciplines of prayer and self-denial than the evidences of astronomy can be properly evaluated without giving attention to the instruments, charts and tables by which celestial observations and computations are made and recorded."

We have noted the theologians' appeal to astronomy before. But this instance is no more persuasive than the other. On the contrary, this writer's argument proves the very point against which he is contending. Most of us know nothing of the devices of astronomy. We have never been in an observatory, never examined any astronomical charts, never seen the sky through anything stronger than a pair of binoculars or a neighbor's homemade telescope. Yet we accept the conclusions of the astronomers without examining their technical evidence because all those who have taken the trouble to look at it agree as to what it is. If those who enter into the disciplines of prayer and self-denial were as agreed upon the data such disciplines yield as the astronomers are agreed as to the distance to the Pleiades or the composition of the Great Nebula in Orion, religion would be a far more useful instrument than it is. But there is nothing in astronomy that corresponds to the strife among the theologians as to the data that are to be derived from the many and varying disciplines of prayer to be found in the several religions. As William James observed long ago, the experiences of religion are self-validating only in the sense that they seem real to those who have such experiences. And they are necessarily personal and private.

That mystical experiences are often very vivid and carry with them a sense of importance and immediacy for transcending ordinary human experience no one can doubt. St. Theresa of Lisieux, yearning to bring the love of God to men, spent the few years of her adult life in almost solitary contemplation and prayer. As a result, she had the most profound and convincing inner experience of the person of Jesus. Speaking of him, the year before her death at age twenty-four, she wrote: "Never have I heard Him speak; yet I know that He dwells within me. Each instant He guides and inspires me. I discover a light not before seen at the very moment of my greatest need. It is not usually during prayer that these illuminations come to me, but when I am in the midst of my daily tasks. . . ."

Nevertheless, those who offer religion to contemporary-minded men and women must understand that the disciplines of modern prayer, like medieval mystical experiences, may be impressive, but they leave the most important question still unanswered. How is the circle to be broken? How is the experience to be trusted? If I enter a church and its disciplines feel good to me, how am I to know that my experience is valid? There has been much criticism lately of religion that *feels* good. If such a subjective experience is bad, why are not mystical experiences?

To argue that you must enter a religion, accept its beliefs, and submit to its disciplines if you would know its truth is again to argue in a circle. For what does the validity of such an experience depend upon but the authority of the church which provides it. But you were advised to enter the church and take up its disciplines in the first place in order to experience at first hand the truth it held. An experience of the truth of a teaching cannot prove its truth if that teaching depends for its truth upon our experiencing it. Again we have truth which stands upon no firmer ground than its assertion by those who hold it.

This method of substantiating religious truth is not, however, confined to the clergy. A popular American picture magazine, *Life,* has from time to time run religious editorials of unmistakably orthodox stamp. Apparently after each such essay into theology there is a prompt response from the readership, for the "Letters" column is soon filled with replies, all from laymen, except those that commend the editorial. Typical was a letter from Philip Wylie which read in part as follows: "Life is uninformed when it tries to give a metaphysical slant to the uncertainty principle. Quantum mathematicians have tried to explain the nature of their logic in such a fashion as to stop philosophers and theologians from making *Life*'s blunder in their subject, but the mathematically naïve continue to do so. *Life*, when it points out as evidence of "mystery" the unpredictability of the behaviour of any one molecule in a gas, is still more naïve. That fact by itself would indicate that pure chance, not divine rule, governs nature. Fortunately we have more data than that."

The magazine replied: "Let tractarian Wylie forget what his fore-fathers thought about science and re-examine what they knew about God," which of course proves the point Wylie was making. What man knows about nature and what he knows about God must be measured by the same standards. The one is not opinion because it concerns science and the other knowledge because it concerns God. To say that we ought to examine what our ancestors "knew" about God is no different from saying that we ought to examine what they "knew" about witches. And if we distinguish what they "knew" about the one from what they "thought" about the other, we have begged the question before we begin.

The difficulty is "Truth" as contemporary theologians understand the word has a different meaning than when used in any other area of life. One of the multitudinous books attempting yet again to tell the faithful how they may believe the Apostles' Creed says: "Christian truth is not primarily a set of true propositions or state-ments that we have merely to accept, but rather a reality of life in God that confronts us in Jesus Christ. To be in the truth or to have the truth dwelling in us, is to be united by faith with Jesus Christ in a relationship in which he is Lord and we, acknowledging our-selves as subjects, are accepted as friends with whom he shares the fullness of his life. We can know the truth only insofar as we know him and have our life from him."

Anyone who wishes may define his terms, and he may take old words and endow them with such new meanings as suit his pur-pose. With philosophers and theologians it is an old and well-established habit, as we have seen. But it is also a slippery device at best, and we have to watch carefully when we meet it in order that we may be clear as to what is really happening. The foregoing defender of the Creed, for example, offers us a new concept of truth

—truth of a particular kind: Christian truth. On examination it turns out to be something quite different from what we had supposed. For him truth is not a set of true propositions, says the author. It is "a reality of life in God that confronts us in Jesus Christ." Granting for the moment that we know what those words mean, we need to be aware that whatever they mean, "truth" in this paragraph is something other than what we ordinarily take truth to be. In Christianity, this author is saying truth is not truth. It is something else, masquerading under the same name. It is a "reality of life in God. . . ."

The fourth faith would not deny to a man the right to resort to this kind of lap dissolve if he thinks it the best way to get his idea across. But the fourth faith would insist upon the importance of being aware as to what is happening here. One of the primary concerns of the fourth faith is truth, and for that reason it would insist that the fading of "truth" into Christian dogmatics be made far more explicit than it is in the foregoing paragraph. It would then add: If the foregoing refers to truth in the familiar sense of the word, then whatever is "Christian" truth, is also scientific truth or truth of any other kind. Unless there is one kind of truth in this universe, it is not a universe but chaos and truth is but a hope and an illusion.

A few other examples chosen at random further illustrate the position of present-day Protestantism. J. B. Phillips writes in *God Our Contemporary,* "I believe that modern man can never possess a faith which can both command his intelligent loyalty and influence every part of his thinking and feeling until he discovers the unique authority of Jesus Christ." Is further comment necessary? Religious faith is to be gained only at the price of submission to external authority. It cannot be had through the assent of a persuaded mind, the only kind of faith that would seem to many to be either intelligent or safe.

Most Christian theology is lost upon the people of the fourth faith because it appears not even to be aware of its own circularity. Their writers seem not to know that they talk as if the truth were what they say is true, a position which gives equal validity to Christianity, communism, fascism, and the single tax. A popular interdenominational weekly deplored the inadequate concept of man held by social workers. "If social workers are obsessed by Enlightenment notions of the goodness, dignity and freedom of man," lamented the editor, "if they are handicapped by the 'inadequate appraisal' that man has the 'intrinsic ability to love his neighbor,' where did they acquire such ideas?" Plainly implicit in his question is the view that belief in the dignity of man, and the ability of man to love his neighbor, constitute some kind of Christian heresy, the origin of which must be unearthed. "It is the job of the churches," the editorial concluded, "to address themselves to the ministry of proclaiming the truth." And what is the truth? Why it is what the churches teach, and social workers who disagree are not merely ill-advised, they are in error. They believe and act upon propositions which are false.

Sometimes eager defenders of the faith fall into the simple assertion of the patently false. One of the reports submitted at the meetings of the World Council of Churches at Evanston, Illinois, in 1954, spoke of "the dignity of independent human thought only at the foot of the cross." Yet any student of human history knows that independent thought appeared long before the Galilean died a terrible death because he was one of its greatest exemplars. And any student of ecclesiastical history knows the extent to which independent thought has been crushed in those who stood at the foot of the cross.

A favorite device of the believer is to address his words to the secularist, the agnostic, the skeptic, the unbeliever, and so on. One such volume entitled *Epistle to the Skeptics,* a fair sample of this body of semipopular religious writing, begins by praising skepticism, and quite rightly pointing out that it is a necessary part of all constructive thinking. The author persuades the reader that he too is ready to make the inquirer's questions his point of departure in presenting Christian beliefs. But then, very early (p. 17) he slips a cog apparently without being aware that he has done so. "Whether we are atheists or theists," he asserts, "we live from first to last within the sustaining, correcting and directing hand of God." This may well be true. The author deeply believes that it is. But he seems to miss the fact that this is the point at issue. And as a matter of fact in making it, he has left out the very people to whom he addresses his words, for most of them would not think of themselves as either theists or atheists.

"God breaks through into every system of thought," continues the

Epistle. "He breaks through into history." Does he? the skeptic would ask simply. If you wish me to believe it, I am ready to have you say why I should. But to affirm such beliefs is not to address an epistle to the skeptic. An epistle directed to him must begin where he now is; it must begin with the questions that bother him. If instead it begins with affirmations, it is a letter not to the skeptic but to the believer. There is no reason why a book should not begin so. Most do. But such a book cannot do the job to which this one addressed itself.

Examples of theological substantiation of truth by nothing more than self-assertion could be multiplied without end. One more set of examples of such efforts must suffice, the my-God-is-better-than-your-God argument. Karl Barth, speaking at the University of Chicago at the time he received an honorary degree in 1962, described the God he believes in and worships as follows: "He is no lonely God detached from everything and enclosed within Himself—He is not only the Lord of man, but his Father, Brother and Friend. This is the God who reveals Himself in the Gospel, who Himself speaks to men and acts among and upon them."

Such a statement, like a great many of those made by the Swiss theologian, leaves adherents of the faith of adventure open-mouthed with astonishment. Can it be that the Barthians construct out of the Gospel the kind of God they find congenial and then fall down and worship him? Surely it is a fine God that Barth worships and we are glad that his divinity boasts so many desirable characteristics. But does this make the deity Barth derives from the Gospels any more certain to exist? Are we to argue, as Barth seems to be doing here, that we should be his kind of Christian because he has derived from the Gospels a God who is father, brother, and friend?

Another contemporary theologian argues in much the same vein that orthodoxy is better than liberalism because it is "more exciting. . . . There is adventure in orthodoxy," he writes, "a sense of expectancy. The God of orthodoxy does not sit calmly in heaven waiting for men to find him. Rather, he invades the earth, is born as a babe, eats, drinks, suffers and dies." This man may be right, but he has altogether missed the point. He or someone else might be able to contrive a far more exciting faith than orthodoxy—the doctrine of the Black Muslims, for example. But most of us would ask first whether that faith is true. If it is, all well and good. But if it is not, the fact that it is exciting is a cause not for rejoicing, but for alarm.

A church does not possess the answers to man's ultimate questions because it is arrogant enough to say that it does. Neither is a church "God's church" because it unashamedly makes that claim for itself. Too many churches make this claim. Consequently, no one is convinced by it. Nor is the Bible "Holy" because it claims to be in its own pages, or because some learned divine makes the claim on its behalf, or because some church says it is, or because men have believed this to be so for some three thousand years. To admit any of these claims would be to fling all religion into a morass of conflicting avowals and declarations. It would be to ask the religions to invite choice among them, not on the basis of a common standard by which all are to be judged, but on the basis of the vehemence with which each asserts its superiority over the rest. To allow self-assertion to have anything to do with the presentation of religion is to degrade it. Insofar as such dynamism characterizes the three standard American faiths today, just insofar does the need become apparent for a faith whose dynamism denounces such a procedure and whose vehemence issues in the demand that all the claims of all the religions be judged by the same standard.

We, in our time, have had a frightening exhibition of the self-assertive dynamism that now passes under the name of religion. Fascism and Nazism were a rejection of the basic Western philosophy that requires careful examination of every claim, to know the truth by one and the same standard. As Roland Bainton has pointed out, the great gulf that developed between Germany and the West was a result of Germany's rejection of the classical ideal of natural law as the basis of unity of mankind, valid for all, and available through reason. Germany, and in particular the Nazis, replaced this concept with a self-assertive dynamism that was nonrational. They asserted their right to forge their own morality. This was the true secularism. It is emotional, not rational. It demands loyalty, not justification, and its final appeal is to the welfare of the group, if necessary at the expense of the welfare of men more generally. The classical and Christian ideal, on the other hand, was the welfare of mankind.

William Ernest Hocking, in a classic phrase, once spoke of the need for an "outside purchase" upon religious affirmations. It is a need the men and women of the fourth faith would also proclaim. If this requirement were kept in mind, it would quickly bring all circular reasoning to an end, to the enormous benefit of the religions of men.

★ ★ ★

CHAPTER VI

The Faith of Adventure

We have now seen the impact of the Copernican revolution upon the church. We have seen the effort of the church, in particular Protestant liberalism, to meet the challenge that revolution involved for Christian theology. We have seen that liberalism did not succeed, that its attempted crusade became first a retreat, then a rout. We have reviewed the neo-orthodox effort to re-establish the faith, always keeping a weather eye on the Copernican revolution in order not to seem either ignorant or irrelevant to man's ever-increasing body of knowledge. We have seen the weaknesses in many of the arguments employed by the churchmen to sustain their case.

We have also seen that the emergence of religious pluralism in America resulted in the formulation of the fact that there is a fourth faith to be found along with the three standard faiths, Protestantism, Catholicism, and Judaism. Eschewing much of what has been thrown into that convenient catchall the "fourth faith," we have undertaken to speak on behalf of a very genuine and significant aspect of it. We have said that the fourth faith is primordial, that it antedates the several historic faiths which have in turn claimed superiority or supremacy. We have also asserted that it is contemporary, and have compared it to Paul Tillich's Protestant principle which transcends all historic religions but may find expression at a particular time in any of them, provided of course the necessary conditions are met.

We have called the fourth faith the faith of adventure. The name, cumbersome though it is, has been chosen because it suggests the contrast with the faith of stability which it stands over against. The fourth faith declares that man is now and always has been engaged in a continuing effort to state his religious faith in the clearest terms possible, to celebrate it in the most meaningful way possible, and to clarify it, correct it, amplify it, and nurture it to the uttermost of his ability. For this reason, man has never been able or willing to confine the expression of his faith within any particular historic religion. Yet the faith of adventure does not reject tradition. It says with Alfred North Whitehead: "The art of a free society consists: first, in the maintenance of a symbolic code; and secondly, in fearlessness of revision to secure that the code serves those purposes which satisfy and enlighten reason. The society which cannot combine reverence of their symbols with freedom of revision must ultimately decay either from anarchy or from the slow atrophy of a life stifled by useless shadows." The fourth faith, like all the faiths, recognizes the value of a symbolic code. It differs with the historic faiths in its readiness to enact revisions of that code in accordance with enlightened reason and fresh insight.

We are not attempting a full-length statement of the fourth faith here. It is our purpose rather to say that those who purport to have found a fourth faith in the socioreligious structure of American life are right. It is our purpose to show why such a faith has emerged, and how it relates to the three standard faiths as well as to such other faiths as may lay their claim to man's attention. In this concluding chapter we turn to some of the principles that characterize the faith of adventure and try to see them in relation to the contrasting tenets of the faith of stability.

1. A Second Look at Adam

Oddly enough, we owe our understanding of Adam and Eve and the Garden of Eden not so much to the Book of Genesis where it is told as to its retelling in the letters of the Apostle Paul. Paul had two basic problems to solve in his effort to convert both Jews and Gentiles to his new faith and in his effort to sustain the churches he founded in that faith. He had in the first instance to deal with Judaism: he had to show why Judaism was insufficient as a religion. He had in the second place to make some of the bizarre teachings of the Christians acceptable to the sophisticated Hellenistic mind. In this effort the story of Adam and his fall proved a very useful tool. In fact, the Eden story became pivotal in Paul's theology.

Paul hit on the notion that Christ was the new Adam who had come to take the place of the old. As sin had entered the world through one man Adam, he said, so the world was now redeemed from sin through one man Christ. He developed this theory in his letter to the Romans and expanded it further in his first letter to the Corinthians. Struggling to persuade his doubting Greek converts that bodily resurrection was possible, he said: "As in Adam all die, so in Christ shall all be made alive." A little later on he contrasts the first man Adam, as a living being from the earth, with Christ, the last Adam who is a life-giving spirit, a man from heaven.

It was a brilliant conception and a genuine achievment for a mind of the first century A.D. It was particularly so for a man who was ignorant of Greek philosophy, a religious convert, and a tent-maker by trade. Paul had no theological system to fall back on and only rabbinical training. He had to hammer out his own explanations of the problem that troubled his converts.

Of course, he was not entirely without precedent for the theory he developed. He did not fashion it out of the air; no man ever does, no matter how original a mind he may have. In the later Jewish writings, the Apocrypha and the Pseudepigrapha, the theory had been developed that no one had ever really understood the story of Adam. In the light of Israel's domination by Babylon, Syria, and Rome in succession, the rabbis began to exalt Adam's state before his fall. Paul, who was a realist, also knew that in another strain in latter-day Jewish lore, great emphasis had been placed where it belonged, namely, upon Adam's sin and guilt. In this view, all mankind's evil and sin was laid to Adam's initial transgression. Philo, for example, distinguished between the first man of Genesis, the heavenly man, not created but formed after the image of God; and the second, the earthly man, the historical Adam who became the father of sinful mankind. Paul, who we have every reason to think was well-trained in this lore, transmuted this concept into the first man Adam and the second man Christ.

The Pauline interpretation of the Eden story is legitimate, not only on the basis of the text as it stands but also on the basis of human nature and destiny as many ancients understood it. Man's pessimism about himself is at least as old as his own history. "The lot of man is to suffer and to die," sang Homer, and Pindar, echoing his words half a millennium later, wrote in his Pythian Ode: "We are creatures of a day. What is one? What is one not? Man is the dream of a shadow." James Breasted has laid before us one of the great periods of pessimism of man about himself, that in Egypt about 2500 B.C., after the fall of the ancient line of kings whose pyramids endure to the present day.

From the time man first became self-conscious enough to record his own feelings, his estimate of himself ran low. The reason was he found himself so helpless in the face of the forces against which he had to contend. He was subject to an unending succession of calamities he could neither prevent nor control. War, famines, floods, earthquakes, plagues, hunger, injury, suffering, disease, and death all came upon him unbidden.

Recall the 91st Psalm. Here the poet sings of the mercies of his God. Our theology and his are not the same, but in the list of things against which he seeks protection we get a picture of the precarious life he led. Think of the meaning of the words: "The pestilence that walketh in darkness" or "the destruction that wasteth at noonday." Few of us have been where a thousand might fall at our side or ten thousand at our right hand, and to hope that it might not come nigh to us, although now we can foresee such a possibility in nuclear warfare.

To account for his difficulties and his failures, both Hebrew and Greek blamed the gods, not themselves. The Book of Psalms is immediately preceded in our Bible by the Book of Job. All of that poor man's misery is clearly due to the will of the Almighty. The Psalms themselves are filled with references to the misfortunes as well as the benefits that God sends upon men. Among the Greeks it was the same. "My son, the end of all things is in the hands of Zeus the Thunderer," writes Semonides, "and he disposes as he wills." And Sophocles in *Oedipus at Colonus* writes: "Never to be born is, past all reckoning, best: next best by far, when a man has come into the world, that, as soon as may be, he should return thither whence he came. For when the days of his youth are gone, and the foolish delights thereof are fled away, the stroke of affliction smites him and spares his not; he is weary and has no rest from envy and strife, faction and warfare and the shedding of blood."

The genius of Euripides penetrates through to the real meaning of these explanations of man's misery. He, almost alone among the ancients, is able to see that man is really seeking to escape responsibility for his suffering by shifting it all onto the gods. Euripides is unwilling to do this. "If the gods do anything base," he cries in a fragment of the lost play *Bellerophon,* "they are no gods." And his *Iphigenia* asserts that the evil gods of the Taurians do but reflect the evils of the Taurians themselves. "I do not believe any divinity is evil," Iphigenia declares with finality in the *Iphigenia in Tauris.*

There was also a strong strain in Judaism that took from God's hands the blame for man's woes and placed it squarely on man's own shoulders. That is what the Eden story attempts to do and it was upon this aspect of it that Paul fixed his attention. The central fact of the story was man's disobedience, said Paul. This is why he was punished and this is why his redemption through Christ was necessary.

For Paul there was no sense of anomaly in saying that Adam was the first man. But there is with us. We expect such statements from the Fundamentalists, but in the light of modern knowledge about the origins of life in its many forms on this planet; in view of our rapidly accumulating body of knowledge regarding primitive cultures; in the face of the discoveries in Mesopotamia regarding the beginnings of civilization there some ten thousand years ago; considering the cave paintings at Lascaux in France and others in Africa, not to speak of the discoveries of Louis B. Leakey in the Olduvai Gorge in Tanganyika we do not expect educated men and women nowadays to assert that Adam was the first man. And if we cannot speak of Adam as the first man, then we cannot speak of Christ as the second. And neither can we say that as sin entered the world through the first man, so the world is redeemed from sin through the second. If the parallelism breaks down, the entire structure falls, for the concept of the second man Christ and the belief that he redeemed us from sin is based upon the mischief done by the first man Adam.

It hardly seems necessary to say that in the light of modern knowledge Christian theology ought to take a second look at Adam and ask itself whether there is any sense in which he may still be said to have been "the first man from whom all mankind is descended." If he was not, then it is of historical but not theological interest to note that the Bible said he was.

We have seen how modern theology deals with these questions. There are several levels of truth in the Genesis story, say today's theologians. There is the surface account, a pretty story which no one takes literally any longer. But there is a deeper meaning lying beneath the surface: in fact there are several levels of meaning. One level obviously is the attempt of less sophisticated minds than ours to grapple with questions that troubled them: Why cannot man live in joy and bliss in a garden? Why must he labor for his bread in the sweat of his brow? Why must women bear children in pain? Here is a kind of mythological answer.

At a deeper level, we can say that the story addresses itself to the question: Why is there so much evil in the world? Modern theologians carry the process yet further. At their hands the story becomes the means by which we are made to see the truth that we are fallen creatures, lost in sin, helpless without God's grace shed upon us through Jesus Christ. This is really what Paul said the story meant. He did not talk about levels of meaning or stages of truth, but this is what he meant. The true meaning of the Garden of Eden story is not to be found in Genesis but in the New Testament: in the crucifixion and resurrection of Christ. As Reinhold Niebuhr has said, the story of the fall of Adam serves us as a constant reminder of man's fallen state—of the evil and sin which he commits in spite of his good intent.

Now this is all very well. A vast amount of time and energy has been spent in recent years in developing this theory. And it has the happy result, so far as Christian orthodoxy is concerned, of making a basic yet strange part of the Bible believable. But I would ask these men a different question. Granted that we need to be aware of man's evil, I would ask them why we need the charming myth of Eden to remind us of it. Wouldn't Dachau, Belsen, and Buchenwald do better? Wouldn't Hiroshima and Nagasaki be more persuasive?

But let us take contemporary theology on the basis it has itself chosen: that there are levels of truth in the Genesis story. Now if we are going to play hide-and-seek with Bible meanings, we have entered upon a game at which anyone can play. If there are levels of truth in these stories which await only the ingenuity of a penetrating mind, then we can all re-examine these tales and see what levels of truth we can discern. Perhaps the deepest meaning, like the diamonds at the lowest levels of a mine, yet remain to be unearthed and brought to the surface.

Ancient man set up a second defense for his helplessness and his misery. He early came to believe that he should not try to understand too much. Very early he came to believe that he should not attempt to penetrate the realm where the answers to his deepest questions lay. Man must not overreach himself, the ancients believed. He must not, in pride, seek to know more than the gods desire him to know, to go where they do not wish him to go, or to do what they do not want him to do.

Uncounted myths testify to this anxiety, and it is the nub of the Garden of Eden story. Man was driven from paradise because he disobeyed the commandment of God, says Christian theology. He ate of the fruit of the tree that was forbidden and this was his sin. But according to the Bible account itself, he was driven out of the Garden not as punishment for wrongdoing but because of God's fear of what he might do next. The story as it is in Genesis reads: "Then the Lord God said [after Adam had eaten the fruit], 'Behold, the man has become like one of us, knowing good and evil; and now, lest he put forth his hand and take also of the tree of life, and eat, and live for ever'—therefore the Lord God sent him forth from the garden of Eden, to till the ground from which he was taken."

The language could not be clearer. Christianity may emphasize man's disobedience if it chooses, and it is to be neither doubted nor denied. But if we ask what the Bible authors thought moved God against Adam, it was not his disobedience so much as God's anxiety that man might learn too much.

The story, of course, reflects man's thought about himself, not

God's thought about man. And the anxiety it expresses is repeated again and again in ancient literature. The Eden story, in fact, is by no means the only instance of it in the Bible. The story of the Tower of Babel bears an identical message. Don't venture too far. Don't try to find out too much, or the gods will be angry. When men had succeeded in building a tower that rose up toward the clouds, so the story goes, God grew anxious. "This is only the beginning of what they will do," he said to himself; "and nothing that they propose to do will now be impossible for them," and brought the project to an abrupt end.

This story, as it is recorded in Genesis, appears to have as its purpose, accounting for the many languages that are found in the world. It also explains how men came to be scattered all across the face of the earth. But it has a far more profound meaning. The confusion of tongues is but an incidental flourish on the central theme. The story of the Tower of Babel is primarily concerned with the problem of man's striving for knowledge and for material achievement, but it clearly reflects his constant fear that in his strivings he might overreach himself, displease the gods, and be punished.

Today it is still the same. The areas within which we think investigation is permissible have infinitely broadened. But the age-old anxiety that we may learn too much for our own good lingers on. The ancients expressed their anxiety in theological terms. We are more apt to state ours in terms of cause and effect. Our fear of retribution, divine in some sense, if we really face up to what we are thinking, is no less real. Perhaps it is more so. We have split the atom, and now we tremble before it. Already we know how to reduce our Eden to a blackened cinder, and we shudder to think that we might do so in spite of ourselves. While we develop newer and ever more subtle ways of destroying the lives of men, we tremble— tremble as the ancients trembled—because of the wrath that may fall upon us because such knowledge is ours, because of the punishment that will be visited upon us if we ascend too high and learn too much. We feel the same anxiety as we explore the secrets of life itself, and realize that one day we may be able to build it in the laboratory.

Our exercise in level-of-truth analysis of the Bible should have made one thing clear. It is a method which does not reveal the truth lying at the deepest levels of Scripture so much as it is a device by which the interpreter, like the Essenes of old, reads out of the text that which he is able to find there. In level-of-truth analysis, the orthodox of today are twice guilty of the sin of which they found the liberals of yesterday guilty. As the liberals read into the historical Jesus they reconstructed, their own ideals of social justice, pacifism, and piety, so today's orthodox read out of Scripture their concern for man's sin and guilt, his sense of estrangement, and his need for redemption. The one is no more nor less justified than the other. It is time for Christianity to take a second look at the Adam it has for its own purposes, read out of Genesis, and for all the rest of its biblical outreadings as well. This is the truth we can find if we take a second look at Adam.

But what nonsense is this! Why should we expend our energy in searching out levels of truth in Genesis? We are told it is to enable us to understand the nature of man. If this is true, then I would like to ask a second question. Why do we think that in a document written between twenty-five hundred and three thousand years ago we shall find a better understanding of the nature of man than in the thought of our contemporaries? It is interesting and instructive to probe for levels of truth in Genesis, for it reveals the depth of understanding the ancient mind achieved. It is interesting and instructive to do it with Homer and Plato too, with the Upanishads and with Milton. But let us not lose sight of what we are up to. Christian theology in its game of levels of truth is not trying to show how wise the ancients were. It is showing us that the Bible, because of the truth it contains, should remain central for us today, and should continue to be regarded as God's Word, especially revealed, and continually revealing.

2. The Heaven Stormer

According to the biblical account, the forbidden tree that stood in the center of the garden was the tree of the knowledge of good and evil. The punishment for eating its fruit was death. Nevertheless, Eve took the fruit and ate it, at the serpent's suggestion to be sure. But she did it, says the Bible, because it "was good for food . . . a delight to the eyes . . . and desired to make one wise."

Now these are all good and worthy purposes. Our orthodox friends find man's sin, not in these purposes but in the fact of his disobedience. In eating the fruit, man transgressed the Lord's command, and it was for this that he was punished. I suggest that we take a second look at Adam in this connection. With equal propriety we can lay our emphasis, not upon the fact of his disobedience, but rather upon the purpose for which he ate the fruit, and the result he achieved in eating it. If we are to find the truth for our time by searching out the meaning of the deepest levels of this ancient tale, I suggest that we shall find it in the fact that Eve had the courage to break an ancient religious taboo. Adam joined her in it, and as a result the world was not lost in sin. As a result the world advanced in knowledge although it also paid the price that new knowledge always brings, the price, for example, that we have paid for splitting the atom. A second look at Adam reveals him to us not as the evil progenitor of the race who brought suffering upon all humanity, but as a daring adventurer, thirsting for knowledge and ready to pursue it to the uttermost of his ability. If we will take a second look at Adam, we will see that we are not the victims of his sin, but the benefactors of his desire to know.

It is just as valid to say that the Garden of Eden story means the one as the other. Both elements are present in the ancient story, and to me, the readiness of man to risk all in his desire to know stands out more clearly than anything else. And so I would take Adam out of the role in which Christianity has cast him. I would take off his back the burden of the world's sin which Pauline theology has placed there. I would instead offer Adam as a hero, and his wife Eve as a heroine greater than he. Both are pioneers. Both—in the biblical context—brought us the knowledge we have to have in this sordid world—knowledge of the difference between good and evil.

When we take a good look at poor old Adam we find he was neither the weakling nor the monster we had generally supposed. He is bone of our bone and flesh of our flesh. He is a rebel. No slave to arbitrary authority is he, and no citizen of the paternalistic state. He did not want the ease and comfort of a garden in which he was happy because he was ignorant. He preferred to know good and evil and to pay whatever price that knowledge had upon it, and then to take the steps his new responsibility entailed as we at last have begun to do with atomic power. In short, although neither Judaism nor Christianity has chosen to do so, it is quite as legitimate to look upon Adam as a Promethean as it is to view him as a Pauline figure. Adam brought to earth from heaven, where the secret was held, knowledge of good and evil, and suffered for his audacity. Prometheus brought fire from heaven where it was hidden and gave it to the men of earth, for which he too was punished.

Neither the calamities that constantly beset ancient man nor the admonitions of the priesthood deterred him from his attempt to find meaning in his own life and in the world of which he was so obviously a part. With all his setbacks and all the obstacles that were put in his path, man knew that he had long been engaged upon a process of discovery. We can see it extending far back of the Hebrew Psalmists and myth writers, far back of the Greek classical playwrights, back of Homer, back of the earliest Egyptian and Sumerian writings. Ancient man sensed this too.

The process of discovery, of the widening of the horizons of understanding, has been a process of self-discovery also. And in the course of it, man has occasionally stopped to reflect. And when he has done so he has been astonished at himself. Occasionally he has said so and said why. When the author of the 8th Psalm asked himself why God was mindful of man, the answer he gave to his own question was exultant:

> Yet thou hast made him little less than God,
>   and dost crown him with glory and honor.
> Thou hast given him dominion over the works of thy hands;
>   thou has put all things under his feet,
> all sheep and oxen
>   and also the beasts of the field,
> the birds of the air, and the fish of the sea,
>   whatever passes along the paths of the sea.

The Psalm concludes with a paean of praise to the Almighty for so thoughtfully designing the world for man's pleasure:

> O Lord, our Lord, how majestic is thy name
>   in all the earth!

Certain of the Greeks were even more emphatic in the high estimate they placed upon man. Recall the first choral ode in Sophocles' *Antigone:*

Many the wonders, but nothing walks stranger
    than man.
This thing crosses the sea in the winter's storm,
making his path through the roaring waves.
And she, the greatest of gods, the earth—
ageless she is, and unwearied—he wears her
    away
as the ploughs go up and down from year to
    year
and his mules turn up the soil.
Gay nations of birds he snares and leads,
wild beast tribes and the salty brood of
    the sea,
with the twisted mesh of his nets, this clever
    man.
He controls with craft the beasts of the
    open air,
walkers on hills. The horse with his shaggy
    mane
he holds and harnesses, yoked about the neck,
and the strong bull of the mountain.
Language, and thought like the wind
and the feelings that make the town,
he has taught himself, and shelter
    against the cold,
refuge from rain. He can always help
    himself.
He faces no future helpless. There's only
    death
that he cannot find an escape from. He
    has contrived
refuge from illnesses beyond all cure.
Clever beyond all dreams
The inventive craft that he has
which may drive him one time or another
    to well or ill.
When he honors the laws of the land and
    the gods' sworn right
high indeed is his city; but stateless
    the man
who dares to dwell with dishonor.

All the alarms of all the theologians, both ancient and modern,
have been sounded in vain. Today, more than ever before, man as-
saults the ramparts of whatever heaven he knows. He searches out

Eden, he builds his Tower of Babel as high as he can, and he strives to bring down yet more fire from heaven. This includes all knowledge, all truth, and all religion. Denounced for his belief in progress, he strives on to progress as far as he is able. Accused of holding to an empty optimism, he still seeks to build Utopia right here on earth where he lives. Dismissed as a dreamer, he goes right on dreaming of a world better than this, and he goes right on bending his efforts toward bringing it to pass.

This is man the heaven-stormer. This is man the adventurer. He is man spiritual, standing in awe before the wonders of the universe in which he finds himself. He is man religious, filled with wonder, thinking, yearning to know, aspiring to understand. He is the heretic, the seeker, the everlasting questioner. He is man the inquirer, whose restless mind constantly re-examines all the knowledge he possesses, testing it, seeking to discover whether it really is knowledge, or whether perchance it is the kind of superstition that so often passed as knowledge in earlier times.

The ancient heavens he both feared and yearned after have vanished like the dreams of the night. The Olympus whence Prometheus once stole fire disintegrated with the rise of Greek philosophy and science. The heaven the builders of Babel hoped to see has been removed from up over our heads, out of space and out of time until only the alchemy of theology can make it seem real any more. No longer does man seek Paradise in a lost Eden. He seeks it here. He would build it now and in the time that is to come. He dreams of it by night. He labors for it by day and he is determined to bring it to pass.

This is man the heaven-stormer, and it is the first and most important thing we can say about man. It is the first and most important thing we can say about the meaning of life itself and of the universe in which life finds its home. In spite of its evil, it is marvelously good. In spite of its decay, it is filled with promise. In spite of all our failures, we are men of hope. In spite of the fact that the heavens of our ancestors have vanished, we are still heaven-stormers. From this fundamental fact our religion takes its rise. We would make this earth an Eden and all men brothers.

All this we can say, even while the threat of atomic war hangs over our heads. Though we destroy ourselves, though we pass from the earth and are no more, it may still be said of man that he was a heaven-stormer. Knowledge is power, for good or evil. If we would attain the good that knowledge brings, we must run the risk of its perversion to evil ends.

In saying this, we do not overlook man's evil and his sin. We have not forgotten that man is also a bumbler and a glutton; that he can destroy the souls of thousands for his own personal profit; that he can degrade and enslave both men and women. He can enslave their minds as well as their bodies, starve their spirits, and pervert all that it means to be a man. All this we know.

But we know, too, that having done these things, man can become aware of the wrong he has done. Having despoiled himself, he can know guilt. Having brought bodily pain to others, he can know anguish of soul. Having lived in frustration, he can turn to hope. Having lived in squalor, he can dream of plenty. Having slaughtered in war, he can yearn for peace. Having done grievous wrong, he can seek to do the right.

We men of earth, limited in our vision, in our understanding, and even in our hope—we who are finite while dwelling amidst the infinite, mortal while dwelling amidst immortality—we human creatures are a jumble of seemingly impossible contrasts. Even while we dream of heaven upon earth, we seize our neighbor's goods, his livelihood, perhaps even his life. While we save life in our myriad hospitals, we maim and destroy it with the instruments of war. While we sing of righteousness, teaching honorable ways to our children, we corrupt, corrode, and debauch them with our chicanery and evil. We preach love and foment hate: we praise kindliness, yet lack the power or the will to do unto others as we should like them to do unto us.

Miserable, happy, blaspheming, praying mortals that we are, twisted and pulled apart by all the emotions and all the yearnings that swirl through us, we are rent in twain when we try to believe even as we are divided against ourselves in everything else we do. We believe what we doubt: we doubt what we believe. We are credulous to the point of stupidity and stubborn unbelievers in the face of overwhelming evidence. We live our lives in accordance with opinions which our minds have already rejected as the veriest nonsense, while refusing to live by demonstrable facts as clear as the light of the sun.

Heaven does not lie about us in our infancy. It lies beyond us in our maturity. It is not a place where good people go when they die. It is a present vision, so wondrous that, beholding it, we are set on fire. And thereafter we cannot rest. We are not merely seekers; yet more we are stormers. We shall not knock on the door and wait. If heaven does not yield to us we shall take it by assault. Indeed, we know this is the only way it can ever be won.

But it is not man's success or failure in besieging the ramparts of heaven that distinguish him from the creatures of earth to whom he is otherwise so closely akin. It is the fact that man alone has lifted his head from the ground and wondered whence came the sun, the moon, and the stars. Man alone has asked what they are, how they were made, why they are there, and how to reach them. Finding himself a creature of earth, man alone has thought to ask what the earth is and what it means to be a creature who walks upon it. He alone has thought to ask whence he himself came and whither he shall go. He alone has been able to transform the earth's surface and to venture out into the space that surrounds it. Man alone wants to know what it means to be born, to die, and to live the life that has been given to him.

This is man the heaven-stormer and it is this aspect of his nature that gives rise to the faith of adventure. The life after death, of which man has dreamed since first he was able to distinguish his thoughts from his experience, is but a small part of the heaven he reaches toward. For his dreams of heaven, in the beyond of both time and space, have always been matched by dreams of a heaven in the here and now. His belief that sometime, somewhere, all his questions will be answered, all mystery and all knowledge will be his, has been matched by his determination to learn as much as he could during the course of his life on earth. His vision of a time and place where the righteous prosper and the ungodly are like chaff which the wind drives away; his hope for a time and place from which sorrow and sighing, pain and suffering, have fled, has been matched by his determination to make this earth an Eden, to establish righteousness, joy, and peace among men here and now.

3. THE HERETIC

If Adam were a Promethean, rather than a Pauline figure, the fourth faith would seem to be greatly strengthened. But it is not, for the fourth faith rests neither upon Greek insight into the nature of man reflected in the Prometheus myth, nor in Paul's insight into the nature of man reflected in his reconstruction of the Eden myth. The fourth faith readily acknowledges the genius of both and that in any attempt to understand man and his destiny, both insights have to be taken into account, but it is interested in a different question.

The faith of adventure asks, What can I today say about man that will help him to understand himself, to avoid the pitfalls that clutter his path, and to choose the right and the good, the just, the true, the kindly, and the beautiful? It is glad to get what insight it can from Christianity, from Paul, from Aeschylus, or from any other source. But it does not ask, as Christian theology does, What truth can I find in Genesis that will be meaningful to men today? The fourth faith asks, What can I in my time say about man that is as true as I can make it and will also be of most benefit to him? Let me make what use I can of whatever statements have preceded mine, but let me not feel bound by any of them, no matter how many people, now, and before my time, may have believed those statements to be completely and finally true.

We live in the atomic age or the space age, as you will. Neither concept touched the imagination of the greatest seer when Genesis was written. It was written in a time when the only motive power known was that of men and oxen, when the world was supposed to be flat and not many hundred miles square, when men still believed the future could be foretold by interpreting dreams, when disease was cured by incantation, and when the monarch had the arbitrary power of life, death, and welfare over all his subjects. And you and I are invited to discern the nature of man through the writings of a mind so circumscribed. Barth, Niebuhr, Tillich, Bultmann, Brunner, and the rest have done well in making modern sense out of ancient myths. But they have given their efforts to the wrong enterprise. Their result was doomed at the outset to be distorted or insignificant in the long run, for they have taken as their norm the thought of a day that is dead.

It is our task to seek truth in our time as the Bible writers sought truth in theirs. It is our task to state what we believe to be the truth in the concepts of our time, as the Bible writers stated it in the concepts of theirs. It is for us to remember that as Adam rebelled in the Garden of Eden, and sought dangerous knowledge, so also must we. We have sought truth within and without the Christian tradition. We have sought it wherever we might find it, and in doing so, have been faithful to another and oft-neglected principle of the Judeo-Christian tradition: that of the rebel against arbitrary authority.

Prometheus, Adam, man the heaven-stormer, is man the seeker after knowledge and understanding. Man the seeker after knowledge is also man the questioner for he is never satisfied with the answers that are given him. Always he seeks to know whether the "knowledge" others offer him is true knowledge or whether perchance it is false. Man is a questioner because life makes him so. It constantly teaches him to doubt the wisdom of authority and by yielding answers to his questions invites him to ask more of them.

We can see this in every aspect of life but perhaps nowhere so well as in children. Suppose that an eight-year-old is getting ready for school on an overcast morning in the fall. It is not raining, but it certainly looks as though it were going to. Both the newspaper and the radio emphatically predict that it will rain throughout the day. The eight-year-old's mother cocks a weather eye at the sky and concurs with the official forecast.

Now the boy has the natural abhorrence of rubbers and a raincoat characteristic of all boys. On this particular morning he objects as usual, and chooses as his ground the fact that it is not raining now and that it may clear up. His mother is adamant, but so is he for a while. Then, because he has been taught to believe that "mother knows best," and because his limited experience has pretty well corroborated the maxim, he yields in part to her wisdom, but mostly to her authority, and wears the full rain apparel to school.

But let us suppose that on the day in question the sun comes out around ten o'clock in the morning. Let us suppose also that most of the other third-grade mothers had been able to anticipate the sudden shift in the weather, although his mother had not. And let us suppose what surely would have happened—that the rubberless, raincoatless boys and girls would have made our eight-year-old's life miserable all the way home from school. The result is the discovery that mother does not always know best. The seeds of skepticism are sown, and life has begun to teach one more of her children that the judgments of those in authority who are supposed to know are not always accurate. Life has begun the lesson which it never ceases to teach—that wider knowledge, and a better understanding of things, is to be gained by questioning old answers and old authorities as well as by asking new questions.

What happens at this point in a child's development has an incalculable influence on his mental habits and attitudes throughout life. If, as he begins to think for himself, his parents and teachers encourage him, then he will acquire the habit of testing all the assertions that are made to him, no matter who makes them; no matter how high and holy he may be. He will learn to turn over in his mind every avowal of every kind, to think about it, and to re-examine it. If he does this, by the time he has accepted any statement the idea it presents will have become wholly his, and he will know why he has made it a part of his body of knowledge.

A young man of my acquaintance told me how his father had taught him such habits of independent thought. One Sunday when he was about twelve years of age, he returned home from Sunday School following a session in which the teacher had given the class a pious account of the traditional heaven. It had all seemed very plausible and lovely to the boy as she described a world almost exactly like ours, except that the people had wings, and there was no work, no pain, no suffering, and everybody was good to every body else. The father listened with great interest as the boy recounted it all. When the story was concluded he made but a single comment. "Heaven must be a pretty big place," he said.

Then they talked about all the people in their community who presumably would go to heaven. They spoke of the number that had lived there before them and who had already died. They moved from that to the population of their city, their state, the United States, and finally the entire world. From that they moved back through history and tried to think of the number of people who must have lived and died since life first began upon the earth. Then they looked ahead to all the people that would be born in the future.

When, after that, they tried to locate the heaven the Sunday School teacher described, the problem became even more complicated. The teacher had said merely that it was up in the sky somewhere, which had seemed all right when she said it. Now, however, with untold billions of people to care for, and considering the fact, on second thought, that there are only planets and stars in the sky, it all seemed not merely remote, but highly improbable. When they had finished talking, a boy who was accustomed to come home from Sunday School merely accepting what he had been told, had begun the practice of testing whatever was told to him, a practice which remained with him throughout his life.

This habit of mind produces a Galileo dropping stones from the Leaning Tower of Pisa to see whether large ones fall faster than small ones. It accounts for all science constantly checking and rechecking what is already supposed to be known. It explains De-Wette analyzing the Pentateuch to see whether Moses really wrote it and David Friedrich Strauss analyzing the Gospels to see what they really tell us about the life of Jesus. The habit of checking supposed knowledge, once established, applies in every aspect of life, and therefore in religion also.

We owe this approach to the ancient Greeks, and although they may be said to have established it, their efforts were soon lost in the social and political upheavals of the classical world. It was not until modern times in Western Europe that the mood of inquiry really set in again and the astounding results that the process could yield first became apparent. It was inevitable that so fruitful a line of endeavor should eventually be applied to religion; that the Western mind should want to ask of its religion the same kind of questions it was learning to ask about the natural world. When this happened a new kind of heresy was born, not the heresy of the ancient world where different interpretations of Christianity warred with one another for supremacy, but the heresy of independent thinking which brought the Inquisition into being. Thus, the faith of adventure is heresy because it denies the first premise of orthodoxy—that either a church or a man can authoritatively know the truth. It affirms, by contrast, the validity of the questioning process. Its faith is more in questions than in answers. Man the heretic, man the inquirer, spends his energy not in defending his faith but in improving it; not in interpreting it but in restating it so that defense, exposition, exegesis, and commentary are not necessary.

Because the habit of independent thinking has become increasingly characteristic of the West, and because we have long been asking questions of our religions and testing every religious assertion, we have grown used to it in spite of its heretical implications. No one expects censure today if he says with a sly smile: "You know, I'm a bit of a heretic myself." Rather, he looks around for the approval he usually gets, as G. K. Chesterton observed many years ago. Many a theologian serving an officially orthodox church gains praise today for his "courage" in saying he does not believe what his church officially teaches. He is commended for being so broad in his outlook. Consequently, the profession of heresy causes pain today in an ever-narrowing circle: almost none at all if it is presented in the trappings of the ancient faith. If the old language is kept, the old forms used, the old ceremonies observed, the familiar clerical garb worn, and the old books read and still said to be holy, there are very few to object.

Is heresy then but a pale thing, the vitality of which belongs to a day that is dead? It is, if you can call it heresy to reinterpret words in order to make them mean what you want them to mean. But to be a heretic is not to try to put new wine in old wineskins. It is to declare the faith that is in you boldly and to contrast it with the traditional faith you wish it to modify or to replace. "Ye have heard that it hath been said by them of old time," Jesus said, quoting an accepted part of the Jewish tradition of his time. But then he went on: "But I say unto you . . ." and then he gave his new interpretation of God's commandments for men. "What new teaching is this?" asked those who heard him. Was the Law now to be displaced? Jesus was perfectly clear that the tradition of his people was not to be discarded. "Think not that I have come to abolish the law and the prophets," he said. "I have come not to abolish them but to fulfill them." Walter Nigg, after compiling a good representative list of heretics, characterizes Jesus as the "worst," by which he means the most thoroughgoing.

To be a heretic is to thrust aside that which seems to us to be inadequate or mean or unworthy, in the faith of the fathers. It is to fail to conform to the expected when the expected seems to us to be unjust, ungenerous, or in error. Above all, to be a heretic is to reject the claims of the churches to know the truth. It is to hold that the truth in religion, as in all things, is never wholly in our possession; that it slowly unfolds before us as we press on in pursuit of it.

The heretic listens with amazement while some churches say their teachings are derived from a Book containing the very Words of God: while others say the Book contains not so much the Words as the Revelations of God: while yet others say their teachings are derived from church councils, the conclusions of which represent divine inspiration: while yet others say their church is capable of speaking on God's behalf even today. Unconvinced by any of these claims, he is convinced on the contrary that all of them are futile, all are in error, and that all would confine man's thought and expression in an area where he ought to be the most free—his religion.

Nor does heresy tinker with trivialities. In 1961 the Church of England received a report from a commission charged with preparing a new modern language version of the catechism. The commission omitted from its revision the words, "I would renounce the devil and all his works." Since few people believe in the devil any more, this was far from heresy, although it was a departure from one of the tenets of traditional Christian faith. The Convocation approved the proposal, and the devil, after a distinguished if unenviable career, departed officially but almost unnoticed from the Church of England.

But amid the quiet rejoicing at the elimination of so formidable a figure with so little effort, certain friends of his Satanic Majesty made plans to restore him to his vacant throne. After all, had not God himself fought with Satan through some thousand lines of Milton's poetry? Had he not plagued good Christians for two millennia? Was he to be vanquished by the vote of a mere commission? Not so! The commission restored him to the catechism, and the Convocation voted him back into existence again, as a result of which the faithful in the Church of England have once more to renounce him, though, oddly enough, not his works. The new words are: "I would renounce the devil and fight against evil." But Satan has only a seven-year reprieve. If at the end of that time the Church of England decides it does not want him in the catechism after all, he will lapse against into the nonexistence whence he was called into life in 1962.

The heretic is one who does not countenance such pottering about with the articles of his faith. The heretic not only renounces the devil and his works: he renounces the doctrine that the devil exists or that he ever existed, not to speak of the whole idea that religious reality can pass in and out of existence according to majority vote. The heretic renounces the idea that there are right and wrong beliefs that a church may accept or reject. He renounces the idea of heresy itself because he first renounced the idea of orthodoxy of which it is the counterpart.

Man is a heretic because he will not be bound down by his own past. His imagination o'erleaps the present to a future that is better. In his imagination he can always transcend even the best thought the ages have bequeathed to him. His imagination is not limited by the sanctions of men. It is as active in religion as in politics: it leaps as far in morals as in natural science. Imagination can no more be bound by the church than by the state. It can no more be limited by an ecclesiastical council than by the legislature.

The heretic has a noble ancestry. We have seen that no one can claim a more distinguished line of descent than the independent thinker.

But we sometimes forget the debt we owe to the "unbelievers" who founded this nation. Or we forget that the founders of this nation were unbelievers. Surely it is no accident that minds independent enough to do their own thinking in religion were also independent enough to do their own thinking in politics and boldly to found a new nation, designed, not in accordance with a previously existing model, but in accordance with high principle carefully, intelligently, and realistically translated into the structure of government. Benjamin Franklin was well known for his agnosticism, Jefferson had to content himself with being "a Unitarian alone," and John Adams in an oft-quoted passage said of theological writings: "I have learned nothing of importance to me [from them] for they have made no change in my moral or religious creed, which has for fifty or sixty years been contained in four short words 'Be just and good.' "

Perhaps the most independent mind of the Revolutionary period, and certainly one of the most influential in crystallizing public opinion in favor of the Revolution, was Thomas Paine. His heretical spirit was so marked that he remains today a shadowed hero of American history, a man whose greatness we seldom acknowledge and whose contribution to our independence is known only in very narrow circles. As one dour observer remarked: "The Post Office Department has never brought out a Paine commemorative stamp although it has paid philatelic honors to Joel Chandler Harris, Virginia Dare, the Pony Express, and the American Poultry Industry."

Since the utterances of these men are more or less familiar, let us turn to a modern thinker, neither churchman nor prophet, who attacked this question, Albert Camus. "Revolt is one of the essential dimensions of mankind," he wrote in *The Rebel*. Phrasing the same thought differently, he said, with characteristic literary flair: "It is better to die on one's feet than to live on one's knees." Camus' own life helped to shape his philosophy. His father was killed at the Battle of the Marne when the boy was still an infant in arms. When France fell before the onslaught of German arms in 1940, he joined the Resistance movement and founded the underground newspaper *Combat*. Through all his adult life he wrestled with the problem of the meaning of what he had seen and what he himself had tried to do.

Camus boldly faced the fact that rebellion, once it is accepted as a principle, must be carried all the way. But total rebellion is nihilism. When every rule is rejected, anything goes. This implication he faced with characteristic forthrightness. But he found his way back from so intolerable an extremity. Once you face the meaning of what you do when you rebel, he wrote, you discover that you have generalized your own protest. You discover that you have rebelled not only on your own account but on account of all who suffer as you have suffered: on account of all who have been imprisoned by the system against which you made your protest.

"The most pure form of . . . rebellion," he concluded, "is crowned with the heart-rending cry of Karamazov [the reference is to Dostoevski's novel]: 'If all are not saved, what good is the salvation of only one?' " He thinks of himself as "preparing a renaissance beyond the limits of nihilism." The nihilists, he added, "have deified themselves and their misfortunes." As a result, "the gods have put their eyes out. . . . The only original rule of life [is] to learn to live and die, and in order to be a man, to refuse to be a god. . . . The rebel rejects divinity in order to share in the struggles and destiny of all men."

Such is the heretic, the rebel, as Camus called him, or the prophet, as he was known in Old Testament times. He is not content that his mind alone should roam free. The great vistas that open before his imagination he must show to others. He must bring others into the green pastures where he himself would dwell. He must lead them beside the still waters, where he has learned to go. As his soul has been restored, he must help to restore the souls of others. This alone justifies his rebellion against a church that would confine him. Through the light that has come to him he would enlighten everyone else if he could.

Camus began where we begin—with the absurdity of the situation against which we feel ourselves compelled to rebel. For him the absurdity was a world which, in the course of thirty years, had slain thirty million men and women through the legal device called war. We rebel against that, but as religious people we also rebel against the absurdity of trying to cram the spiritual life of modern men into the religious thought and practice of the ancients. Would we attempt to conduct our economic life according to ancient Roman rules? No more should we guide our spiritual lives by those standards. We rebel against the absurd notion that the science of Rome may pass away while the religion she bequeathed to us must be kept intact.

Rather, we say, it should be the other way around. If we had to choose we should develop our moral and spiritual life first: then perhaps we should be able to control the machines our science devises and turn them not to our destruction but to our advantage. What could be more absurd, we ask, than to open wide the gates of discovery concerning the comforts and pleasures of the body while keeping the gates locked against all moral and spiritual progress? What could be more incredible than to encourage free thought and investigation into the means of mass murder, while insisting that our moral and spiritual life be anchored to the thought patterns of the ancient world?

Because of the difficulties heretics have always suffered, and because the churches still give no real place to the independent mind in religion, some have leaped to the easy conclusion that the religion of the free mind is only to be achieved outside the church. A self-styled heretic of the present day, for example, writes caustically of virtually all organized religion. Another, after contrasting religion and skepticism—he really means Christianity vs. science—concludes that a layman's religion is the answer. But such men fail to sense the true character of heresy. The true heretic is neither a dissenter only, nor is he a malcontent, nor is he a nihilist, nor is he merely indifferent to the concerns of religion. He cares very deeply about the things of the spirit, and he seeks to nurture and celebrate this aspect of human life in a human institution because he knows that only so can he make religion real in the lives of men: only so can he keep it from degenerating into its more primitive and corrosive forms.

The faith of adventure seeks to make heresy orthodox. It seeks to canonize the inquiring mind in religion. If man is to realize his spiritual potential he must take the conforming mind from the central place it has always held in his churches and put the independent mind in its place. In religion, if nowhere else, the mind should be given full opportunity for expression. The faith of adventure holds that a church is no church where the free mind does not hold sway; that man can commit no greater folly than to deny to himself the right to search out God in the illusion that he already knows what God is like. There is no greater blasphemy than for man to declare that he knows the nature of God when he must know, if he knows anything, that the nature of God is the one thing above all else it is not given to him to know. The time has come to set the free mind at the heart of the religions of men.

Down through the ages man has suffered from this kind of confusion of thought. He has worshiped idols of his own construction. He has reared up the best conception of God he could, declared that this God had revealed this conception to him, and then he has fallen down and worshiped at the feet of what he himself has constructed. He has gone further. When he has worked out a conception of God that satisfies him, he has forbidden anyone else to think differently. He has said that God is who some man has said he is, and asserted that no man had the right to a different opinion. Man has made God in his own image, and worshiped himself in what he has made.

Against all this the heretic calls man to rebel; against man's tendency to hide God from himself. Surrounded by the figments of his own imagination, not daring to tamper with the work of the past, he does not try to look for God himself. He is content to say that God is who and what his ancestors said God is. He believes his ancestors when their writings say that God himself revealed what they wrote, and he thinks it nothing strange to do so. He stops questioning because his ancestors tell him to, because they tell him God came to earth once upon a time and told them all man needs to know in such matters.

Man has lost God today because he has allowed the past to pull down a curtain in front of God's face. It is a beautiful curtain, to be sure. But on it is the delineation of the thoughts and hopes and dreams of another age, not ours. On it is a picture of the God the ancients saw—a truly heroic God, to be sure, a magnificent figure—but it is their vision, not ours. It is drawn in the lines of their time and it is expressed in terms of their hopes, their difficulties, their struggles, their failures, their needs and aspirations, not ours.

4. THE LAST QUESTION

Man is an unbeliever, not only because his constant questioning exposes errors made by other thinkers, but because of the errors he himself makes. He knows, among other things, that he is capable of believing the most outrageous lies and clinging to the most preposterous superstitions. He believes in flying saucers today as his ancestor once believed in witches. He believes that his future is foretold by the planets as he once believed his future was foretold by the liver of a sheep. He believes in the power of charms and amulets, medallions and statues, as he once believed there was power in the teeth of tigers and the blood of bulls.

Man is also an unbeliever because he knows he is subject to delusions. He can be mistaken even when he is aware of his own fallibility and seeks to guard against it. The delusion is a well-recognized psychological phenomenon. When he develops a firm conviction, based upon misrepresentation or unwarranted inferences, and proceeds to act upon this convicition as if it were an established fact, he suffers from what the psychologists call a delusion. It is the basis of both paranoiac and schizophrenic disorders. Delusions also play an important role in mania and in depressions, so important a role in fact that some authorities would discard the term "paranoid" al-together.

We who like to think of ourselves as healthy-minded, or hope we are, cannot escape them. Physical injury to the brain can cause delu-sions. Excessive fatigue can cause them; starvation, a high fever, dehydration, or systemic disease. Whoever wishes may easily provide himself with a first-rate set of delusions. He has only to get drunk. Moderate intoxication can make a man believe himself to be a whiz at the wheel, a raconteur of consummate skill, a beautiful singer, or a veritable Don Juan.

But the man who is a questioner and a doubter because he knows he can be so easily deceived is not a nihilist. He is not the profes-sional skeptic who doubts everything or the cynic who holds that there is nothing to believe in at all. He is a man who has ceased to believe in the doctrines and dogmas of tradition because another and deeper set of convictions has taken their place. His approach to religious belief is neither debonair nor casual. He is a so-called un-believer because he is first a believer. He is a heretic because he be-lieves in principles which call in question the principle of orthodoxy itself. He is an unbeliever because he no longer believes any church may declare what beliefs are right and what beliefs are wrong.

The unbeliever believes what he must because it commends itself to him as believable, not what he is asked to because some religion holds it to be true. In this sense the unbeliever more deeply believes than the believer. He believes not because he has at last surmounted doubt and achieved faith. He believes because all the doubts he could fling at his beliefs have not dislodged them. He believes, not what church or state demands, but what truth requires.

There was a day when the Christians themselves were looked on as unbelievers. Justin Martyr about A.D. 150 wrote in his defense of Christianity, the *Apology:* "We are not atheists since we worship the creator of this universe . . . With good reason we honor Him who has taught us these things and was born for this purpose." Who of to-day's Christians would not argue that the Christians of Roman times were called unbelievers, not because of their skepticism, but because of their beliefs? Who of today's Christians would not argue that the early Christians were stronger believers than the tolerant urbane Romans who at best paid only lip service to their gods?

The inquirer or the doubter—the man of the fourth faith—believes that belief cannot be casual: it must amount to commitment or it is no belief at all. He makes a distinction between the words "belief" and "opinion." A belief is a conviction, lying deep enough within us so that it affects what we think and do. Such, for example, is our belief in the law of gravitation, our belief in the rule that we pass to the right (or to the left in England) and our belief in the ideal of justice, to which we must conform insofar as we are able.

Opinion, on the other hand, often called "belief" in orthodox religious circles, is much more lightly held. It does not affect conduct, and, although often clung to stubbornly, is more easily given up. Such, for example, is the opinion that Jesus the Christ or Gautama the Buddha was divine in some special sense: or the opinion that heaven and hell are real places: or the opinion that a particular church has divine authority it can exercise on earth: or the opinion that God's will for you may be gathered by a moment's silent meditation: or that Jesus walked on the water: or that Moses divided the Red Sea. This distinction holds, even though there comes a point at which opinion and belief imperceptibly merge.

The unbeliever like the believer believes that religion is fundamental in the life of men. He believes that man must believe something; he believes that what he believes is of the utmost importance. So, of course, do all the religions. But the difference is that those who are called unbelievers believe that religion is so important, its beliefs must not be ambiguous. They think beliefs should not be subject to any misrepresentation. They think they must be stated with all the clarity possible.

The men of the fourth faith reject the notion that a man can believe what he wants to. They hold that a man can believe only what seems to him to be true, and that if he is honest with himself, he will test his beliefs in open encounter. It is for this reason so many of them have left the churches in which they were reared. They have left the churches and temples of their youth because they believe with such conviction those things that seem to them to be true. They find they can no longer remain in a church which professes a set of official beliefs the obvious meaning of which has all been explained away.

For example, those who are attracted to the faith of adventure would find it difficult to say, in the course of reciting the Apostles' Creed, that Jesus descended into hell. It would not matter to them how we interpreted the statement. We could call it an allegory, a myth, a symbol, a truth lying at the second, fifth, or tenth level down —it would not matter. The inquirer would suspect that we might be deceiving ourselves if we recited those words each Sunday morning, unless we really believed there is a hell and that Jesus Christ descended into it. The inquirer would also suspect that it did not really matter which of these alternatives we accepted. Our thoughts and actions would not be affected in any case.

But suppose a man were to attend a church service which required him to say each Sunday morning: "I believe in honesty." He could easily discover, before the next Sunday rolled around and he found himself ready to say it all over again, whether this was one more irrelevant theological opinion, or whether he had really meant what he said. Maybe that is why no creed of any church has ever required its members to stand up each Sunday morning and say: "I believe in honesty." Maybe no church ever will.

Because the beliefs of the unbeliever thrust him into the questioning process, he pursues it with a will. Yet he does not suppose himself to be the only one engaged upon it. All faiths in one sense or another encourage questions. All re-examine this premise to a greater or less degree and all take account of the credulity of man as well as his proneness to endure. It is of the essence of the fourth faith as against the other three, however, that it asks the *last* question, whereas the faiths of stability conclude their questioning somewhere short of it.

Revelation is the point at which the questioning process in religion usually ends. When we confront an alleged revelation, there are only two possible things we can say. We can accept it as a revelation, in which case we also accept its total competence. After all, a revelation from on high is no ordinary kind of truth and ought not to require the emendation of men. If, however, the alleged revelation is said to be but a vehicle through which truth is revealed, then a quite different point of view prevails. Then we may ask, What part is revelation; in what sense is it a revelation; why that much—why not more, or less; how do you know? and so on, ad infinitum.

A revelation is like those things in life which are perfect or total or complete. One error, one blemish, is enough to change the character of the whole. After that, a thousand errors or blemishes may be detected, but the situation itself does not change—except quantitatively. Qualitatively, the change comes with the first blemish.

It is like an eclipse of the sun. To see even a partial eclipse is a remarkable sight. To see an eclipse that is nearly total is remarkable indeed. No one who has seen such a phenomenon will ever forget it. Nevertheless, the difference between 99 per cent and a total eclipse is all the difference. Only when the sun is completely hidden behind the sphere of the moon does the corona—in all its glory—appear. It is the same with the doctrine of revelation. There are, of course, partial, imperfect, or incomplete revelations. This is the kind that most of the religions talk about most of the time. The difference has to do with whether or not we claim a revelation. If we do, we at once remove our claim from the realm of question and argument. Truth that lies at the end of the questioning process carries with it only such authority as its own persuasive power can command. Truth, however imperfectly presented, if it is revealed to us, carries its own authority. We are to believe it, not because it makes sense, not because we are persuaded by it, not even because we understand it, but because it comes from God. The statement that a truth is revealed brings the questioning process to an end, except insofar as it may elaborate or defend the truth revelation has given us.

The doctrine of revelation is perhaps the most pernicious idea ever invented by the human mind. It admits to advanced standing whatever is alleged to have been revealed. Hence it is not tested as other statements are, and its falsity or distortion, if any, is thus not shown. If man is ever to attain truth, he will do so only when he has given up the idea of special revelation. The general idea is not harmful. If all discovery may be looked upon as God's revelation to men, then all ideas stand alike, with no distinction between them based upon God's alleged activity. It is when an idea or a fact is said to be true because God said so, that the trouble starts. Then men begin trying to live in two worlds at the same time, and it cannot be done.

The weakness in the doctrine lies in this: once it is admitted that God speaks directly to men, who is to deny the claim of any visionary, no matter how fanciful, that he has had a revelation direct from God? How can such a claim to divine revelation be disproved? The

Apostle Paul himself, while he favored prophesying, nevertheless insisted that it be done decently and in order. He knew the difficulty and had to meet it at first hand.

The Canadian Government recently faced such a problem in connection with the Doukhobors in the Province of Saskatchewan. The Doukhobors are a religious sect which meets every attempt to integrate them into the Canadian civil state with the statement: "We want only to be left alone! We want only to follow Jesus!" They believe that Jesus lives among them, telling them what to do, and they believe that they must follow him, no matter what happens to them. There is no logical basis on which the Canadian Government can refute this claim.

Many churches have undertaken to deal with such problems by declaring officially that certain alleged revelations were mere delusions. The false prophet has always been the bane of organized religion. How do you tell the true bearer of God's revelation to men from the deceivers and those suffering from hallucinations? The Roman Catholic Church, which explicitly holds the doctrine of revelation, has very elaborate machinery by which it separates what it considers to be the truth in this area from what it holds to be error. A detailed investigation is conducted, and a long period of time is allowed to elapse before a vision is accepted as having been authentic, as was the case, for example, with the vision of St. Bernadette at Lourdes.

We can, of course, resort to the formulas of Paul Tillich in an attempt to escape from the dilemma in which the doctrine of revelation places us. He rejects any doctrine of revelation by which a church claims final truth or authority. But he saves the word or the concept by asserting that the content of revelation is God. Religion is man's answer to that revelation. God is the spirit that breaks through the several churches' claims to authority. The fourth faith would agree. But when Tillich attempts to solve the problem created by the authority any revelation must be admitted to bear within itself if it is a revelation, we find him of little help. Tillich asks: "How is it possible to accept revelation as coming from God who is the 'highest being with absolute power, knowledge, goodness, who is the source of everything that is and ought to be [who] seems irresistible and all-devouring,' and at the same time to accept revelation as coming from a God with the other qualities, namely, love and mercy . . . a Lord who makes his law dependent on obedience to his will and his mercy on complete self-surrender."

We may choose which God we will give ourselves to, says Tillich, "because God is not a being, but the ground of all being, because as the creative ground of all being he is also the ground of my being and does not stand against me. In my self-affirmation he affirms himself. Participation conquers authority. That in me which wants to kill God is God himself, namely, the ground of my being, my meaning, my self-affirmation. One could call this the God beyond God, that is, beyond the God who is the highest being and the source of heteronomy and hypostatized authority. The true God beyond the God who is a being liberates us from the total authority of the last polytheistic God who is in reality a demon.

"Truth liberates because truth makes us participate in itself as truth. The truth of revelation is the truth of that God who participates, the central symbol of whose participation is the Christ. Revelation is the permanent struggle against a demonic authority which breaks man in order to save man. But only he is saved who is free and through whose self-affirmation God himself affirms himself."

Apart from the question of what such writing may mean lies the further question which is uppermost in the minds of the people of the fourth faith. When Tillich is all through, does he have anything left but the empty word "revelation" with all its customary meaning taken away? He has condemned what the religions call revelation, and he has condemned the authority they claim as well, which we can only applaud. But we have then to ask him what he gains but confusion when he empties the word of its traditional and current meaning. And so the last question remains unanswered, in religion as in all things.

Will this infinite regress of questions bring us to an ultimate non-religion, as is so often said? Will it result in secularism, skepticism, atheism, and the abandonment of religion, as so many think? Yes, it will, if your definition of religion requires a belief in the Supernatural and the special intervention of the Supernatural in the natural. But if our notion of religion is not so narrowly construed: if we think of religion not as the acceptance of an alleged revelation, but as the attempt of man to find meaning for his life, to find a home in the cosmos so to speak, then the process of inquiry does not end in skepticism and doubt: rather it marks the beginning of a spiritual pilgrimage. Then religion becomes a matter, not of learning in modern times the meaning of an ancient tradition, but a process whereby the meaning of the universe and of life is increasingly made plain.

The faith of adventure is a process of constant seeking. It never ceases to question. Always it asks of every assertion that anyone may make: "How do you know?" It asks the question again and again, as often as an assertion of any kind is made. At last there must come a time when the question, How do you know? has been asked long enough, and the answer must come. When that time comes, we still will not have asked the last question, for those with sufficient imagination will always have another to ask.

5. The Battle of the Assumptions

Astronomers tell us that the universe appears to be flying apart at a prodigious rate of speed. Galaxies near and far seem to be fleeing from each other at velocities approaching half that of light. The farther away these astral bodies are, the faster they seem to be fleeing from us and from each other. All the evidence is by no means in as yet. At best, such an observation is an educated guess. But there it stands nevertheless, and it gives us a good deal to conjure with as to what it may mean if it is true. It also gives us a very apt comparison for the situation in which man finds himself as he tries to understand himself and his world.

None of the answers which man has been able to give to eternal questions has ever satisfied him. Something is always left out. An abiding mystery always lurks just beyond everything he has been able to say in answer to the fundamental questions that gnaw at his soul. "Man is a creature who cannot find a true norm short of ultimate reality," says Reinhold Niebuhr. He "has always been his own most vexing problem . . . every affirmation which he may make about his stature, virtue or place in the cosmos becomes involved in contradictions when fully analyzed. The analysis reveals some presupposition or implication which seems to deny what the proposition intended to affirm."

When the experiments have all been made, when the data are all in and tabulated, when the broadest generalizations possible have been stated, the most important things still remain unknown. What is the meaning of life and death, of good and evil, of joy, suffering, and loneliness? Whence comes the moral law and why should I obey it to my own hurt? These are the questions man must answer and yet cannot. These are the things his anguished soul would know. "All religious writings, pre-Christian and Christian, unite in trying to express the unexpressible," wrote E. R. Goodenough. It is their purpose to explain the inexplicable. Thus man the inquirer, man in pursuit of eternal truth, is as we have seen involved in an infinite regress. Behind every answer to every question there lurks yet another question. The process is never completed because man is never able to fashion an explanation that suits him. No sooner does an intellectual giant draw up something like a total synthesis of the thought of his day, than some new problem arises to show him he has failed. Others agree that the system falls short of its goal and the hunt for the complete and perfect explanation is taken up again. But it goes on. Always it goes on.

The greatest scientists have always insisted that this is so. "I do not know what I may appear to the world," wrote Sir Isaac Newton, "but to myself I seem to have been only like a boy playing on the seashore, diverting myself in now and then finding a smoother pebble or a prettier shell than ordinary, while the great ocean of truth lay all undiscovered before me."

Through the night of his life upon earth, man is condemned forever to yearn to know. He knows his inquiries will bring him no final answers. He knows the widening rim of knowledge is also the widening edge of ignorance. "Our knowledge is a torch of smoky pine," wrote Santayana, "that lights the pathway but one step ahead across a void of mystery and dread."

Are we then doomed only to increase our ignorance about the most fundamental things? If true knowledge forever drops out of sight beyond the horizon of the conscious mind, does this state of affairs not condemn us to a permanent guesswork and uncertainty in the area of the ultimate where we most need to know? In fact, does this not reduce us to impotency and hopelessness in the matter of religious belief?

We can, of course, look at this process from the opposite point of view. We can observe the enormous mass of knowledge man has accumulated and the rapidity with which it is being increased. We can observe the degree to which the knowledge accumulated in the past is being clarified, corrected, related to other areas of experience, and its deeper meanings understood. Perhaps we have here another description of the difference between the optimist and the pessimist: the pessimist gazes upon the vast sea of ignorance around him and is cast down when he realizes that he will die without ever knowing the answers to the most basic questions. The optimist gazes upon the knowledge man has accumulated: he contemplates the process of rearranging, clarifying, and correcting it, together with the constant probing to ferret out its deeper meanings; he is excited by what man has accomplished already, what he is now accomplishing; and extrapolating the process, he is exhilarated by what man seems likely to be able to accomplish in the future.

Some have guessed that if we could ever reach the ultimate we should find that it was irrational. In our time notably Arthur O. Lovejoy and most of the neo-orthodox have taken this position. Nevertheless the majority of thinkers, Christian and non-Christian, have supposed that ultimately everything would prove to be rational. We need not resolve this issue for it lies beyond our province. It is enough for us to note that the concept of man's expanding knowledge does not conflict with either view. Human understanding may go on broadening and deepening whether or not rationality or irrationality lies at the end of the process. Only a few dare so much as to guess what radical reconception of our fundamental ideas may be necessary in the future. Occasionally a writer has the hardihood to try, as when Charles Galton Darwin published a book entitled *The Next Million Years*. Yet as we read this book we suspect that despite its ambitious title, it will be outdated in all too short a time.

No one has stated the conception of truth as something that grows better than Sir James Frazer. In the preface to his *Golden Bough* he wrote: "Whether the explanation which I have offered . . . is correct or not, must be left for the future to determine. I shall always be ready to abandon it if a better can be suggested." And echoing him, E. A. Burtt, in our time, remarked: "The most soundly established law . . . will prove to be but a limited approximation to the truth as later disclosed." Charles Péguy sharpened the dilemma that this principle lays before us when he pointed out that we cannot come to rest upon any set of principles because none is final. "The life of an honest man must be an apostasy and a perpetual desertion," he wrote in one of his inimitable little essays. "The man who wishes to remain faithful to the truth must make himself continually unfaithful to all the continual, successive, indefatigable renascent errors." F. S. C. Northrop concluded a lifelong concern with man in society in a similar vein. He finds as a basic meaning of life the fact that the quest for that meaning is never over.

It is for this reason that the fourth faith must always state its answers to ultimate questions in terms of quandary. This is not to say dogmatically or even philosophically that ultimate questions are unanswerable. It is only to say that so far as we are concerned, such questions will not be answered with finality. It is to say that basic theological matters will for us always remain as questions. The faith of adventure is not agnostic in the sense that it maintains a dogmatic skepticism. It is agnostic in the sense that Thomas Huxley had in mind when he first coined the word. In theological matters we don't *know*, and since others are sure they do know, it is important for us to emphasize our conviction that no one can know with the certitude the religions are accustomed to claim for their "knowledge."

The belief that theological questions belong in the area of quandary has a second aspect. Man's approach is not one of permanent perplexity, but of exultation in the continuing process of investigation and discovery. The importance of theology is not minimized. Rather the sense of its importance is enhanced if its affirmations are kept as quandaries. If theological matters are looked upon as living continuing questions, rather than as unquestionables or final credal statements, there is less danger that they will cease to be discussed and eventually become inert. But the fact of quandary in the face of ultimate questions does not permit us to suspend judgment on important questions. Religion cannot conclude with questions, for true religion is the basis of life. As William James observed, we may not know the final answers to the questions we ask, but we cannot avoid giving some kind of answer by what we decide to do. He very appropriately called this dilemma the "forced option." We have to act while we live, and our actions, he reminded us often, imply one kind of basic philosophy or another. If, then, we must make some kind of choice, how does the faith of adventure propose that we do it? It is on this issue that religion enters upon the battle of the assumptions.

The religions traditionally have solved this problem either by official mystery and miracle declared to lie in the keeping of the church, or by withdrawal into personal and private experience declared by the experiencer to be authentic. In either case the questioning process is brought to a stop by the declaration of a dogma, the truth of which rests upon the authority of the declarer. With the fourth faith, as in most aspects of Western life, what is regarded as truth derives its authority from acceptance by the human community of open and free minds. Such minds may also accept the dogmas of a religion as truth and they often do. In fact, most Protestants maintain that their acceptance of the dogmas of their churches rests upon their free and open decision, not upon the authority of the church that holds the dogma in its keeping.

It is here that we make one of our most fundamental mistakes in theology. We think that selecting a set of assumptions is something like buying a new car. There is quite an assortment to choose from. Each has some features the others lack: all have certain basic features in common. None completely suits our purpose. A noted theologian, a warm advocate of the faith of stability, once asked me: "Why aren't my assumptions as good as yours?" He was really attempting to force the argument on religious fundamentals to a draw. He was trying to prove that the Lordship of Jesus Christ was as good an assumption as any other.

But his question showed that he had not grasped the nature of the battle of the assumptions. It is not a contest to see whose assumptions are better. It is not the difference between the surmise that Christ was the Son of God or that Mohammed was his prophet or that Gautama was the "anointed one." It is the difference between the surmise that life has the meaning it seems to have or that it does not; that values are the values they seem to be or that they are not; that truth is something man discovers and demonstrates, not something handed down out of the skies. This is where the battle of the assumptions must be fought out. It is not a contest between the

Judeo-Christian tradition and Islam; it is not a contest between Protestants, Catholics, and Jews. The issue lies between the faith of stability and the faith of adventure; between the historic faiths that claim to hold the truth and the faith that believes truth transcends all the historic faiths.

Both Tillich and Niebuhr come very close to this position in their thinking. But both, as we have seen, are in the final analysis apologists for Christianity, defenders of the faith of stability, not advocates of the faith of adventure. Both find truth in a particular religion and a particular revelation. Either might have taken Protestantism and drawn it into the position of the faith of adventure toward which it has been moving for more than four centuries. But both chose to lead Protestantism back into the fold of historical orthodoxy and their legacy to us is a religion that is an anachronism—a religion that does not possess the concepts through which the moral and spiritual qualities of life may adequately be interpreted to the modern age. Though they introduce a host of new terms and redefine all the old ones, they do not lead man into a bright new day of religious hope; they lead him back to the faith of his fathers in which he would dearly like to believe but cannot, even with a manual of the new orthodoxy at his elbow to explain how it is possible.

The faith of adventure neither accepts nor rejects the assumption that God was in Christ, that he revealed his divine will to Moses, or that he anointed the Buddha or called Mohammed to be his Prophet. The faith of adventure assumes that how you carry on the assumption-making process is more fundamental than the assumptions from which you proceed, for that process determines the validity of the assumptions you make. The faith of adventure assumes that it is better not to choose any of the assumptions the religions have set up but rather to make the more basic assumption that they all are faulty, and that one day each will yield to a new formulation which is better able to interpret man's experience. The faith of adventure holds that the truth in religion, as in all things, does not lie in one particular assumption or another, but in the continually changing product of the assumption-making process. In this view faith lies in the validity of the process by which truth is separated from error. The fourth faith assumes that truth emerges as the various assumptions we make are tested against eath other.

Men have long known that to ask the right questions is the way to achieve valid and significant statements about the nature of things. Applying this principle to contemporary religion, the faith of adventure holds that the ancient and honored religious question, "What is the truth?" will always yield the wrong answer. That question carries within itself the false assumption that the truth in religion can be known once and for all. But it cannot. There is no infallibility among men, however high the ecclesiastical office they may hold, and however narrowly their alleged infallibility may be construed. The question we must ask is this: "How best may we state what we now believe the truth to be?" That question should be followed by a second: "How could we state it better?"

The faith of adventure proposes as a method, constant probing, constant inquiry, constant testing of all concepts, and the constant formulation of new concepts deemed to be more adequate. It proposes as an answer to the fundamental questions which concern all faiths, the concept of the open mind that never supposes it has all the truth in hand. In the faith of adventure the nature of reality is revealed not by any statement we may make about it but by the continuing series of questions we ask.

To sum up, we may assume that truth is revealed from heaven; or we may assume the opposite, that truth is slowly pieced together by the minds of men here on earth. We may assume that man is a helpless creature, lost in sin, awaiting God's grace; or we may assume that great achievement lies behind him, and that the promise of yet greater achievement lies before him. We may assume that some men under certain circumstances are infallible; or we may assume that all men are fallible—that even the best of us are capable of the grossest errors and that therefore we must constantly check and recheck whatever we believe to be true. We may assume that certain books are different from all others because they represent, in some sense, God's will; or we may assume that all books are human documents, however exalted their content may be.

We may assume that one particular church (our own) was established by God, and that it continues to be His instrument on earth; or we may assume that churches are established by men and are therefore subject to all the foibles of men. We may assume that a clergyman who has been duly ordained may, under certain circum-

stances, act on God's behalf, that when ordained by certain pre-
scribed rites, he may bind and loose upon earth what will later be
bound and loosed in heaven; or we may assume that a clergyman is
a man like anyone else, whose professional calling is the church
rather than medicine, engineering, or law. We may assume that God
himself once came to earth in the form of a man; or we may reject
such an assumption. We may assume that that God-man performed
miracles, and that miracles happened to him—such as birth by a
virgin, and bodily resurrection from the dead; or we may reject those
assumptions too.

It all boils down in the end to two alternatives: we can assume
that a supernatural being called God directs and controls a vast
amount of what happens on earth, particularly in the area of religion; or we can assume that what happens on earth, human achievement and human misery, all are the result of human aspiration,
human insight, human hope, human avarice, and human stupidity.

If we take the second of these assumptions—that the causes of our
human lot are human, not divine—we can stop there. But we can go
on if we wish and make a third assumption. We can hazard the guess
that all the wonders our human endeavor has laid before us are but
a glimpse of a totality we neither know nor understand. And we can
assume that in that totality, whatever it is, our human lives find
meaning, and our human values are seen to be ultimately real. We
can assume that any experience we designate by the word "spiritual"
reflects this totality, and that in some sense we can participate in it.

In a word, to reject the assumption of supernaturalism is not to
be forced into the assumption of materialism. There is another and
a better alternative. We can assume the possibility of human accomplishment and assume also that there is a dimension of the universe which makes all such accomplishment meaningful. This is our
most basic assumption within the assumption-making process. Why
do we make it? Not because we think man the most important being
in the universe. In anything so vast as the spatiotemporal continuum
in which we find ourselves, it is extremely unlikely that man plays
the most important role. His planet is surely a very tiny object. His
star, the sun, is not very large, and it occupies no particularly significant place in the galaxy to which it belongs. The dominance and
superiority man has achieved over all the other beings on his own

planet could give him the exaggerated notion of his own importance he now enjoys. But man need not be victimized by his own achievements. The native endowment by which he has been able to accomplish so much should also give him a sense of proportion in the light of which to assess his new knowledge of the universe around him.

Why do we assume that human life has meaning? To that question we turn in our final chapter.

6. THE QUEST FOR ULTIMATE MEANING

If the meaning of life is to be found in the questioning process, what then is religion? Religion is man's attempt to deal with ultimate questions. Philosophy has the same purpose, but there is an important difference. Philosophy constructs varying speculative systems and seeks to assess critically the merits and faults of each of them. Religion constructs systems of thought also, but it goes far beyond philosophy in the use to which its thought systems are put. Where philosophy is speculative, religion is positive. Where philosophy is critical of itself, religion is critical of other religions, not of itself. Where philosophy says it seeks, religion says it knows. Where philosophy calls for inquiry, religion invites assent. Where philosophy remains in the university, religion moves into life. Philosophy is an intellectual discipline. Religion is also, but it goes on to prescribe a mode of living as well. Religion requires commitment.

Perhaps for this reason religion has organized man's effort to understand himself and his universe, and it has organized his commitment to a way of life. While many different enterprises of man are devoted to his understanding of himself—perhaps more than we suspect—it is his religion which almost alone has organized the effort. Man is by nature a doer as well as a thinker. He not only meditates upon the meaning of life, he proposes to do something about the meaning he finds in it, and he searches for meaning because he wants some kind of guidance by which to decide what to do.

Since prehistoric times this is what man has sought to do through his religions. The savage is not motivated by curiosity only. He is not content to try to identify the various spirits that inhabit his environment. He believes that they influence what goes on around him and so he seeks to placate them. By his obsequies he seeks to persuade them to act in a friendly manner. Man's religion has changed little since prehistoric times. Now as then, it is basically a combination of beliefs, usually in mythical form; of ritual by which he attempts to influence the course of events, and a social organism whereby the tribe or band is held together, and through which its deepest needs find expression.

Religion has been defined in a thousand ways, but this is its true purpose. It is an expression of the organized search for the meaning of life, and the celebration of whatever result that search may be thought to have disclosed. This is why religion must concern itself with God. God is ultimate meaning. The Name, whatever word may be used, denotes the concept whereby a people seeks an ultimate explanation of the mystery that lies just back of every fact of our existence. Yet God is not mystery. He is not the unknown. He is not the as-yet-unexplained. He is the meaning that constantly unfolds before us. This is why questions about the existence of God are as futile as questions about the existence of the universe. The universe *is*, and so also its meaning *is*. To try to prove the existence of God is only to attempt to demonstrate the undemonstrable. In practice, it usually turns out to be nothing more than an attempt to prove that *your* notion of God is the true one. The unbeliever is only the man with other gods than yours.

In the words of Paul Tillich: "Being religious means asking passionately the questions of the meaning of our existence and being willing to receive answers, even if the answers hurt. Such an idea of religion makes religion universally human, but it certainly differs from what is usually called religion. It does not describe religion as the belief in the existence of gods or one God, and as a set of activities and institutions for the sake of relating oneself to these beings in thought, devotion, and obedience. No one can deny that the religions which have appeared in history are religious in this sense. Nevertheless, religion in its innermost nature is more than religion in this narrower sense. It is the state of being concerned about one's own being and about being universally."

Religion concerns the goals of our individual lives as we are living them out right now. Religion is concerned with the choices we make today in a way that the speculative schemes of Plato, Augustine, or

Tillich himself can never be, except in the most general sense. Philosophy and theology try to guess what the deeper implications of man's more immediate goals may be, and they try to relate those guesses to other guesses they are making about protons and galaxies, the rise and fall of civilizations, and man's age-old yearning for immortality. Religion demands commitment now. Religion, taken in its widest dimension, lifts a man off his knees, draws him out of his armchair or away from his desk and flings him into the midst of life with commitments that not merely guide him but may even drive him in what he does. These commitments are in turn derived from the meanings he has found.

Julius Seelye Bixler once stated the point in capsule form. The call of Isaiah to be a prophet of the Lord contains a profound perception, he wrote. It is that man must worship not what he fears but what he honors. He must worship what he believes to be just and true. Isaiah in his vision discovered that God differs from man in that God is perfect, man is imperfect, God is clean, man is unclean; God is sinless, man is sinful. In the light of Isaiah's vision religion based upon fear of personal hurt and celebrated through correct rituals is transformed into religion based upon devotion to the ideal and celebrated in personal righteousness. Thus we do not worship the unknown and strange. We worship the known moral ideal. As he remarked in another connection, we begin with God as the unknown or mystery. "But we do not stay with the mystery. Like Isaiah we find that the call of the unknown is ultimately the call of fear."

The principle applies today, Bixler said. He was writing in 1944 at the depth of World War II. The worship of blood, race, soil, and force is based on fear of the dictator's arbitrary will, as the worship of the tribal God Yahweh in ancient Israel was based upon fear of his caprice. But, continued Bixler, the worship of the ideals of democracy—freedom, and justice—is based upon personal commitment for those ideals that appeal directly to the rational mind and the sensitive conscience. Democracy and justice apply not to one nation in one place and one time, but universally to all men always. The basic contrast is between the statement "I have a feeling . . . [of fear or desire]" and the statement "This is true." I recognize it to be so. Doubt it, test it, check it as I may, it still commends itself to me as truth. This truth is taken intimately into us, Bixler concluded. God is our name for it. It (He?) is independent of us. We do not create truth. We find it. Justice is its counterpart in practical affairs, as its emotional counterpart is love in our hearts toward our fellow men.

Religion thus broadly conceived, attempts to explain beauty and to invite its enjoyment, but it also demands that whoever would explain or enjoy beauty must extend the same opportunity to everyone else. Religion reminds the individual man that he is not alone. It demands to know why one man should enjoy privileges another man is denied. Religion is concerned with the problems of metaphysics and epistemology, but it also demands to know why the individual man should not honor the self that he is—why he should not eschew self-indulgence and debauchery, sloth, deceit, and ignorance. Religion demands to know why the things that go with the side of his nature man calls "spiritual" are not better and more important than those he calls "material."

Religion gives emphatic answers to questions like these, and it has always done so. It often expresses itself in terms that are metaphysical and epistemological—in short, in terms of theology. And of these explanations there are as many as there are religions. But the consistent and common factor in them all has been the attempt to deal with the lives of men, their relationship to the universe, and to one another. It is this common factor, which most men instinctively recognize, that accounts for the underlying common faith expressed by contemporary American pluralism.

Is it not the task of the state to order the lives of men? we may ask. Of course. But religion and state are partners in this undertaking. They are not competitors, and except when nationalism becomes a religion, or religion becomes chauvinistic, religion is concerned with the same purposes as the state. It is not concerned with the survival of a particular state. It is concerned with the survival of the kind of state that promotes human values. Religion deals with the hearts of men and points their lives in the direction of the ideals toward which the laws of the state are directed. It creates in men not only the desire for rules of good conduct, but the desire to conform to them without which all such rules are vain.

The one thing that sets religion apart from all other aspects of human experience and activity is this: the religions of men have always insisted that there is more meaning to the life of individual men and women than the eye can see, and the mind may know. This is true of primitive religion. It is true of the more highly developed religions of the present time. Again, the explanations offered by the various religions vary enormously. But this special quality belongs to them all. They all teach that man is not alone in the universe. The teaching may or may not be personalized. But all alike hold that there is a dimension of existence transcending our present knowledge which we cannot forget if any true sense of the meaning of life is to be grasped.

These principles are often lost sight of by particular historic faiths, their eyes fixed upon their own problems. In their zeal for their own answers to religious questions, and in their confidence in their own mode of expression and practice, the historic faiths have tended to grow rigid. The faith of adventure, on the other hand, the fourth faith, the primordial religious faith of man, begins with the constant necessity to break out of those traditions. The fourth faith, as it emerges in Western culture, seeks to establish a form of religious expression which has as its first principle freedom from the fixed answers of tradition. The fourth faith believes this ideal can be achieved only when men are unimpeded in the effort by the traditionalism that characterizes America's three officially recognized faiths, for always they try to hold to the tradition of the elders, in form if not in substance, in word if not in deed.

As civilizations advance and cultural patterns grow more complex, areas of thought and activity once thought to fall exclusively within the province of religion move out into the nonecclesiastical realm. In primitive societies religion and medicine were not distinguished from each other. The shaman, the tribal priest, whoever held the post of religious authority, performed whatever duties were necessary in the two fields we would designate "religion" and "medicine." As a matter of fact, this dual pattern of the shaman is so ingrained in human thought the distinction between the two is not yet entirely clear. Even today prayers for the good health of a patient are said, religious medals are pinned to the pillow of the sick and candles are burned, in the belief that these acts are as likely to effect a cure as the efforts of the doctors and nurses. With the Christian Scientists, the prayers of the practitioner are as often relied upon as the services of a medical doctor.

As medicine is increasingly separated off from religion, a new cleavage appears in the area of mental health. At the moment, there are sharp differences between the clergy and the psychiatrists on this issue. Where begins the science of the mind considered as a mechanism and subject to malformation and malfunctioning like the body, and where ends the province of religion? Right before our eyes today we can see the steady retreat of religion in the face of the steady advance of psychiatry. With natural science, social and political science, it has been the same: art, music, education, drama, the dance, literature—each has slowly emerged from the religion that nurtured it, and each in turn has then taken its place as an independent human activity, protected, and advanced by its own group of specialists. Perhaps even more conspicuous than the shift of the care of the mentally troubled from the church to the hospital has been the shift of the care of the indigent from the church to the state. Few people today are aware how new the public welfare programs in this country really are.

The aspect of the fourth faith which most clearly sets it apart from the other three concerns another shift out of the ecclesiastical realm which has been going on in Western culture for more than two thousand years. It has always been the province of religion to declare officially that certain things happened in the past which no living man witnessed and to declare with finality that certain meanings are to be found in those events. Christianity has been nothing loath to engage in this practice. Nor has Judaism. Both do so today. Both declare officially that certain events, of which no man can now know, did take place in the past, and both declare that meanings of high import are to be found in those events.

The fourth faith stands with modern culture and against Christianity and Judaism at this point. The religions of the West are slowly giving up to science the right to determine what did and what did not happen in the past. The fourth faith would hasten the process. It would give to contemporary science the authority to seek out and state what happened in the past. But it would stand with Christianity and Judaism in their attempt to assert the values by which

man should live, to nurture those values, and to lay them as commandments upon the mind and heart. The faith of adventure stands
against the faith of stability in the reluctance of the latter to break
through its own traditions and assert within its own structure the
values it proclaims to the world.

The faith of stability is like a book that is printed, bound, and may
be read and consulted at any time. It is always available, always the
same, and for this reason it is always dependable. The faith of adventure, on the other hand, is like a flower that unfolds before the
eyes, or like a path through the forest you have never followed
before, like a story, or like life itself that slowly, piece by piece,
comes to you. In immersing yourself in that kind of faith, you may
know religious ecstasy, not of the trance or the stigmata, but the
ecstasy of experiencing the discovery of truth, the exultation of per-
ceiving new meanings never before caught by the mind of man; the
perception of beauty you did not suppose existed, the sensation of
love that calls from you deeds of generosity and self-sacrifice you
had not supposed lay within your power. And in it all, you find, too,
a sense of awe creeping over you as you stand in the presence of
so much, a sense of wonder at the mounting complexities of things,
and a sense of reverence before the majesty of the whole. You need
no more revelation than this; if indeed it can be called revelation
at all; in fact, you cannot encompass half the meaning such an experience contains.

It is as if, having spent the night on a mountaintop, you watch
incredulously while the broad invisible earth beneath you slowly
takes form as the dawn comes on; you watch as the scene slowly
takes color while the morning light advances, until, at last, you are
overwhelmed with the beauty of the panorama spread out before
you. Beholding such loveliness, feeling more than understanding its
meaning, like the inquirer who stands before unfolding truth, you
would speak, but no words come, for no words can serve your purpose. Then a Name rises to your lips, an ancient name, a name as
old as man. And so you speak the Name, not knowing quite what
you have said or why you have said it. But you have known what
man has always known when he has come close to the infinite and
the eternal—that he must speak of it. He must find words for his
thoughts, answers for his questions, and somehow share them with

his fellow men. The fourth faith grows articulate today because Protestantism primarily, and Judaism secondarily, both of which had been moving out of traditionalism, have reverted to a new emphasis on orthodoxy. Out of the demand that man's religious spirit be completely free, the faith of adventure has emerged as an historic faith in our time.

Notes

These notes serve primarily to indicate the sources of material quoted in the text. A few entries are for more general reference purposes. The citations will also serve to give the reader some indication of the area of reading that lies behind the text. Bible quotations are from the Revised Standard Version, except where noted.

INTRODUCTION

Page Line
xiv 14 A. N. Whitehead, *Science and the Modern World* (New York: The Macmillan Company, 1925), p. 299.

xv 31 Will Herberg, *Protestant, Catholic, Jew* (Garden City, N.Y.: Doubleday & Company, 1955), pp. 254-270.

CHAPTER I. CONTEMPORARY UNBELIEF

1 12 Walter Lippmann, *A Preface to Morals* (New York: The Macmillan Company, 1929), p. 3.

1. SOME SOBERING STATISTICS

2 17 Editorial: "What Do Christians Actually Believe?" *Christian Century*, June 6, 1951, p. 676

3 22 Raymond G. Kuhlen and Martha Arnold, "Age Differences in Religious Beliefs and Problems During Adolescence," *Journal of Genetic Psychology*, Vol. 65, 1944, pp. 291-300.

4 21 *Time* magazine, June 22, 1959, p. 56.

4 34 *Intelligence Digest*, Bucks, England, Feb. 1960, p. 16.

5 28 *Emmanuel Church Bulletin*, Boston, Mass., Mar. 13, 1955.

6 17 *New York Times*, July 30, 1961.

7   8 Quoted in Editorial: "Backlash of Revival," *Christian Century*, Apr. 26, 1961, p. 507.

7 19 Roy W. Fairchild and J. C. Wynn, *Families in the Church* (New York, Association Press, 1961).

7 22 Louis Schneider and Sanford M. Dornbusch, *Popular Religion* (Chicago: University of Chicago Press, 1958).

8   3 Gibson Winter, *The Suburban Captivity of the Churches* (Garden City, N.Y.: Doubleday & Company, 1961).

8   4 Peter Berger, *The Noise of Solemn Assemblies* (Garden City, N.Y.: Doubleday & Company, 1961).

8   5 A. Roy Eckardt, *The Surge of Piety in America* (New York: Association Press, 1958).

8   6 Martin E. Marty, *The New Shape of American Religion* (New York: Harper & Brothers, 1958).

8   6 For a kind of Protestant dirge on the low estate of the church see David W. Soper, ed., *Room for Improvement: Next Steps for Protestants* (Chicago: Wilcox & Follett Co., 1951).

8 19 II Tim. 4:7.

8 31 Quoted by O. Hobart Mowrer, "Science Religion and Student Values," *Christian Century*, Oct. 2, 1963, p. 1202.

9   2 William Hordern, "The Jittery Generation," *The Lutheran*, Sept. 11, 1963, p. 11.

Page Line

2. UNBELIEF AMONG THE CLERGY

9　24　*Time* magazine, Aug. 24, 1959, p. 62.

10　5　*New York Times,* Jan. 20, 1960.

10　22　*Idem,* Aug. 11, 1963.

10　29　*Washington Post,* Feb. 1, 1960.

11　2　William Hordern, "Young Theologians Rebel," *Christian Century,* Mar. 12, 1952, p. 307.

11　12　Robert Rankin, "Strengthening the Ministry," *Christian Century,* Apr. 27, 1955, p. 497.

11　15　*Christian Century,* Oct. 29, 1947, p. 1312.

11　32　Jhan and June Robbins, "The Surprising Beliefs of Our Future Ministers," *Redbook,* Aug. 1961.

12　12　"Uproar Over the Modern Minister's Beliefs," *Redbook,* Nov. 1961, p. 50.

14　5　Editorial: "The Hopes and Fears of All the Years," *Christian Century,* Dec. 25, 1957, p. 1534.

3. HERESY TRIALS

15　13　J. W. Thompson and E. N. Johnson, *Medieval Europe* (New York: W. W. Norton, 1937), p. 641.

16　6　Charles M. Jones, "Statement on the Occasion of his withdrawing from the Presbyterian Ministry," pamphlet.
Summer Meeting, Orange Presbytery, Synod of North Carolina, Presbyterian Church of the United States, held at New Hope Presbyterian Church, Chapel Hill, N.C., July 6, 1953.

18　11　Rufus M. Jones, *Studies in Mystical Religion* (London: Macmillan & Co., 1909), p. 143.

18　15　News item: "Lutheran Pastor Ruled Heretical," *Christian Century,* Aug. 17, 1955, p. 952.

19　11　Letter to *Christian Century,* Sept. 14, 1955, p. 1060.

19　21　Editorial: "Heresy-Hunters Hew to the Line," *Christian Century,* Nov. 2, 1955, p. 1260.

19　33　Theodore A. Gill, "Lutheran Answers Leave Questions," *Christian Century,* Feb. 8, 1956, p. 166.

19　36　*New York Times,* Jan. 21, 1960.

20　17　Virgie Bernhardt, "McCrackin Before the Presbytery," *Christian Century,* Sept. 7, 1960.

21　5　Editorial: "Synod Sustains McCrackin," *Christian Century,* Oct. 11, 1961, p. 1196.

21　18　Letters to the Editor, *Christian Century,* Oct. 18, 1961, p. 1243.

21　38　Martin E. Marty, *op. cit.,* pp. 158, 163.

22　9　John Henry Newman, *Apologia Pro Vita Sua* (New York: Catholic Publishing House, 1864), p. 264.

4. THE ECUMENICAL MOVEMENT

23　9　R. L. Calhoun, "Christ the Hope of the World," Opening Address at

Page Line

World Council of Churches, August 15, 1954, *Christian Century*, Aug. 25, 1954, p. 1011.

23   29   Robert S. Bilheimer, *The Quest for Christian Unity* (New York: Association Press, 1952).

23   36   William A. Wright, "Is Denominationalism a Delusion?" *Christian Century*, Aug. 15, 1951, p. 938.

24   5   Charles Clayton Morrison, *The Unfinished Reformation* (New York: Harper & Brothers, 1953), p. 44.

24   13   H. P. Van Dusen, "Our Gravest Heresy," *Christian Century*, July 20, 1955, p. 683.

24   13   See also W. E. Garrison, *The Quest and Character of a United Church* (Nashville: Abingdon Press, 1958).

24   28   *Zion's Herald*, Vol. 131, Oct. 6, 1964, p. 3.

26   6   *Time* magazine, July 12, 1955, p. 59.

26   11   *Infallible Fallacies*, pamphlet (London: SPCK, 1953).

CHAPTER II. THE FOURTH FAITH

1. The Copernican Revolution and the Church

29   14   See Thomas S. Kuhn, *The Copernican Revolution* (Cambridge: Harvard University Press, 1955).

29   14   See Herbert Butterfield, *The Origin of Modern Science* (London: Bell, 1950).

29   14   Galileo Galilei, *Discoveries and Opinions of Galileo*, trans. and introd. by Stillman Drake (Garden City, N.Y.: Doubleday Anchor Co., 1957).

30   4   Alexandre Koyré, *From the Closed World to the Infinite Universe* (Baltimore: Johns Hopkins University Press, 1957).

30   37   W. E. H. Lecky, *Rationalism in Europe* (New York: D. Appleton and Co., 1888), Vol. I, p. 71, n. 1.

31   17   Averroës, *On the Harmony of Religion and Philosophy*, trans. and ed. by George F. Hourani, printed for the Trustees of the E. J. Gibb Memorial (London: Luzac and Co., 1961).

31   17   Averroës, *Epitome of Parva Naturalia*, trans. and ed. by Harry Blumberg (Cambridge: Medieval Academy of America, 1961).

31   35   Walter Nigg, *The Heretics* (New York: Alfred A. Knopf, Inc., 1962).

31   35   Fred Gladstone Bratton, *Legacy of the Liberal Spirit* (New York: Charles Scribner's Sons, 1943).

32   12   Arthur O. Lovejoy, *The Great Chain of Being* (Cambridge: Harvard University Press, 1939), p. 123.

32   35   See Giorgio de Santillana, *The Crime of Galileo* (Chicago: University of Chicago Press, 1955.)

33   11   J. Bronowski and B. Mazlish, *Western Intellectual Tradition* (New York: Harper & Brothers, 1960), pp. 240-241.

33   24   See Thompson and Johnson, *op cit.*, p. 607.

34   19   Alfred North Whitehead, *Science and the Modern World* (New York: The Macmillan Company, 1928), p. 270.

35   2   Millar Burrows, *More Light on the Dead Sea Scrolls* (New York: The Viking Press, 1958), chaps. 3 and 4.

Page Line

36 14 Norman W. Pittenger, "Christianity and the Modern Man," *Christian Century,* June 20, 1956, p. 747.

36 29 Andrew D. White, *Warfare of Science with Theology in Christendom,* 2 vols. (New York: D. Appleton and Co., 1896).

37   4 Bronowski and Mazlish, *op cit.,* p. 502.

37 13 Robert Strother, "The Concentrations of Isaac Newton," *The Saturday Review,* July 23, 1955, pp. 25-26.

37 23 J. B. Conant, *On Understanding Science* (New Haven: Yale University Press, 1947), chap. 4.

38 32 Thomas H. Huxley, quoted in Edward Mims *Great Writers as Interpreters of Religion* (Nashville: Abingdon Press, 1945), p. 154.

39 13 Oliver Cromwell, quoted in Alfred N. Whitehead, *Science and the Modern World,* p. 24; E. A. Burtt, *Religion in an Age of Science,* p. 79; R. M. Janus, *Preface to Christian Faith in a New Age.*

39 36 Isaac Newton, "Rules of Philosophizing," see Ernst Cassirer's *Philosophy of Enlightenment* (Princeton: Princeton University Press, 1951), pp. 7 ff.

40   9 Bronowski and Mazlish, *op cit.*

40 11 H. J. Muller, *Uses of the Past* (New York: Oxford University Press, 1953).

40 15 Charles C. Gillespie, *The Edge of Objectivity* (Princeton: Princeton University Press, 1960).

40 17 Carlton S. Coon, *The Story of Man* (New York: Alfred A. Knopf, Inc., 1954).

2. AMERICAN RELIGIOUS PLURALISM

41 38 Editorial: "War and Peace," *Fortune,* Jan. 1940, p. 26.

42 23 Edward R. Murrow, *This I Believe* (New York: Simon & Schuster, 1952), p. vii.

42 27 *Ibid.,* p. xviii.

43   6 Will Herberg, *Protestant, Catholic, Jew* (Garden City, N.Y.: Doubleday & Company, 1955), p. 14.

43 25 Will Herberg, "Religion in a Secularized Society," *Review of Religion Research,* Vol. IV, No. 1, Fall 1962, p. 33.

44   1 George H. Williams, "American Critical Pluralism as the Emerging Middle Ground in Interfaith Relations," in a symposium on "Issues between Catholics and Protestants at Mid-Century," *Religion in Life,* 1954.

44 16 John Courtney Murray "Governmental Repression of Heresy," *The Catholic Theological Society of America,* Proceedings of the Third Annual Meeting, Chicago 1948, pp. 31ff.

44 19 *Idem,* "St. Robert Bellarmine on the Indirect Power," *Theological Studies* IX, 1948, p. 528.

44 30 *Idem,* "Contemporary Orientations of Catholic Thought on Church and State in the Light of History," *Theological Studies* X, 1949, p. 224.

45   6 *Idem,* "The Problem of Pluralism in America," *Thought* XXIX, #13, Summer 1954, p. 165.

Page Line

46 31 Louis J. Putz, ed., "The Catholic Church USA," *Fides*, 1957.

46 35 Charles Donahue, "Freedom and Education: the Pluralist Background," *Thought* XXVI, 1952-1953, p. 542.

46 38 John Courtney Murray, "Governmental Repression. . . ," p. 31.

47 16 Eugene J. Lipman and Albert Vorspan, *A Tale of Ten Cities* (New York: Union of American Hebrew Congregations, 1962).

47 32 Alexis de Tocqueville, *Democracy in America,* ed. by Phillips Bradley (New York: Alfred A. Knopf, Inc., 1945), Vol. I, p. 308.

3. SECULARISM

48 20 Edwin E. Aubrey, *Secularism a Myth* (New York: Harper & Brothers, 1954), chap. 1.

49   1 Rufus M. Jones, "Secular Civilization and the Churches' Task," *Jerusalem Meeting of the International Missionary Council,* Mar. 24-Apr. 8, 1928 (New York: International Missionary Council), Vol. I, p. 230.

49 11 J. Richard Spann, ed., *The Christian Faith and Secularism,* Evanston Conference Lectures of 1947 (Nashville: Abingdon Press, 1948).

50   6 Gerald O. McCulloch, "How Christianity Challenges Secularism," in J. R. Spann, *op. cit.,* pp. 232, 233.

51   3 Will Herberg, *Protestant, Catholic, Jew* (Garden City, N.Y., Doubleday & Company, 1960), p. 258.

51   6 Will Herberg, "Religion in a Secularized Society," *Review of Religious Research,* Vol. IV, No. 1, Fall 1962, p. 44.

51   6 See also Gabriel Vahanian, *The Death of God* (New York: George Braziller Co., 1961), pp. 230-31.

51 12 J. K. Jessup, "The World, the Flesh and the Devil," *Life,* Dec. 26, 1955, p. 140.

51 22 Arnold B. Rhodes, ed., *The Church Faces the Isms* (Nashville: Abingdon Press, 1958).

51 30 See also Georgia Harkness, *The Modern Rival of the Christian Faith* (Nashville: Abingdon Press, 1952), pp. 11 ff.

51 30 Cornelius Loew, *Modern Rivals to Christian Faith* (Philadelphia: Westminister Press, 1956).

51 31 Walter Nigg, *The Heretics* (New York: Alfred A. Knopf, Inc., 1962), p. 401.

52   1 Will Herberg, *Protestant, Catholic, Jew,* pp. 1, 82.

52 22 John Courtney Murray, "America's Four Conspiracies," in John Cogley, ed., *Religion in America* (New York: Meridian Books, 1958). This essay also appears in John Courtney Murray, *We Hold These Truths* (New York: Sheed and Ward, 1960, pp. 18 ff.

53 10 Martin E. Marty, *op. cit.,* pp. 70 ff.

53 30 Martin E. Marty, *Second Chance for American Protestants* (New York: Harper & Row, 1963), p. 31.

54   2 Robert McAfee Brown in *Stanford Today,* Winter 1962, cited in *Washington Post,* Jan. 5, 1963.

54   8 Robert McAfee Brown and Gustave Weigel: Will Herberg, ed., *An American Dialogue* (Garden City, N.Y., Doubleday Anchor Co., 1960).

Page Line

4. THE FOURTH FAITH

55 34 See Duncan Howlett, *Man against the Church* (Boston: Beacon Press, 1954), Pt. III.

56 29 Sebastian Castellio, *Concerning Heretics,* trans. and ed. by Roland Bainton (New York: Columbia University Press, 1935).

CHAPTER III. THE FAITH OF STABILITY

62 17 Matt. 25:14-30.

1. JUDAISM

64 4 Arthur Hertzberg, ed., *Judaism* (New York: George Braziller, 1961), pp. 11ff.

66 21 Arthur A. Cohen, *The Natural and Supernatural Jew* (New York: Pantheon Books, 1962).

67 9 Will Herberg, *Judaism and Modern Man* (New York: Farrar, Straus, and Cudahy, 1951).

67 36 Will Herberg, *Protestant, Catholic, Jew* (Garden City, N.Y.: Doubleday & Company, 1960), p. 254.

68 4 I Kings 16:29-22:40.

68 25 I. G. Matthews,, *The Religious Pilgrimage of Israel* (New York: Harper & Brothers, 1947), pp. 91, 110.

69 36 G. Ernest Wright, *Biblical Archeology* (Philadelphia: Westminster Press, 1957), chap 7.

72 9 See Pierre Teilhard de Chardin, *The Phenomenon of Man,* trans. Bernard Wall (New York: Harper & Row, 1959).

72 14 Roland Gittelsohn, *Man's Best Hope* (New York: Random House, 1961).

2. ROMAN CATHOLIC FAITH

72 29 See Jaroslav Pelikan, *The Riddle of Roman Catholicism* (Nashville: Abingdon Press, 1959).

72 32 G. D. Smith, ed., *Teachings of the Catholic Church* (New York: The Macmillan Company, 1949), Vol. II, p. 659.

73 21 *Ibid.,* Vol. I, pp. 1 ff.

73 30 Ronald Knox, *A Spiritual Aeneid: A Religious Autobiography* (London: Longmans, Green & Co., 1918).

74 20 G. D. Smith, ed., *op. cit.,* Vol. I, p. 87.

74 33 Richard Ginder, "Are All Churches Equally Good?" *Our Sunday Visitor,* Aug. 18, 1957, p. 1.

75 21 John B. Harney, C. S. P., pamphlet "Is One Church As Good As Another?" (New York: The Paulist Press).

76 18 Roland H. Bainton, *Here I Stand* (Nashville: Abingdon Press, 1950), p. 185.

79 3 John Henry Newman, *Apologia Pro Vita Sua* (New York: Catholic Publishing House, 1864).

Page Line
79 13 William P. Witcutt, *Return to Reality* (New York: The Macmillan Company, 1955).

79 26 John Henry Newman, *op. cit.*, p. 264.

79 29 Willard L. Sperry, in Louis Finkelstein, ed., *Thirteen Americans: Their Spiritual Autobiographies* (New York: Harper & Brothers, 1953), p. 248.

80 7 John Courtney Murray, "Contemporary Orientation," *op cit.*, pp. 222 ff. and 188.

81 11 *Time,* Aug. 3, 1953, p. 41.

82 15 J. C. Murray, "Contemporary Orientation," p. 224.

82 39 *Idem,* "Problems of Pluralism," *Thought* XXIX, 1954, p. 167.

83 11 Charles J. V. Murphy, "The Cardinal," *Fortune,* Feb. 1960, p. 151.

3. PROTESTANT LIBERALISM

85 26 Earl Morse Wilbur, *History of Unitarianism* (Cambridge: Harvard University Press, 1945), Vol. I, pp. 326 ff.

85 38 *Ibid.,* Vol. I, p. 380.

86 35 Ernest Sutherland Bates, *American Faith* (New York: W. W. Norton, 1940), p. 9.

87 16 Ernest Renan, *Life of Jesus* (1863), ed. from the 23rd and final edition by Joseph Henry Allen (Boston: Little, Brown & Co., 1895).

87 25 Washington Gladden, *Who Wrote the Bible?* (Boston: Houghton Mifflin Co., 1891).

88 5 See Vergilius Ferm, ed., *Contemporary American Theology,* 2 vols. (New York: Round Table Press, 1932-33).

89 22 J. H. Randall, Jr., "The Churches and the Liberal Tradition," *Annals of the American Academy,* Vol. 256, Mar. 1948, p. 153.

90 10 A. C. McGiffert, Jr., in *Liberal Theology,* ed. by David E. Roberts and Henry P. Van Dusen (New York: Charles Scribner's Sons, 1942), p. 117.

90 21 Kenneth Cauthen, *The Impact of American Religious Liberalism* (New York: Harper & Row, 1962), p. 212.

91 7 John Lawson, "Theologies without Grace," *Christian Century,* Jan. 2, 1963, p. 15.

92 3 Editorial: *Religion in Life,* Summer 1963, p. 33.

92 7 J. H. Randall, Jr., *op cit.*, p. 4.

92 11 William E. Hocking, in *Liberal Theology,* p. 57.

92 13 Henry E. Kolbe, "What is Liberalism?" *Religion in Life,* Autumn 1954.

4. MODERNISM

93 33 S. J. Case, *The Origins of Christian Supernaturalism* (Chicago: University of Chicago Press, 1946).

94 30 J. Estlin Carpenter, *The Historical Jesus and the Theological Christ* (Boston: American Unitarian Association, 1912).

95 8 Kirby Page, *Jesus or Christianity* (Garden City, N.Y.: Doubleday & Company, 1949), p. 316.

Page Line
95 20 Harry Emerson Fosdick, *The Living of These Days* (New York: Harper & Brothers, 1956), p. 269.
95 28 Harry Emerson Fosdick, *The Modern Use of the Bible* (New York: The Macmillan Company, 1924).
96 7   *Ibid.*, pp. 102 ff.
96 12 Theodore Parker, *The Transient and Permanent in Christianity*, Centenary Edition, Vol. IV, edited with notes by George Willis Cooke (Boston: American Unitarian Association, 1908), p. 1.
96 16 Harry Emerson Fosdick, *The Modern Use of the Bible*, pp. 63 ff.
96 30 *Ibid.*, p. 104.
96 33 *Ibid.*, p. 121.
96 37 *Ibid.*, p. 123.
97 2   *Ibid.*, p. 125.
97 8   *Ibid.*, p. 1.
97 20 *Ibid.*, p. 219.
97 34 *Ibid.*, p. 235.
98 8   Harry Emerson Fosdick, "The Church Must Go Beyond Modernism," sermon preached at The Riverside Church, New York, Oct. 3, 1935.
98 27 Albert Schweitzer, *Quest of the Historical Jesus* (London: A. C. Black, 1910), pp. 397 and 4.
99 27 Charles Harris, *Creeds or No Creeds* (New York: E. P. Dutton & Co., 1922), p. 308.

CHAPTER IV. THE RETURN TO ORTHODOXY

1. KARL BARTH

103 12 See William Hordern, *Layman's Guide to Protestant Theology* (New York: The Macmillan Company, 1955).
103 35 Karl Barth, *The Word of God and the Word of Man* (Boston: The Pilgrim Press, 1928), p. 26.
103 38 Karl Barth, *Epistle to the Romans*, trans. and ed. by Edwyn C. Hoskyns (New York: Oxford University Press, 1933).

2. REINHOLD NIEBUHR

107 5   Reinhold Niebuhr, in Charles W. Kegley and Robert W. Bretall, eds., *Reinhold Niebuhr: His Religious, Social and Political Thought* (New York: The Macmillan Company, 1956), pp. 5-7.
107 19 Karl Barth, *The Word of God and the Word of Man*, Douglas Horton, ed. (New York: Harper Torchbooks, 1957), Foreword.
107 29 Douglas Horton, "God Lets Loose Karl Barth," *Christian Century*, Feb. 16, 1928.
108 8   Reinhold Niebuhr, *Moral Man and Immoral Society* (New York: Charles Scribner's Sons, 1932), Introduction.
108 26 *Ibid.*, p. 79.
109 10 Reinhold Niebuhr, *Nature and Destiny of Man* (New York: Charles Scribner's Sons, 1941), Vol. I, pp. 142 ff.
109 14 Reinhold Niebuhr, *Moral Man and Immoral Society*, p. 82.

Page Line

109 29 Reinhold Niebuhr, *Nature and Destiny of Man*, Vol. I, pp. 147 ff.

110 13 *Ibid.*, p. 146.

110 27 Bernard Iddings Bell, *Crowd Culture* (New York: Harper & Brothers, 1952) , chap. 4.

110 35 Bernard Iddings Bell, "Liberalism: Destination or Transition," address at Charles Street Forum, Boston, Mass., Dec. 1, 1940, MS p. 17.

110 37 Koppel S. Pinson, "Pietism, a Source of German Nationalism," *Christendom*, Winter 1936, Vol. I, No. 2, p. 267.

111 4 Carl Mayer, "The Crisis of German Protestantism," *Social Research*, Nov. 1945.

111 21 Barbara Ward, *Faith and Freedom* (New York: W. W. Norton Co., 1954) , p. 265.

112 26 Will Herberg, "Niebuhr's Three Phases," *Christian Century*, Aug. 10, 1960, p. 927.

3. Neo-Orthodoxy's Debt to Fundamentalism

113 15 See William Hordern, *op. cit.*, chap. 3.

114 28 Walter Rauschenbusch, *Christianity and the Social Crisis* (New York: The Macmillan Company, 1907) .

116 23 Kenneth Cauthen, *op. cit.*, p. 245.

117 2 Editorial: "Fundamentalist Revival," *Christian Century*, June 19, 1957, p. 749.

117 19 E. G. Homrighausen, "Billy Graham and the Protestant Predicament," *Christian Century*, July 18, 1956, p. 848.

117 25 See Sydney Ahlstrom, "Neo-Orthodoxy Demythologized," *Christian Century*, May 22, 1957, p. 649.

118 1 Karl Barth, *The Word of God and the Word of Man* (Boston: The Pilgrim Press, 1928) , p. 43.

118 14 Thomas C. Oden, "Fundamentalism's Weak Christology," *Christian Century*, Nov. 7, 1962, p. 1349.

199 16 Arnold W. Hearn, "Fundamentalist Renascence," *Christian Century*, Apr. 30, 1958, p. 529.

4. Paul Tillich

120 2 Paul Tillich, "Beyond Religious Socialism," *Christian Century*, June 15, 1949, p. 733.

120 20 Paul Tillich, *The Protestant Era*, trans, by J. L. Adams (Chicago: University of Chicago Press, 1948) , Introduction.

121 18 Paul Tillich, "Beyond the Usual Alternatives," *Christian Century*, May 7, 1958, p. 555.

121 20 *Washington Post*, Nov. 21, 1961.

121 38 Nels F. S. Ferré, "Three Critical Issues in Tillich's Philosophical Theology," *Scottish Journal of Theology*, Sept. 1957, pp. 236, 237.

122 21 Nels F. S. Ferré, "To Renew or to Destroy," *Interpretation*, Vol. IX, 1955, p. 465.

123 18 Paul Tillich, *Dynamics of Faith* (New York: Harper & Brothers, 1957) , p. 125.

Page Line

123 31 W. P. Lemon, "Theology Radivivus," *Christian Century*, Jan. 7, 1953, p. 16.

123 32 W. Norman Pittenger, "The Why of Man," *New York Times Book Review*, Jan. 4, 1953.

124 5 See Melville Channing-Pearce, *Søren Kierkegaard* (London: James Clarke & Co. Ltd., 1945).

124 24 H. Richard Niebuhr, *The Social Sources of Denominationalism* (New York: Henry Holt & Co., 1929).

124 27 H. Richard Niebuhr, W. Pauck, and F. P. Miller, *The Church against the World* (Chicago: Willett-Clark and Co., 1935).

124 29 H. Richard Niebuhr, *The Kingdom of God in America* (Chicago: Willett-Clark and Co., 1937), p. vii.

124 34 Karl Jaspers, *The Future of Mankind* (Chicago: University of Chicago Press, 1961).

125 3 Douglas Clyde Macintosh, *Theology as an Empirical Science* (New York: The Macmillan Company, 1919).

125 36 Alfred North Whitehead, *Science and the Modern World* (New York: The Macmillan Company, 1925).

125 38 Alfred North Whitehead, "Harvard: The Future," *Atlantic*, Sept. 1936.

126 12 Alfred North Whitehead, *Adventures of Ideas* (New York: The Macmillan Company, 1935).

126 19 Charles Hartshorne, in *The Theology of Paul Tillich*, ed. by Charles W. Kegley and Robert W. Bretall (New York: The Macmillan Company, 1952).

CHAPTER V. THE HOUSE BUILT UPON THE SAND

127 8 Arthur O. Lovejoy, *The Great Chain of Being* (Cambridge: Harvard University Press, 1936), p. 19.

1. BIBLICAL THEOLOGY

129 22 W. Burnet Easton, Jr., *Basic Christian Beliefs* (Philadelphia: Westminster Press, 1957).

129 24 H. H. Rowley, *The Unity of the Bible* (London: Carey Kingsgate Press, 1953).

129 27 Joseph R. Sizoo, *I Believed in the Bible* (Nashville: Abingdon Press, 1958).

129 34 W. N. Pittenger, "Wanted, a New Christian Modernism," *Christian Century*, Apr. 6, 1955, p. 418.

130 11 W. F. Albright, *Recent Discoveries in Bible Lands*, pamphlet (New York: The Bible Colloquium and Funk & Wagnalls, 1955), p. 132.

130 33 H. H. Farmer, in *The Interpreter's Bible* (Nashville: Abingdon Press, 1952), Vol. I, p. 3.

132 34 *The Interpreter's Bible* (Nashville: Abingdon Press, 1952), Vol. II, p. 594.

133 15 Alan Richardson, *Genesis I-XI* (London: SCM Press, 1953), pp. 7, 27.

134 6 Quoted in Arthur O. Lovejoy, *op. cit.*, p. 121.

134 22 See Frank M. Cross, Jr., *The Ancient Library of Qumran* (Garden City, N.Y.: Doubleday & Company, 1958), chap. 3.

Page Line

135 14   Duncan Howlett, *The Essenes and Christianity* (New York: Harper & Brothers, 1957), pp. 18 ff.

135 21   Robert H. Pfeiffer, *Introduction to the Old Testament* (New York: Harper & Brothers, 1941), p. 765.

135 21   Julius A. Bewer, *The Book of Daniel* (New York: Harper & Brothers, 1955), p. 7.

135 27   Krister Stendahl, *The School of St. Matthew* (Uppsala: C.W.K. Gleerup Lund, 1954).

135 37   Alfred Harbage, "Sweet Will and Gentle Marlowe," review of Calvin Hoffman: *The Murder of the Man Who Was Shakespeare* (New York: Julian Messner, 1954). *New York Times Book Review,* June 12, 1955, p. 1.

136 21   Jack Anderson, "Dramatic New Evidence Confirms the Story of Jesus," *Parade,* Dec. 9, 1962, p. 4.

136 34   G. Ernest Wright, *Biblical Archeology* (Philadelphia: Westminster Press, 1957), p. 19.

137 1   Matt. 7:24-27.

For further examples of theology derived from the Bible, see also:

    L. Harold DeWolf, *The Enduring Message of the Bible* (New York: Harper & Brothers, 1960).

    Alan Richardson and W. Schweitzer, *Biblical Authority for Today* (Philadelphia: Westminster Press, 1951).

    A. Cressy Morrison, *Man Does Not Stand Alone* (Westwood, N.J.: Fleming H. Revell, 1947).

2. The Paradox

137 38   I Cor. 1:18-25.

138 13   I Cor. 2:6-7.

138 24   I Cor. 15:51, 52.

139 13   Arthur E. Murphy in *Religious Liberals Reply* (Boston: Beacon Press, 1947), pp. 29 ff.

140 11   Tertullian, quoted in Vergilius Ferm, *What Can We Believe?* (New York: Philosophical Library, 1948), p. 51.

140 28   C. S. Lewis, *Surprised by Joy: The Shape of My Early Life* (New York: Harcourt, Brace and Co., 1956), p. 229.

140 32   Richard Reinhold Niebuhr, *Resurrection and Historical Reason* (New York: Charles Scribner's Sons, 1957).

142 21   Lewis Carroll, *Through the Looking Glass,* chap. 5.

3. You Can Believe If You Want To

143 38   A. J. Balfour, *Foundations of Belief* (New York: Longmans, Green and Co., 1895).

144 2   F. W. Robertson, *Sermons* (New York: Harper & Brothers, 1864).

144 29   Editorial: "The Greatest Gift," *Life,* Christmas issue, 1949, p. 20.

145 6   James A. Pike and J. McG. Krumm, *Roadblocks to Faith* (New York: Morehouse-Gorham Co., 1954).

Page Line

145 9 Frank W. Hanft, *You Can Believe* (Indianapolis: Bobbs-Merrill & Company, 1952).

145 19 J. B. Bury, *History of Freedom of Thought* (New York: Henry Holt and Co., 1913), p. 19.

145 21 Martin E. Marty, *Second Chance for American Protestants* (New York: Harper & Row, 1963), p. 166.

146 3 Charles Journet, *The Primacy of Peter*, trans. from the French by John S. Chapin (Westminster, Md.: Newman, 1954).

146 26 E.g., W. E. Garrison, *Protestant Manifesto* (Nashville: Abingdon Press, 1952), p. 86.

146 34 Joseph A. Seiss, *A Miracle in Stone*, The Great Pyramid of Egypt (Philadelphia: Porter & Coates, 1877), pp. 152 ff.

146 34 Conor MacDari, *Irish Wisdom*. Preserved in Bible and Pyramids (Boston: The Four Seas Press, 1923).

4. GOD IN HISTORY

147 28 Reinhold Niebuhr, *Beyond Tragedy* (New York: Charles Scribner's Sons, 1937), p. ix.

148 13 Judg. 5:1, 3, 4, 5.

148 16 Judg. 4:23.

148 22 Judg. 4:1.

149 2 G. E. Wright, *Biblical Archeology* (Philadelphia: Westminster Press, 1957), p. 17.

149 25 *Ibid.*, pp. 27, 28.

150 14 J. N. Geldenhuys, *Supreme Authority* (Grand Rapids: Wm. B. Eerdmans Publishing Co., 1953).

151 10 T. Herbert Bindley, *The Oecumenical Documents of the Faith* (London: Methuen and Co., 1950). Revised from ed. of 1899 by F. W. Green, p. 1.

151 18 M. C. D'Arcy, S.J., *The Meaning and Matter of History* (New York: Farrar, Straus and Cudahy, 1959).

153 19 A. J. Jackson, "God's Promises Demonstrated," *Wells Way*, Sept.-Dec. 1954, p. 5.

153 33 "St. John's-by-the-Gas-Station" was made famous by Halford E. Luccock. See his *Like a Mighty Army* (New York: Oxford University Press, 1954), pp. 3 ff.

154 6 C. S. Lewis, *The Case for Christianity* (New York: The Macmillan Company, 1954), p. 55.

5. THE AUTHORITY OF SELF-ASSERTION

155 30 Henri Frankfort, *The Art and Architecture of the Ancient Orient* (Baltimore: Penguin Books, 1955), Hammurabi stele Plates 65 and 59.

157 34 Robert N. Bellah, "Religious Aspects of Modernization in Turkey and Japan," *American Journal of Sociology*, Vol. 64, July 1958, p. 1.

158 33 Charles J. Wright, *Modern Issues in Religious Thought* (London: Epworth Press, 1937).

Page Line

159 1 Anders Nygren, *Agape and Eros,* trans. by A. G. Herbert (London: S.P.C.K., 1932), Pt. I.

159 37 Vergilius Ferm, *What Can We Believe?* (New York: Philosophical Library, 1948), pp. 136-137.

160 19 L. Harold DeWolf, *A Theology of the Living Church* (New York: Harper & Brothers, 1953), p. 20.

160 33 See Cecelia Payne-Gaposchkin, *Stars in the Making* (Cambridge: Harvard University Press, 1952).

160 39 William James, *Varieties of Religious Experience* (New York: Longmans, Green and Co., 1902).

161 12 Lucie Delarue-Mardrus, *Sainte Therese of Lisieux,* trans. by Helen Younger Chase (London: Longmans, Green & Co., 1929), p. 99.

162 8 Philip Wylie, Letter to the Editor, *Life,* July 14, 1947, p. 7.

162 31 James D. Smart, *The Creed in Christian Teaching* (Philadelphia: Westminster Press, 1962), p. 23.

163 27 J. B. Phillips, *God Our Contemporary* (New York: The Macmillan Company, 1960).

163 38 Editorial: "Theological Education of Laymen Needed," *Christian Century,* May 22, 1957.

164 27 David Wesley Soper, *Epistle to the Skeptics* (New York: Association Press, 1956), p. 17.

165 19 Karl Barth, University of Chicago Lectures, April, 1962. *N.Y. Times,* Apr. 24, 1962, p. 38.

165 35 William Hordern, "Young Theologians Rebel," *Christian Century,* Mar. 12, 1952, p. 306.

166 31 Roland H. Bainton, "Unity of Mankind in the Classical Christian Tradition," in *Schweitzer Jubilee Book,* ed. by A. A. Roback (Cambridge, Mass.: Sci-Art Publishers, 1945).

CHAPTER VI. THE FAITH OF ADVENTURE

1. A SECOND LOOK AT ADAM

170 15 Rom. 5:12-21.

170 17 I Cor. 15:22.

171 2 Philo, *Allegory of the Jewish Law,* I, 31-32.

171 9 Homer *Odyssey,* line 117.

171 12 Pindar, Pythian Ode, 8.

171 15 James Breasted, *Dawn of Conscience* (New York: Charles Scribner's Sons, 1933), p. 181.

172 1 Semonides, Fragment I, F.M. Cornford, ed., *Greek Religious Thought* (Boston: Beacon Press, 1950), p. 37.

172 8 Sophocles, *Oedipus at Colonus,* line 1224.

172 14 Euripides, *Bellerophon* fragment, line 292, F.M. Cornford, *op. cit.,* p. 151.

172 17 Euripides, *Iphigenia in Tauris,* line 391.

174 32 Gen. 3:22-23.

175 4 Gen. 11:1-9.

176 38 Gen. 3:6.

Page Line

2. THE HEAVENSTORMER

179 41 Sophocles, *Antigone*, trans. Elizabeth Wyckoff in David Green and
         Richard Lattimore, eds., *The Complete Greek Tragedies* (Chi-
         cago: The University Press, 1959), Vol. II, p. 170.

3. THE HERETIC

187 11 G. K. Chesterton, *Heretics* (New York: John Lane Company, 1905).
187 28 Matt. 5:17 ff.
189   3 *Washington Post,* Jan. 18, 1962.
189 33 On Jefferson's Unitarianism and his religious views generally see
         especially:
         Lester J. Cappou, ed., *The Adams-Jefferson Letters,* two vols.
         (Chapel Hill: The University of North Carolina Press, 1959).
190   9 Robert Bendiner, "Our Right Not to Believe," *Saturday Evening
         Post,* Feb. 10, 1962, p. 10.
190 13 Albert Camus, *The Rebel,* trans. Anthony Bower (New York: Alfred
         A. Knopf, 1954), p. 8.
190 15 *Ibid.,* p. 21.
190 35 *Ibid.,* pp. 271 ff.
192   3 Walter Kaufmann, *The Faith of a Heretic* (Garden City, N.Y.: Dou-
         bleday & Company, 1961).
192   5 F. S. Bauman, *Religion and the Rise of Skepticism* (New York:
         Harcourt, Brace & Co., 1960).

4. THE LAST QUESTION

193 33 Norman Cameron, *The Psychology of Behavior Disorders* (Boston:
         Houghton Mifflin Co., 1947), pp. 388 ff.
194 33 Justin Martyr, quoted in J. N. D. Kelly, *Early Christian Creeds*
         (London: Longmans, Green & Co., 1950), p. 72.
198   5 Marcus Bach, "The Douks Are At It Again," *Christian Century*
         Dec. 16, 1953, p. 1453.
199 20 Paul Tillich, "Authority and Revelation," *Harvard Divinity School
         Bulletin,* 1952, p. 36.
199 20 See also Paul Tillich, *Systematic Theology* (Chicago: University of
         Chicago Press, 1951), Vol. I, pp. 106 ff.

5. THE BATTLE OF THE ASSUMPTIONS

200 32 Reinhold Niebuhr, *Nature and Destiny of Man* (New York: Charles
         Scribner's Sons, 1941), Vol. I, p. 146.
200 37 *Ibid.,* p. 1.
201   8 E. R. Goodenough, *Religious Tradition and Myth* (New Haven:
         Yale University Press, 1937), p. 96.
201 24 David Brewster, *Memoirs of the Life, Writings, and Discoveries of
         Sir Isaac Newton* (Edinburgh: T. Constable and Co., 1855), Vol.
         II, chap. 27.

Page Line

202 18 Arthur O. Lovejoy, *The Great Chain of Being* (Cambridge: Harvard University Press, 1936), pp. 331, 332.

202 29 Charles Galton Darwin, *The Next Million Years* (London: R. Hart-Davis, 1952).

202 36 J. G. Frazer, *The Golden Bough,* one-vol. ed. (New York: The Macmillan Company, 1922), p. vii.

203 1 E. A. Burtt, *Religion in an Age of Science* (New York: F. A. Stokes Co., 1929), p. 87.

203 8 Charles Péguy, *Basic Verities* (New York: Pantheon Books, 1943), p. 51.

203 9 F. S. C. Northrop, *Man, Nature and God* (New York: Trident Press, Simon and Schuster, 1962), p. 256.

203 37 William James, *The Will To Believe* (New York: Longmans, Green and Co., 1896), pp. 19 ff.

6. THE QUEST FOR ULTIMATE MEANING

210 12 Julius Seelye Bixler, "The Search for Reasonable Authority, *Christian Register,* Aug. 1944.

210 13 Isa. 6.

210 25 J. S. Bixler, *A Faith that Fulfills* (New York: Harper & Brothers, 1951), p. 59.

Index

A number of authors are quoted or cited in the text of this book whose names appear only in the Notes (pp. 218-232). The index reference in each such case includes the page on which the citation appears and the letter *n*.

Abelard, 30, 56
Adam, 115, 169-177
Adams, John, 189
Adventism, 51
Agapé, 122, 158
Agnostic, 38, 99, 164, 189
Ahlstrom, Sydney, 117 n.
Akhenaton, 56
Albright, W. F., 130
Amos, 56
Anaxagoras, 31
Anaximander, 31
Anaximines, 31
Anderson, Jack, 136 n.
Angels, 96
Annunciationists, 25 ff.
Anthropology, 40, 129
Apostolic Succession, 25
Aquinas, St. Thomas, 30, 124
Archimedes, 31
Aristotle, 74
Arnold, Martha, 3 n.
Atonement, doctrine of, 109
Aubrey, Edwin A., 48 n.
Augustine, St., 18, 106, 124, 151, 209
Averroës, 30-31, 56

Bach, Marcus, 198 n.
Baillie, John, 24

Bainton, Roland, 166
Balfour, A. J., 143
Barth, Karl, 103 ff., 107, 111, 117, 124, 128, 137 ff., 165, 183
Barton, Bruce, 144
Bauman, F. S., 192 n.
Bayle, Pierre, 33
Bates, Ernest Sutherland, 86
Beliefs: discrepancy between creeds and, *see* Creeds; heresy trials related to, 21; man can have, 143; man's need for, 41-42; opinions distinguished, 195
Bell, Bernard Iddings, 110-111
Bellah, Robert N., 157 n.
Bendiner, Robert, 190 n.
Benedict, Ruth, 40
Berger, Peter, 8
Bernhardt, Virgie, 20 n.
Berrill, N. J., 72
Bestsellers, religious, 7
Bewer, Julius A., 135 n.
Bible: Authority of, 148-151; Barth on, 104-5; Biblical Theology, 128-137; Bultmann on, 124; Congregational ministers' views on, 11; England, views of in, 4, 5, 10; Essenes' interpretation of, 134-135; Fosdick on, 95-96; Fundamentalist view, 114 ff;

Interpreter's Bible, 130-132; Liberalism, role of, in, 90, 114; Modernism, treatment of, in, 93-97; Neo-orthodox view of, 114 ff.; reading, frequency of, 3; Reformation, use of, in, 83-85; stories, 132-133; youth, views on, 3; *see also* Biblical Criticism, Jesus

Biblical criticism, 85, 87-88, 95-96

Biblical theology, 128, 137, 147 ff.

Bilheimer, Robert A., 23 n.

Bindley, T. Herbert, 150

Bixler, Julius Seelye, 210

Black Muslims, 165

Bonhoeffer, Dietrich, 124

Brake, Tycho, 32

Bratton, Fred Gladstone, 32 n.

Breasted, James, 171

Brewster, David, 201 n.

Bronowski, J., 37, 40

Brown, Robert McAfee, 53

Brunner, Emil, 124, 183

Bultmann, Rudolf, 124, 183

Burrows, Millar, 35 n.

Burtt, E. A., 202

Bury, J. B., 145

Butterfield, Herbert, 29 n.

Calhoun, Robert L., 23

Cameron, Norman, 193 n.

Calvin, John, 40, 84, 106, 124

Calvinists, 112

Camus, Albert, 190-191

Carpenter, J. Estlin, 94

Case, Shirley Jackson, 93-94

Cassirer, Ernst, 39 n.

Castellio, Sebastian, 56

Catholicism, Roman: 72 ff.; Church, founded by God, 73-74; conversions to Protestantism, 6; discrepancy between dogma and belief, 5-6; exclusiveness of, 26, 74-75, 80-82; power of, 83; revelation in, 73, 198; pluralism accepted by, 44; secularism equated with, 51; stability, as Faith of, 72 ff.; State, relation to, 44; students, 4; tolerance, effect of American on, 45-46; *See also* Inquisition and Murray, John Courtney

Cauthen, Kenneth, 90-91, 93, 97, 116

Channing-Pearce, Melville, 124 n.

Chesterton, G. K., 187

Christ: Barth on, 103 ff., 147; beliefs about, 3, 4, 11, 162-163; biblical theology, 129 ff.; Fundamentalist view, 114; Kierkegaard on, 124; Reinhold Niebuhr on, 147; Richard Reinhold Niebuhr on, 140-141; Pauline theology, 170; Tillich on, 120 ff; *see also* Jesus

Church: Catholic doctrine of, 72 ff.; Congregational ministers' views on, 11; Fourth Faith, view of, 60, 206; governing authority of, 60; secularism within, 50; unbelief in, 8

Church of England: Annunciationist controversy, 25-27; creed, 10; devil, view on, 188

Clergy: Apostolic succession, 25; authority of, 206; Congregational, 11; Episcopal, 9-10; Methodist, 9; unbelief among, 9 ff., 187

Cohen, Arthur A., 66-67

Columbus, Christopher, 40

Communion, Holy, 9, 18

Communism, 51

Conant, James Bryant, 37

Coon, Carleton S., 40

Copernican Revolution, 29-30, 39, 40

Copernicus, 29, 32, 87

Creeds: discrepancy between, and beliefs, 2 ff., 42, 187; effect of ecumenicity on, 25; *see also* Polls

Crist, George P., 18

Cromwell, Oliver, 39

Cross, Frank M., Jr., 134 n.

Daniel, Book of, 135

D'Arcy, M. C., 151

Darwin, Sir Charles 38, 87

Darwin, Charles Galton, 202

David, Francis, 86

Dead Sea Scrolls, 35, 134-135, 138

Deborah, Song of, 147

Deists, 33, 56, 87, 100

Delarue-Mardrus, Lucie, 161 n.

Democracy, 86

Denominationalism, 51
Denominations: differences, 22 ff; merger of, 25; *see* specific denominations by name
Descartes, René, 32, 124
Devil, 188
DeWette, Wilhelm Martin, 186
DeWolf, L. Harold, 137 n., 160 n.
Dispensationalism, 51
Divorce, 27
Doctrines: declining importance of, 27; denominational differences, 23; effect of science on, 33-36; obstacles to ecumenical movement, 23-27
Donahue, Charles, 46
Dornbusch, Sanford M., 7
Doukhobors, 198

Eastern Orthodox Church, 24
Easton, W. Burnet, Jr., 129 n.
Ecclesiasticism, 60
Eck, Johann, 75-78
Eckardt, A. Roy, 8
Ecumenical Movement, 22 ff: Apostolic succession in, 25; doctrinal differences, 23-27; effect on creeds, 25; obstacles to agreement, 23-27
Ecumenism, 51
Einstein, Albert, 38
Enlightenment, The, 48, 87
Episcopal Church, 2, 10, 139
Erasmus, Desiderius, 85
Eschatology, 115
Essenes, 134-135, 138
Euripides, 172
Evanston Conference of World Council of Churches, 23, 49, 164
Existentialism, 120

Fairchild, Roy W., 7 n.
Faith, 42, 58, 117; *see also* Fourth Faith
Faith of Stability, 62 ff.; 101 ff., 119, 124, 214; *see also,* Judaism, Catholicism, and Neo-Orthodoxy
Farmer, H. H., 130-132
Fascism, 51, 166
Ferm, Vergilius, 144, 159
Ferré, Nels F. S., 121-122
Fourth Faith: on authority of religion, 158; existence of, recognized, 52-54;

nature of, 54-61, 126 ff., 169, 183-184, 186, 192, 195, 204 ff., 213-215; on Reinhold Niebuhr, 112; on Richard Reinhold Niebuhr, 141; relation to secularism, 154-155; on Tillich, 122; why it arose, 1
Fosdick, Harry Emerson, 95-98
Franklin, Benjamin, 189
Frazer, Sir James G., 202
Freedom: religious, in U.S., 45-46; effect of, on Catholicism, 46
Fundamentalism, 51, 108, 113 ff., 129 ff., 146

Galilei, Galileo, 29, 32, 87
Garrison, W. E., 24 n., 146
Gelasius XIII, Pope, 80
Geldenhuys, J. N., 150
Genesis, 115, 133, 169-177
Germany, 103, 111, 112, 166, 174
Gilkey, J. G., 144
Gill, Theodore A., 19 n.
Gillespie, Charles C., 40
Ginder, Richard, 74 n.
Gittelsohn, Roland B., 72
God: Barth on, 104, 138 ff., 165; Bible as record of, 148-155; in biblical theology, 129 ff.; children's beliefs about, 3; college students' beliefs about, 4; contemporary writings on, 162-165; in Fundamentalism, 114 ff.; in history, 147; "Mighty acts of," 147-155; nature of, 209-210; Niebuhr on, 147; personal beliefs about, 2; Tillich on, 120 ff., 199, 209
Goodchild, Frank M., 144
Goodenough, E. R., 201
Gore, Charles, 144
Grace, 115
Graham, Billy, 116-117, 128
Greeks, 31, 170, 171-172, 186
Gregory IX, Pope, 14
Ground of being, 121, 199

Habakkuk, Book of, 135
Hammurabi, 155-156
Hanft, Frank W., 145 n.
Harbage, Alfred, 135 n.
Harkness, Georgia, 51 n.
Harnack, Adolf, 103, 105

Harney, John B., 75 n.
Harris, Charles, 99 n.
Hartshorne, Charles, 126
Hearn, Arnold W., 118 n.
Hell: beliefs about, 3; theological students' views on, 11
Herberg, Will, 43, 47, 48, 50, 51-53, 55, 67
Heresy: Medieval, 14-15; modern cases, 15 ff.
Heresy Trials: Crist, George P., 18; Gerberding, John, 19; Jones, Charles M., 16-18; legal procedures in, 20-21; Lutheran, 18-19; McCrackin, Maurice, 20; Quigley, Harold, 19-20; Presbyterian, 16-17, 19-21; Wrigley, Victor, 19
Heretics, 187-193
Hertzberg, Arthur, 64-66, 67
Hesiod, 31
Hocking, William Ernest, 92, 167
Homer, 31, 171
Homrighausen, E. G., 117 n.
Hordern, William E., 8, 165 n.
Horton, Douglas, 107
Hus, John, 56
Huxley, Thomas Henry, 38, 203

Immorality, 3, 4, 138
Incarnation, 115, 147
Inquisition, 14, 29, 33
Interpreter's Bible, 130-133
Isaiah, 56
Islam, 31, 157

James, William, 160, 203
Jaspers, Karl, 124
Jefferson, Thomas, 189
Jessup, J. K., 51 n.
Jesus: beliefs about, 3, 4, 11; Fosdick on, 95; Fundamentalists' view of, 117; "historical," 88, 94-95, 98-99; life stories of, 87; Lutheran doctrine of, 18; in Modernism, 94-95; as rebel against authority, 56, 63; Richard Reinhold Niebuhr on, 140-141; *see also* Christ
Jews, 4, 6; *see also* Judaism
John of Paris, 80
John XXIII, Pope, 27, 81
Johnson, E. N., 15 n.

Jones, Charles M., 16-18
Jones, Rufus, 18, 48
Joshua, Book of, 132-133
Journet, Charles, 146 n.
Judaism, 63 ff.; on Adam, 170; "Chosenness," 65, 66; history of, 67-71, 147 ff.; "particular" nature of, 65, 66-69; revelation in, 65; as secularism, 51; Torah, 64, 66; "universal" aspect of, 64

Kant, Immanuel, 124
Kaufmann, Walter, 192 n.
Kelly, J. N. D., 194 n.
Kepler, Johannes, 32
Kierkegaard, Søren, 124, 137-138
Knox, Ronald, 73-74
Kolbe, Henry E., 92
Koyré, Alexandre, 29
Krumm, J. McG., 145 n.
Kuhlen, Raymond G., 3 n.
Kuhn, Thomas S., 29 n.

Lawson, John, 91 n.
Leakey, Louis B., 172
Lecky, W. E. H., 30
Legal procedures, used in heresy trials, 20-21
Lemon, W. P., 123 n.
Lercaro, Giacomo, Cardinal, 6
Lewis, C. S., 140, 154
Liberalism: Barth on, 105, 107; defined, 88-93; Fundamentalism, relation to, 113 ff.; Nazism and relation to, 111-112; Neo-orthodoxy, relation to, 102-103, 113 ff.; Niebuhr and criticism of, 108-110; retreat of, 99-100
Lindstrom, David E., 9
Lipman, Eugene J., 47 n.
Lippmann, Walter, 1
Loew, Cornelius, 51 n.
Lovejoy, Arthur O., 127, 202
Luccock, Halford E., 153 n.
Luther, Martin, 75-78, 84, 106
Lutheran trials of Pastor Crist and others, 18-19

MacDari, Conor, 146 n.
Machen, John Gresham, 113

Macintosh, Douglas Clyde, 124-125
Malinowski, Bronislaw, 40
Man: Barth on, 107; as Heaven stormer, 179-182; liberalism's view of, 107; Niebuhr on, 108-110; as pessimist, 171-172; Tillich on, 120 ff.
Marty, Martin, 8, 21-22, 53, 145
Martyr, Justin, 194
Materialism, 207
Matthew, Book of, 135
Mayer, Carl, 111 n.
McCrackin, Maurice, 20
McCulloch, Gerald O., 50 n.
McGiffert Jr., A. C., 90
McKee, Elmore M., 144
Mead, Margaret, 40
Merger of denominations, 25
Methodist ministers survey, 9
Miracles, 18, 97, 116, 207
Morrison, A. Cressy, 137 n.
Morrison, Charles Clayton, 24 n.
Mowrer, O. Hobart, 8 n.
Muller, Herbert J., 40
Murphy, Arthur E., 139
Murphy, Charles J. V., 83 n.
Murrow, Edward R., 42
Modernism, 51, 93 ff., 124, 144
Murray, Father John Courtney, 44, 46, 52-53, 79-81
Mystery, Doctrine of, 138
Mysticism, 161
Myth, 124, 174, 175, 183

National Council of Churches, 22
Naturalism, 51
Nazism, 110-111, 166, 174
Neo-orthodoxy, 102 ff., 202
Newman, Cardinal John Henry, 22, 77-78
Newton, Sir Isaac, 37, 38, 39, 87, 201
Niebuhr, H. Richard, 124
Niebuhr, Reinhold, 106 ff., 137 ff., 147 ff., 153, 173, 183, 200, 205
Niebuhr, Richard Reinhold, 140-141
Nigg, Walter, 51, 187
Northrop, F. S. C., 203
Nygren, Anders, 158

Oden, Thomas C., 118 n.
Ostow, Mortimer, 144

Ottariani, Cardinal, 80-81
Otto, Rudolph, 104

Pacifism, 99
Page, Kirby, 95
Paine, Thomas, 190
Paradox, 104, 112, 137 ff.
Payne-Gaposchkin, Cecelia, 160 n.
Parker, Theodore, 96-97
Pascal, Blaise, 33
Pasteur, Louis, 37
Paul, 8, 106, 137-138, 170-171, 198
Paul VI, Pope, 81
Peale, Norman Vincent, 128
Péguy, Charles, 203
Pelagius, 18, 56
Pelikan, Jaroslav, 72 n.
Perfectionism, 51
Pessimism, 171-172
Pfeiffer, Robert H., 135 n.
Phillips, J. B., 163
Philo, 170
Pierce-Higgins, Canon John, 10
Pike, James A., 145
Pindar, 171 n.
Pinson, Koppel S., 110 n.
Pittenger, W. Norman, 36 n., 124 n., 129 n.
Plato, 124, 209
Pluralism, 43 ff.
Polish Minor Church, 85-86
Polls, religious: Catholics, 5-6; children, 3; college students, 4, 8; Congregational ministers, 11; England, 4-5; Episcopal clergy, 10; Harvard, 4; Jews, 6-7; lay people, 2 ff.; Methodist clergy, 9; Radcliffe, 4; Redbook, 11; Richmond, Va., 2; Ripon College, 4; Syracuse University, 3; Theological students, 11
Pratt, James B., 144;
Presbyterian: investigation of Charles M. Jones, 16-17; heresy trials in, 19-21
Prayer: Lutheran position on, 18; U.S. Supreme Court decisions, 45
Prayer of General Confession, 2
Pride, 109
Priestley, Joseph, 33
Protestantism, 114, 116-117, 128;

ecumenical problems, 22-27; Herberg's view, 52; Tillich on, 120 ff.
Psalms, 171, 178
Psychiatry, 12, 213
Pyramid cult, 146
Pythagoras, 31

Quigley, Harold, 19-20

Racism, 51
Randall, Jr., John Herman, 89, 92
Rankin, Robert, 11
Rauschenbusch, Walter, 99, 114
Redbook poll, 11
Reformation, 15, 83-86
Reformation, Medieval, 33
Religion: described, 208-210, 211-213; man's need of, 210
Renan, Ernest, 30, 87
Resurrection: Congregational ministers' views on, 11; Lutheran position on, 18; Methodist ministers' views on, 9; Neo-orthodox view on, 115; Richard Reinhold Niebuhr on, 140-141
Revelation: in Fourth Faith, 55, 57, 60; in Fundamentalism, 114, 116, 129; in Judaism, 65; nature of, 196-199; in Neo-orthodoxy, 114, 116, 129; in Roman Catholicism, 73; Tillich on, 120
Rhodes, Arnold B., 51 n.
Richardson, Alan, 133
Ripon College, 4
Ritschl, Albrecht, 103, 125
Robbins, Jhan, 11 n.
Robbins, June, 11 n.
Robertson, F. W., 143
Rockefeller Bros. Theological Fellowship Program, 11
Rowley, H. H., 129 n.
Ryan, Edward A., 46

Scambler, John H., 153 n.
Schleiermacher, Friedrich, 125
Schneider, Louis, 7
Schweitzer, Albert, 98-99
Schweitzer, W., 137 n.
Science: doctrine, modification of, by, 33, 36; Fourth Faith, relation to, 57;

religion, relation to, 32-36, 38-39, 72, 87-88
Scientific method, 30, 37, 125
Scientism, 38, 51
Secularism, 42, 48-54
Secularity, 53
Seiss, Joseph A., 146 n.
Semonides, 172
Separation of Church and State, 45, 79 ff.
Servetus, Michael, 56
Shakespeare, William, authorship, 135-136
Sin: Bell on, 110; Congregational ministers' views on, 11; Neo-orthodox view on, 108; Niebuhr on, 110; Original, 110, 115, 170-177; popular belief in, 2
Sizoo, Joseph W., 129 n.
Smart, James D., 162 n.
Smith, G. D., 72 n.
Social gospel, 99, 111, 114
Socinus, Faustus, 56, 85
Sockman, Ralph W., 144
Socrates, 31, 56
Soper, David W., 8 n., 164 n.
Sophocles, 172, 178-179
Spann, J. Richard, 49 n.
Spencer, Herbert, 38
Sperry, Willard L., 79
Stendhal, Krister, 135 n.
Strauss, David Friedrich, 97, 186
Stability, Faith of, see Faith of Stability
State, separation of Church and, 45, 79 ff.
Strother, Robert, 37 n.
Students: college 4, 8; theological, 11
Supernaturalism, 93, 116, 122, 199, 207
Supreme Court decisions, 45
Syracuse University survey, 3

Teilhard de Chardin, Pierre, 72
Ten Commandments, students' views on, 4
Tertullian, 140-141
Thales, 31
Theresa of Lisieux, St., 161
Thirty-nine Articles, 10
Thompson, J. W., 15 n.

Through the Looking Glass, 142
Tillich, Paul, 119-124, 126, 183, 198-199, 205, 209
Tocqueville, Alexis de, 47
Tolerance, 45, 47, 113
Totalitarianism, 51
Tradition, 59, 169
Tri-partite faith: *see* Pluralism
Troeltsch, Ernst, 125
Truth: in Fourth Faith, 55-57, 163, 205-206; in Neo-orthodoxy, 106, 197-199; Roman Catholic, 73-75; theological, 162 ff., 197-199

Unitarians, 75, 86, 87, 96, 99, 100, 189

Vahamian, Gabriel, 51 n.
Van Dusen, Henry P., 24
Vatican Council, 81
Virgin birth, 9-11, 18
Voltaire, 33
Vorspan, Albert, 47 n.

Ward, Barbara, 111

Weigel, Gustav, 54
White, Andrew D., 36
Whitehead, Alfred North, 34, 36, 124, 125-126, 169
Wilbur, Earl Morse, 85 n.
Williams, George H., 43-44
Winter, Gibson, 8
Witcutt, William P., 79
Wobbermin, 125
World Conference on Faith and Order, Second, 49
World Council of Churches: 22; Evanston meetings, 23, 49, 164; Eastern Orthodox Church, 24
Wright, Charles J., 158 n.
Wright, G. Ernest, 136, 148-150
Wright, William A., 23 n.
Wrigley, Victor, 19
Wynn, J. C., 7 n.
Wycliffe, John, 56
Wylie, Philip, 161

Xenophanes, 56

Youth, 3, 4, 8